Paws to Reflect

PRAISE FOR *PAWS TO REFLECT*

"When I read Devon O'Day's first book, *My Angels Wear Fur*, it awakened a new purpose in life for me. It sent me on a path that introduced me to helping thousands of homeless animals that were dying in southern shelters and on roadsides. Due to those inspirational stories of personal rescues, I formed Critter Cavalry Rescue in 2006. The journey of rescue work is hard but so profoundly rewarding. I now find that Devon and Kim are providing me with the daily devotionals and spiritual depth that I need as I help stay the course with Critter Cavalry Rescue. Devon and Kim have a voice that speaks to us from God's Word and his heart. Their gift of words from God's Spirit carries so many of us through life with hope, purpose, and inspiration. These devotions will change and redirect many lives with their crisp focus on God's lessons to us all."

—CANDACE SIMPSON-GILES
Founder of Critter Cavalry National Animal Rescue and Transport

"Paws to Reflect is an intimate and personal journey through Scripture and life as shared with our best friends—our pets. I begin each day by focusing on the positives—my Lab at my feet, the pasture where our horses stand, our cat waking up—while reading *Paws to Reflect*. You would do well to do the same."

—DR. JOEY FAUCETTE
bestselling author of *Listen to Life with Your Pets*

"I am very excited about *Paws to Reflect,* and and I feel that it will be a blessing as well as provide words of revelation and knowledge to readers. Thank you, Devon and Kim, for bringing new thoughts and ideas by means of God's animal kingdom to the body of Christ."

—GEORGINA BEARDEN
Solid Rock Family Worship Center,
Religion News Columnist, Columbia, TN

"You will be enlightened and blessed by the daily insights in *Paws to Reflect*, even if you do not consider yourself an animal lover. Whether Devon O'Day and Kim McLean are singing, speaking, or writing, they plant God's Word in your mind and, like the animals they love, put smiles in your heart."

—PATSY LEWIS
Author of *Simply Praying, Simply Listening*
and Come to the Fire Testimonies,
and International Coordinator/Speaker for Lydia Prayer Groups

"Devon O'Day and Kim McLean have channeled their lifelong love for animals into a wonderful, faith-based book called *Paws to Reflect*. This is an uplifting read and an ideal holiday gift for all the pet lovers in your life."

—PHIL SWEETLAND
Music & Radio Contributor, *The New York Times*
and Editor, *Country Insider*

365 DEVOTIONS

FOR THE ANIMAL LOVER'S SOUL

Paws to Reflect

DEVON O'DAY

AND

KIM McLEAN

Abingdon Press / *Nashville*

PAWS TO REFLECT
365 DEVOTIONS FOR THE ANIMAL LOVER'S SOUL

Copyright © 2012 by Abingdon Press

This book is printed on acid-free paper.

Library of Congress Cataloging-in-Publication Data has been requested.

ISBN 978-1-4267-4417-4

12 13 14 15 16 17 18 19 20 21—10 9 8 7 6 5 4 3 2 1

MANUFACTURED IN THE UNITED STATES OF AMERICA

To
William McLean Johnston

Chief Dog-Chaser, Cat Whisperer, Pony Wrangler,
Fence Mender, Hay Pitcher, Farm Explorer,
and Environment Protector
at Big Sky Heaven Blue Farm

Thank you for your love of God's creation.
You are the future . . . lead on!

Contents

A Reflective Paws from Devon O'Day

More than twenty-five years of loving animals that have found their way into my life has blessed me beyond measure. Perhaps it's because seeing the lessons of life taught through the practical application of animal care has helped constantly renew my spirit.

A dog's loyalty will certainly teach unconditional love. A purring kitten will certainly bring one peace. Watching a horse come to grips with immeasurable fear the first time under saddle can help us realize the fear we all seek to harness.

In the presence of God's creatures, I am given new insight. I *feel* faith in the company of the faithful. I *see* with new eyes of innocence what is good, true, and healing as I am surrounded by humble animal hearts. I *hear* love in the barks, whinnies, and purrs of a menagerie or in the wild night sounds of the woodland blessings.

God has always spoken to me through animals. Sometimes human communication has fallen short in conveying spiritual truth to me. But God somehow knows how to reach me. He knows how to reach all of us. Some feel closer to God when they see beautiful scenery. Others feel closer to God when they see children playing. God wants to commune with each of us so much, he'll speak whatever language we need to hear. For me, God has often spoken through the language of the animal kingdom.

Following is a book of some of those stories—a gentle daily reflection for those who seek a simple path and understand how much we can grow spiritually by observing the animal kingdom and the lessons it teaches.

A Reflective Paws from Kim McLean

Numerous times I have heard someone tell me they like dogs and cats better than people. "People always let you down," they say, or "My dog appreciates me" or "At least my cat is honest with me." True, you can count on a cat to be honest with you. Nothing about their moody independence or their affectionate cuddles is contrived. And there's nothing quite like the faithfulness and loyalty of a dog. Dogs, cats, horses, hamsters, parakeets, and goldfish . . . whoever the fine, feathered, feline, four-footed friend may be, born of land, sky, or sea, there is no doubt that we humans have much to learn about life and love from them all. You might say animals teach us how to be better humans. Ironic, isn't it? I've always suspected that it's not that we don't like people; it's that we want our faith in our own species restored.

We animal lovers are all a bunch of crazy Dr. Doolittles, huh? We love ascribing human qualities to our animals, but just because our cat, Monkey Face, can't form words, does not mean that she cannot communicate. She is quite jealous of my dog Veronique, and it is clear that jealousy is not species specific. And so we make the leap: the heart connection between people and animals as God gives us a way of seeing the hilarity, the joy, the sorrow, the triumphs, and the shortcomings of God's crazy creatures.

Something about caring for my pets helps restore my faith in myself. They bring out my unselfish streak. They remind me how to care, and how to take it easy. They remind me of my humble link with creation and of my place in the grand scheme of things. They remind me that God loves and cares for us. "Consider the sparrow," Jesus said. Without even trying, it knows that God is taking care of it. Consider the other animals, as well.

We can be reminded of God's love for us by cherishing the gift of our animals. We can be reminded of how to love one another too.

I am so glad that Devon invited me to participate in writing these devotions; these reflections have me realizing once again just what a blessing all of my animal friends have been. Their gift to me has been in demonstrating the kind of patience, forgiveness, and wisdom that it takes to get along with the human race. Their gift has been one of connection, with God and humankind.

We hope that these devotions inspire you, encourage you, heal you, and teach you God's word in a unique way. May everyone who reads these pages find a closer walk with God and experience the joy of his creation a little more keenly than before.

January 1
Let Sleeping Dogs . . . DREAM!

Awake, awake, arm of the LORD, clothe yourself with strength!
Awake, as in days gone by, as in generations of old.
—Isaiah 51:9

Some days, Daisy, our three-legged Dalmatian, is curled in sound sleep, when Henry, the miniature schnauzer, comes along to torment her with a curious sniff. Henry's curiosity and agitation can rouse Daisy from a dead sleep to a ferocious attack in zero to six seconds.

As humans, we have a metaphoric sleep as well, spending a lot of time in a comfortable "coast" in life's holding pattern. We fail to live up to our potential and forget to heed our calling. We need to be awakened to a fresh new life, without taking the heads off those around us, being jolted, as it were, out of our day-to-day rut. How to respond? How do we change and come fully aware and awake? We have to let go of the old habits and let ourselves forge a new path in obedience. When we empty ourselves of the world, we can be filled with God's light. We must let go of comfort—something that can be truly terrifying.

When you see a sleeping dog lash out, it's not usually out of a mean spirit. It's out of fear. We react just as ferociously as a sleeping dog sometimes because we are afraid to become new—afraid to become God's full potential for us.

On this first day of the year, let us wake up into a new day, where we have love all around us to encourage us. Let last night's nightmare fall away and become today's glorious dream. Be courageous in God's new world for you!—d.o.

January 2
Pink Slips and Chew Bones

Grace and peace to you from God our Father and the Lord Jesus Christ.
—Philemon 1:3

I watched the golden retriever I had fostered for six months ride away with her new "mommy" as she stared at me through the back windshield of that little red Honda. She had come such a long way from the frightened abuse victim placed in my care. Her eyes never left me as the car left for the horizon. There was a chew bone in her mouth. Her tail was wagging. This dog knew she was going to a new home. Yet, somehow, she wanted to let me know she was grateful. She knew the dark place she'd come from and where she was now going, and I was just the spot in between.

Some things are not meant to be forever. They are just meant to get us there. Every friendship, every job, every place we live, is just a bridge to learning something we need in order to become who we are to be. People leave us because their part in our journey is finished. We never complete anything without having a lesson to be learned. Good-byes always leave us with a piece missing, don't they? Change is always difficult.

If you are saying good-bye to someone, something, or some place, reflect on what you have gained from the time you have spent. Let it be woven into the fabric of who you are becoming. Just remember, nothing is taken without being replaced by more of what you need. Just as I had been a temporary caregiver for that beautiful golden retriever, she now has a permanent place to curl up and call home. Say good-bye with grace and hello with hope, and leave with a lesson. Nothing leaves until it is time to let go. Accepting loss only comes with God's help and the wisdom of time.—d.o.

January 3
Shane

I will repay you for the years that the swarming locust has eaten.
—Joel 2:25

When I was ten years old, my parents decided that I should have a collie. My dad negotiated with the breeder, who apologized for the one imperfect one left. My parents paid thirty-five dollars for her. I named her Shane. She was my princess, and to me, she was worth a million dollars.

I think of Shane and remember a lifetime. She represents my whole childhood. She was always by my side, a loyal companion, but I let her down when the pressures of growing up pulled me away. I moved away for school, and she died while I was gone. My parents were in a painful divorce, and I was gone—Shane must have wondered where I was. I carried the broken heart of never having said a final good-bye, and I was filled with the regret of knowing that she must have been terribly lonely when I was suddenly not there.

When we are hurting or struggling or striving to get ahead, we tend to let down the ones we love. Someone once said that hurting people hurt people. Sometimes hurting people hurt their furry friends too. The pain of that regret was a secret hurt in my heart for a long time, until one day my daughter and best friend gave me a collie. I named her Veronique. In Shane's honor, I would take care of another. I would give now what I didn't know how to give then. Regret cannot heal. Love can. Love does.

We can break the sad cycle that compels us to create hurt from hurt, and instead we can let the broken places in our hearts become places where there is more room for love.—k m

Dog-Eared Promises

Then Job replied: "How long will you torment me and crush me with words?"
—Job 19:1-2

I remember reading about a man who cut the ears off his dog, so that "when he was fighting other dogs, they couldn't pull him down by his ears." The dog almost bled to death. Even as they removed the dog from the home and took the man into custody on animal cruelty charges, the dog fought to get back to his master.

People who are cruel are often blessed with undeserved loyalty from an animal. The look from the eyes of an abused animal at its master is often sad, pleading—yet never angry. The eyes of an abused person are much the same toward a perpetrator.

In today's scripture, we meet Job, who was hurt by a friend's rudeness and constant badgering of "you deserve what you're getting." So-called friends and family can be more hurtful than the evil we meet in the world. We take this abuse hoping the repetition might lead to a different outcome. This is an unrewarding way to live.

Or maybe we expect God to effect a change in the people who hurt us. Perhaps, though, the change is supposed to be in us. Are we to remain loyal to the world that hurts us, expecting a miracle of change? Or are we to ask God to deliver us, fully ready to make a change if he asks?

God wants us to live in light, love, and joy. He will offer a way out, in peace and compassion, allowing the person inflicting pain on us a chance to change—because this person is hurting too. Maybe God has a plan for this person to learn tolerance, patience, and love through the loss of companionship. What if loneliness helps this person become who God wants him or her to be? Ask God to guide you to a compassionate solution.
—d.o.

January 5

The Songbird

"But get me a musician." And then, while the musician was playing,
the power of the LORD came on him.
—2 Kings 3:15

I n the daily reading from 2 Kings, we meet Elisha, who was in need of an answer. But first, he asked for a song.

A Chinese proverb says a songbird does not sing because she has an answer; she sings because she has a song. Today, I am seeking a song of peace, hope, courage, and love. The song must break forth, seemingly out of nowhere, but it is not out of nowhere. It is a gift. It is as natural as the song of the songbird.

The gift we receive is the Spirit. The Apostle Paul writes, in 2 Corinthians 3:6, that the Spirit gives life. It is the Spirit who puts the song inside you. Interestingly, the Spirit in Scripture sometimes comes in the form of a bird.

"Take delight in the LORD, and he will give you the desires of your heart," the psalmist wrote (Psalm 37:4). Maybe we take delight in our accomplishments, or in the number of errands we can scratch off the list in a day, or in a bank account that offers some sense of security, but these things are no answer to our happiness. Maybe they are the answer to a temporary good mood, but they are not the song-givers. What brings happiness is something quite invisible and difficult to describe. Jesus compared it to the wind. You can't see it, but you know it's there by the way you feel it brush across you. This is the Spirit that gives the songbird her song.

Are you waiting for a song? There are a thousand ways to seek the song. You can be still and wait. Take a walk. Say a prayer. God is listening for your call. Nothing pleases the Lord more than a heart that longs for true happiness. However you search for the song, know that you are not seeking an answer; you are seeking the true song, the design of your life, shaped by the Spirit. You are the songbird. Your life is the song.—k.m.

January 6
A Spotty Politician

You are always righteous, LORD, when I bring a case before you.
Yet I would speak with you about your justice: Why does the way of the wicked prosper?
Why do all the faithless live at ease? You have planted them, and they have taken root;
they grow and bear fruit. You are always on their lips but far from their hearts.
—Jeremiah 12:1-2

Have you ever wondered why, as Jeremiah writes, "the wicked prosper"? This came home to me when I witnessed at a public event accolades being given to the wife of a prominent politician for saving children and calling for humane treatment of animals.

But the reality told a different story behind the glowing facade: the woman had recently taken their healthy, happy Dalmatian into a veterinarian's office to put the dog down. "This dog is just not fitting into our lifestyle," the woman told the vet.

"But she's healthy," replied the vet. "Couldn't we just find her a good home for you?"

"Absolutely not. I would just rather have her put down right now. I wouldn't want her to be in a shelter," she said as she left, not wanting to be present as the deed was carried out.

The vet assistant took the dog back to the kennel, and instead of carrying out a lethal injection, sneaked the dog into her car and later to her home. She found a beautiful home for the dog with a couple mourning the recent death of their aged Dalmatian.

A few weeks later, on public TV, the same woman who ordered that her dog be put down received an award for community service. Not all bad people lose. Not all good people win. Not everyone gets a spotlight on the truth.

As individuals, we cannot control or determine justice. That's not our job. It's God's job. Perhaps, God was answering the prayer of a mourning couple, and the politician's wife was just part of God's plan. Maybe in the darkness, the couple prayed in pain for a dog to replace the one they had lost. God answered their prayer. This may be the only justice needed.
—d.o.

January 7
Little Foxes

Catch us the foxes, the little foxes,
that ruin the vineyards—for our vineyards are in blossom.
—Song of Solomon 2:15

A t my house teeth marks are on the legs of the wooden chairs. Somehow the rubber gorilla, the yellow bouncy bell ball, and a thousand rawhide bones were not enough to get Veronique through the teething phase. But that's what puppies do. It's like little foxes, always needing to chew things.

Every day you have a vineyard to tend in order to yield a harvest of fruit. It is a vineyard full of dreams, gifts, hope for the future, and joy for today. Maybe you want to write or play guitar or plant a garden. What is in your vineyard? What makes your life beautiful? What is calling that needs your attention?

Ever notice how difficult it can be to get around to the things you really want to do? One trip to the grocery store can turn into a day full of errands. One rushed hour fighting traffic to get to the office can kill your ambition. Peace slips away, and dreams fade. It doesn't happen suddenly. It happens one disappointed thought at a time. Those are the little foxes that spoil our vineyards.

Words misspoken or encouragement withheld can chip away at your confidence and steal your joy. Fears and doubts can blind you from the grace that is right there waiting to give you your heart's desire.

What is your heart's desire? Want to learn a secret? If you pray to have God's desire be your desire, miracles will happen. Love God first, wholeheartedly, and watch the vineyard blossom! Devote every new day to the Lord, and he will catch the little foxes that spoil the vines.

Those little foxes don't mean to spoil the vines. They're just being little foxes. Trust in God as you cultivate your vineyard.—k.m.

Breaking Fences—Breaking Chains

This is what the Lord says: "Although they have allies and are numerous, they will be destroyed and pass away. Although I have afflicted you, Judah, I will afflict you no more. Now I will break their yoke from your neck and tear your shackles away."
—Nahum 1:12-13

I number among my friends those who've broken through fences, sneaked into backyards, and stolen animals away from inhumane conditions after discovering the evil of people who allow the chaining of helpless creatures with no food or water and leave them to the agony of the elements. I have seen the power of humans over the weakness of animals.

Subdued and held captive, the weak animals lose their will to live; their spirits morph into quiet, pain-stricken ghosts of their God-intentioned purpose.

As people, we can also become enslaved and weakened by things that surround us. Jobs can place a yoke on us, keeping us from joy. Individuals in our sphere with impure motives can be controlling, sucking the life force from us.

In the moment of feeling powerless with overwhelming factors in our lives, we can call upon God to become strong within us. There is no bond of captivity in our world that cannot be broken by God. Gaining our freedom over the strength of people who seek to bind us means being willing to become free in the first place. We have to trust that God's way is more rewarding than staying in the captive shadows.

Freedom often involves a surrender. We must surrender our need to be accepted by the "cool" group. We must surrender our desire to have all the things the world says are essential. In that surrender, God can give us the blessings waiting in store for us. Let God break through the fence and into the yard to rescue you.

The dream God has for us is always bigger than the dreams the world has for us.—d.o.

January 9
Bear Chaser

In all that they do, they prosper.
—Psalm 1:3b

Once I chased a bear. My parents and I were in the Smoky Mountains of North Carolina when the baby black bear went running past. I took off after it as my parents yelled for me to stop. They knew a mama bear would be close behind.

Maybe it's best not to catch a wild bear, but the bear offers valuable lessons. She sleeps through the winter and enters the cave of dreams. This reminds me that I need to take time to dream too. In the quiet resting place, dreams are born, and it is by first dreaming that the prosperity of happiness comes. Sometimes, the most productive thing you can do is nothing. But it is not the nothing of negligence—it is the nothing of finding a resting place.

The psalmist writes that those who delight in the Lord are happy. We are created to be happy, but I have to ask, what is happiness? The answer is not wealth or fame, though both may happen for some this year. True happiness comes when you allow God's dream to dream through you.

Delight in the ways of God. Peace. Patience. Kindness. Compassion. Love. Understanding. You know the list. Now it's time to live it. *Really* believe in these things when the world is swirling around you. If these attributes are your goal, just wait and see what miracles will happen!

In this season of winter, as people begin to set expectations, let us set our expectation in God. First things first. The most important thing you can do today is to rest in God. Rest like a bear. Take the time to connect with the Source of your strength, and you will emerge from the quiet cave alive, sure to live the dreams that came in the waiting period.—k.m.

Fleas and Flies

When Jesus saw the crowd around him,
he gave orders to cross to the other side of the lake.
Then a teacher of the law came to him and said,
"Teacher, I will follow you wherever you go."
—Matthew 8:18-19

Teaching any animal to fit into our human existence brings all sorts of challenge. For instance, getting a male dog not to lift his leg on the couch, when everything in his being wants to let the world know it's *his* couch, can be difficult at best. Training cats not to climb on the kitchen cabinet when they know that tuna cans are opened there seems almost impossible. Getting a fifteen-hundred-pound horse to put an annoying, even painful piece of steel over his tongue, allow humans to climb on his back, and take them places is a miracle. We teach our animals, and they acquiesce when all goes as planned. But animals do not ever have to do what we ask. We cannot actually *make* a cat, dog, or horse obey. Animals agree to do what we ask because they want to.

When pets disobey, it's not an act of rebellion. They just figure out how to communicate. They get our attention. Sometimes it's the only way they can. Most of the time, our animals see us as miracle workers. We feed them when they are hungry. We give them comfort and a warm place to sleep. We brush them and treat their ailments. We get rid of their demonic fleas and flies. For this, they look at us with wonderment and follow us wherever we go.

We've been taught by Jesus' example how to be better humans. He taught us how to love each other better and how to love ourselves. Still, sometimes we fall back on old habits and self-harming directions. We create hurt for ourselves and those around us. And creating such havoc, we feel unlovable. We literally separate ourselves from God's love. But maybe with those actions, we are using the only language we know to communicate with God. Maybe in our darkest, most desperately harmful actions, we are crying out to God for love.

The interesting thing about following our Teacher wherever he goes is, he never ever goes any farther away than our heart.—d.o.

January 11
Three Horses

Moses drew near to the thick darkness where God was.
—Exodus 20:21b

M oses drew near to the thick darkness *where God was*. Maybe there was thunder and lightning. Have you ever felt God in a storm? There's something about the rhythm, ancient and strong, as the water and the wind dance together in percussive motion. Storms are amazing—*of course* God is there.

We have winter storms at our farm, the kind that usually happen in the summer. One late afternoon, the sky seemed light and dark at the same time, a strange glow of black and blue. The rain was coming down in sheets, slanting like millions of silver arrows. I watched for a little while contemplating whether or not to gather my family and take refuge in some nook in the house that might serve as a tornado shelter.

Instead, I opened the door, stepped out onto the carport, and saw the most beautiful sight I thought I had ever seen. There on the plateau, in front of the barn, were our three horses, Tucker, Fancy, and Poshee, standing in perfect formation, a triangle with Fancy at the point, all facing the direction of the storm. Their manes and tails blowing straight back and their heads up, they looked as though they were breathing the wind's force into their nostrils. I was moved by the majesty of the scene. I took it in, hoping to imprint it on my memory and impress it on my soul.

Sometimes, we try to wish the storms away, but often, there in the black and blue clouds is the source of your strength, God in control. Let the power of the Creator breathe through you today. Like the three horses and the mighty rushing wind, may you be filled with a Spirit strong and unshakable.—k.m.

January 12

No whining!

Do everything without grumbling or arguing, so that you may become blameless and pure,
"children of God without fault in a warped and crooked generation." Then you will shine
among them like stars in the sky as you hold firmly to the word of life. And then I will be
able to boast on the day of Christ that I did not run or labor in vain.
—Philippians 2:14-16

At the end of a long hard day in the workplace where people are negative and complain all the time, isn't it peaceful to come home to a wet nose, warm fur, and the acceptance of our pets? I've never heard a complaint from my dog or cat when I walk in the door a little late. They've been waiting and waiting, but all they can do when I walk in is greet me with purrs and wagging tails. They light up my world with their excitement to see me. They help me feel better about me.

When we're surrounded by complainers, we begin to see life in a negative light. Nothing is good. Everything is bad. But just a moment in the presence of a light, positive spirit can make the world better. It's kindness. It's joy. It's sharing life without complaining about all we see wrong, but rejoicing in all we see right.

When people walk into the office this week, instead of greeting them with complaints they have to remedy, greet them with a smile and some good news. Even a small snippet of good news can change the environment around us. Instead of being the bearer of bad news, we can become the beacon of good news. Instead of the angel of doldrums, become the angel of light. Even in a "warped and crooked generation," we can shine as lights in the world.

Does bringing kindness to a day mean we are trying to live in a false reality, becoming a fake Mary Sunshine? No, it means putting in the effort to be a solution giver, a problem solver, and an encourager to all we see. Do you think your dog or cat agonizes over being happy to see you? No. They are extraordinary teachers in the "how to treat your neighbor" category!—d.o.

January 13
The White Tiger

I press on toward the goal for the prize of the heavenly call of God in Christ Jesus.
—Philippians 3:14

No tigers live by Lake Ponchartrain. I got the last one. This is no ordinary tiger. I won it at the Mandeville Seafood Festival on a scorching hot summer day. My son was helping man the ball-toss booth in the children's pavilion, an important job for a ten-year-old boy. One ticket got you one basket full of footballs. One ball in the big circle would win a small prize, but to win the white tiger, you had to get a ball through each one of the four circles, from largest to smallest. Of course, I had to give it a try.

Passersby were gathering behind me as I took aim. I put just the right spin on it, and the first ball went straight as a bullet into one of the smaller holes. The second ball went into another circle. Then a third. I was doing so well that when the fourth ball was a near miss, my son set another basket of footballs on the table. I was going to get as many chances as it took to win, which I did . . . several baskets later.

"You did it! You won the white tiger!" my son shouted. "Well," I told him, "I had some extra chances." We gave each other a big hug and left it at that.

Later that afternoon, he brought me the white tiger and said, "You got a football into every single hole, and I won't let you leave without your prize." Standing nearby was the adult in charge of the ball-toss booth. I gave her a concerned glance. She smiled and gave a wink.

I learned an important lesson that day. Press toward the mark, and the Holy Spirit will help you make the mark. Learn the lesson of the white tiger and celebrate your victories!—k.m.

January 14
You Can't Judge a Cocker by Its Spaniel

When they go with their flocks and herds to seek the LORD, they will not find him;
he has withdrawn himself from them.
—Hosea 5:6

Outward appearances can sometimes be very deceiving. As a shelter volunteer, I soon learned that the most evil *looking* dogs were sometimes the biggest sweethearts. And then, there were the cocker spaniels. They had those beautiful brown eyes. Visions of *Lady and the Tramp* came to mind as I would reach to pet them.

With one unanticipated sharp growl, I would get bitten. I was not prepared to be bitten by an animal that was cute. This was a breed that had been animated in Disney movies, for goodness' sake! This misperception happened more than once. The adorable toy breeds would growl and snap with no provocation, while the pit bulls and Dobermans would roll around on the floor with me in play. This is by no means a criticism of any breed, just an observation that outward appearances and public opinion can be wrong.

In ancient times, some Israelites spoke highly of God, while worshiping pagan gods on the side. The Israelites were spiritually hedging their bets, so to speak. Well, it didn't work with God. And hedging bets didn't work with me either at the animal shelter. I stopped trusting those sweet, sad eyes until I knew for sure that the animal in front of me was trustworthy. And I was delighted to find cocker spaniels who were.

If we put our faith in gods that can't be trusted, we can get bitten. But we forget that and often put our faith in careers, money, or material possessions because they look at us with their beautiful brown eyes. Then, when we are least expecting it, they turn and bite us, leaving us wounded and with destroyed spirits. But we have God who loves us always and who knows our hearts.—d.o.

Perfectly Muddy Paws

Be perfect, therefore, as your heavenly Father is perfect.
—Matthew 5:48

These words of Jesus are outrageous. Be perfect. I prefer thinking of myself as a work-in-progress, only human—or fallible but lovable. Who wants to be perfect, anyway? What did Jesus mean?

Our animals teach me something about perfection. They know how to just *be.* Geronimo never wonders what he can do to be a perfect pony. He grazes, struts, eats, and teases the big horses in perfect pony fashion. The dogs are perfect too. Jack guards the parameters of our thirty acres and steals the neighbor's dog food. Veronique rounds up the herd at feed time and scratches the side of my car when she jumps on the door. The cats love to leave fur balls and muddy paw prints on the hood. They're a perfect bunch of creatures, all right.

People are different, right? Higher intelligence. So what is a perfect human? To be perfect is to be complete. God means for his people to be blessed, at peace with God, self, and neighbor, and even our enemies. We are, after all, created in his image. To be perfect is to be whole, and to be whole is to be holy, and to be holy, we must be wholly his.

God doesn't ask us to be perfect on our own. We are perfect as we rest in him. When we are rightly related to God, we begin to see ourselves, our true identity as we are created to be.

Jesus never said it would be easy. Maybe that's why he came to earth and showed us how to live. It's about grace. He gives us the strength to live as he calls us to live. He equips us for what he calls us to *be.*   k.m.

January 16
Don't Eat Yellow Snow

He spreads the snow like wool
and scatters the frost like ashes.
—Psalm 147:16

I will never forget the day my dogs were introduced to their first big snow. More than six inches of cold, wet, exciting joy covered the backyard. The big golden retriever, who lived for icy waters, thought it was the best thing in the whole world. He romped and played, plowing headfirst into the drifts until frost clung to every strand of his fur. He ran to me with steaming breath and a rejuvenation of spirit that made him seem like a puppy.

At the same moment he was experiencing new life in the snow, my miniature schnauzer was touching the cold, white mess with caution mixed with disgust. He wasn't about to run through it, the depth coming up to his chest. It was frightening. It was wet. It was unfamiliar. It was just awful. He lifted his leg and aimed a careful stream at the snow, while his body remained dry and safe under the carport.

What one dog found to be a gift from heaven, the other found to be a curse. Weather is a blessing or a curse, rain or drought, depending on the fields where it falls. God brings us all kinds of weather; just as in life we have storms, perfect days, and outright disasters. No one is free or safe from changeable weather. We can have snug warm homes in the winter and cool comfort in the heat of summer, but ultimately, we eventually have to deal with the changing elements and their effects. Life will dish out all sorts of good, bad, and in-between. No one is immune to life, so how will we deal with it?

Will we jump joyfully in the drifts or stand under the shelter watching life go by? In the deep snowdrifts and hot, waterless days, I see God's hand, and each day offers up something new. Even in the aftermath of a hurricane, I see God's hand, as people reach out in love to help each other. May we always remember that life is for experiencing, and God will see us through every single moment—rain or shine!—d.o.

January 17
Jack Loves Veronique

Though we stumble, we shall not fall headlong,
for the LORD holds us by the hand.
—Psalm 37:24

Our dog Jack fell in love with Veronique the day we brought her home, and she adored him. A full-grown Pyrenees-collie can be as intimidating as a polar bear, with a bark that thunders across the valley, but he was gentle as a lamb with the new collie pup. She jumped and nipped and yapped at Jack playfully, and he would look up at us with a twinkle in his eye that seemed to say, "She's pesky, but she sure is cute!"

Overnight, it seemed Veronique was tall enough to reach the latch on the front door. One day, we were all at home when a neighbor called to say that he had our collie, and she had been hit by a car. We didn't even know she'd gotten out! He drove up a few minutes later, and we rushed her to the emergency vet. Her pelvic bone was broken, but it would mend without surgery.

Our neighbor felt bad. I felt bad. Jack felt bad. Our neighbor was a kind man who had seen Jack and Veronique running around, playing as though on a big adventure. They were having such a great time that he was going to let them play before he checked their collars for a number to call. It was clear that they were a couple of crazy-in-love teenagers who were not supposed to be so far from home. Then a car rounded the bend just as Veronique shot out of the woods. Both neighbor and Jack froze with fright as they watched the inevitable collision.

Jack was beside himself for days, until at last he was allowed to come inside and see that Veronique was going to be all right. She could barely lift her head, but she managed to give Jack a lick on the nose so he wouldn't worry. Jack seemed sorry for not taking better care of his girl, for leading her to a dangerous place. And I learned, too, to keep the door locked even though Veronique no longer tries to dash past the threshold before I've given the okay.

We make mistakes. And sometimes our mistakes hurt the ones we love the most. But we don't have to keep making the same mistakes. As today's verse says, God helps us when we stumble, and that's how we grow in grace!—k.m.

January 18
Dove's Eyes

How beautiful you are, my darling!
Oh, how beautiful!
Your eyes are doves.
—Song of Solomon 1:15

One day, after leaving my prayer group, I stepped out the front door to see two beautiful turtledoves sitting next to a shrub on a soft nesting of straw. They didn't move when I stood near them. They just looked up at me with beautiful soft eyes. They had such a peace about them. I try to pay attention to the Holy Spirit's signposts, and I was moved to tears at this moment because this certainly felt like one.

Usually a human's presence would frighten a wild bird away. But this time, although I was just inches from the soft dove eyes, there was no movement, no fear. I caught one of the dove's eyes and felt God speak to my heart.

In Song of Solomon, the most beautiful words of love ever written appear. In this passage, the first time the words "my love" appear, they mean, "dear friend." Doves' eyes are symbolic of purity, innocence, and beauty. From my firsthand experience, as that dove looked up at me, I saw purity, innocence, and beauty. I believe God wanted me to see those qualities in her—and wanted me to see those also in myself again. In Scripture, God calls us *Beloved* over and over and over. He sees our purity, even if we feel covered with the mud of shame. He sees our innocence, even when we feel the world has stolen it. He sees our beauty when we feel ugly with regret.

God showed me what he sees when he looks at me: dove's eyes. Through things like doves' eyes we are constantly reminded of God's vision of us. We are his beloved. He wants us to know that every time we look in a mirror, we should see dove's eyes. God wants us to see purity, innocence, and beauty. He wants us to see . . . him.—d.o.

January 19
Hollywood Kitty

Now to him who is able to keep you from falling,
and to make you stand without blemish
in the presence of his glory with rejoicing. . . .
—Jude 1:24

If Zsa Zsa were human, she would be a movie star, one of the glamorous, classy ones like Elizabeth Taylor, Sophia Loren, or Rita Hayworth. She is, of course, a cat. And she is a cat who won't socialize with our other thirteen cats. She knows she's different. She's a breed apart from the others. Everything about her ragamuffin personality is unique.

Zsa Zsa introduced herself to us in the wee hours of the morning at a Shell station where we had stopped on our way home from a road trip. She came sauntering up to the gas pump and requested our attention with all the poise of a beauty queen, although she was a mess. Her fur was matted, and she had a serious wound on her neck. She cuddled up to us with affectionate thank-yous as we drove home. That's as nice as she's been since. Once home, she let us know her precocious demands as though we had signed a contract. Feed me this. Don't pet me there. Keep those horrible, disgusting dogs away from me.

I have a special affinity for Zsa Zsa. She's been through some rough times but maintained her dignity. She knows she was born for greatness.

Do you know you were born for greatness? You're a shining star.

Walk in the light of who you were born to be. You are called to be a child of God, his very own. As with Zsa Zsa, it doesn't matter what you've been through, God is waiting with love and healing, ready to bless you with the light of heaven and receive you as his own.

But please remember one thing that Zsa Zsa hasn't yet figured out—be nice to the other cats. They're special too!—k.m.

January 20

Dem Dry Bones

The waters of the river will dry up,
and the riverbed will be parched and dry.
—Isaiah 19:5

There was a horrible drought in the western plains of our country. Cattle were literally dying on the plains. The land was dry. Bones parched in the sun. America, the rich farmland that gives us beef and bread, was becoming a desert. Because there was thirst in the land, there was also hunger, because no food would grow on the drought-laden prairie.

Land's not the only thing that needs water; as humans, we are in great part water ourselves. Our animals are too. We all live because of water. When we look at the "needs" our society says we have to have, like expensive cars, bigger homes, and cooler electronic gadgets, it all pales in comparison to that divine combination of hydrogen and oxygen called water.

When the woman at the well gave water to Jesus, he gave her living water in return so that she would never thirst again. What kind of water *is* that? What is water that quenches upon its first taste? When we drink in the water of the Holy Spirit, it cannot be seen, proved, or broken down into basic elements. It simply washes over us and fills us at the same time. In our core beings, we respond to it. We feel refreshed. We feel new again. We can't hold it in. We have to share it with others. There can be drought from no rain, but the worst drought of all is a dry spirit. Isn't it beautiful to know that God has a raindrop with your name on it?—d.o.

January 21
Prince Poshee

Humble yourselves therefore under the mighty
hand of God, so that he may exalt you in due time.
—1 Peter 5:6

Everything is upside down in God's kingdom. Jesus said the first shall be last and the last shall be first. He said the one who is the greatest is the servant. He himself set the example when, as a king, he was friendly with the outcast, touched the untouchable, rode into Jerusalem on a donkey colt, and died on the cross—between two thieves, no less.

I knew a horse that understood humility better than many Christians I've met along the way. His name was Poshee, and he was a regal white Arabian full of pomp and circumstance but never flaunting it. He was a class act. Trained in dressage, he was the master of his art.

Poshee was the adopted brother, you might say, of Fancy and Tucker, the two rambunctious children of a Tennessee walking horse called Maria. He was much older than his barn-mates, but clearly more powerful. His power was his wisdom. Poshee kept them calm when the storms came, kept them in line at feeding time—even though he waited patiently to be fed last—and reprimanded Tucker on occasion for acting . . . well . . . stupid. Poshee could send out a distress cry if the horses needed help that would rattle your soul and call you to immediate action. Poshee stood by the new pony, Geronimo, the day we brought him home when Fancy and Tucker were giving the "new kid" a hard time.

Poshee was a prince, but he knew that power was not only about strength, but about the subtle movements that make life a dance rather than a stampede.

When I think of Poshee, I am reminded of the humble spirit Christ taught us about, that in God's kingdom the least is the greatest.—k.m.

January 22
Miracle Juice

It is I who made the earth and created mankind on it.
My own hands stretched out the heavens;
I marshaled their starry hosts.
—Isaiah 45:12

Any mother in the lower animal kingdom will fight to the death to protect her young. A mare will feed her foal to her own starvation. A dog will attack a ferocious animal three times her size if it is after her puppies. A cat will teach her babies day in and day out to become self-sufficient. In turn, those young trust their matriarch with their very lives.

We have a Creator who has given us life. Yet, somewhere in between birth and death to this human life, we forget that the divine host had anything to do with our being here. We forget that we've been created in God's image and given the divine gifts far beyond earthly measure.

In human scope, we are limited and unable to accomplish miracles. However, just as the young animal trusts in the parent to provide and accomplish the impossible, we have that same advantage. Our earthly parents might give up when the going gets tough, but our heavenly father never does. Our parents can never put limits on the endless flow of miracle juice God gives us.

We believe in the finite earth, yet forget the Infinite One who created it and us along with it. When we have an unbelievable task at hand and stand in fear of proceeding, we can be reminded of Jesus calling to Peter, telling him to walk on water. In the world's eyes, a feat such as walking on water or the curing of cancer is inconceivable. But if you are called to the feat, God will equip you. God made the earth and you, and all the universes beyond. Surely one who is capable of that kind of fatherhood will help us along our path.—d.o.

Receiving Love

You have seen what I did to the Egyptians,
and how I bore you on eagles' wings and brought you to myself.
—Exodus 19:4

There is a theme throughout the Old Testament of God reaching out, seeking relationship with his children. He tells them again and again that he wants to treasure them. God promises his people love and a peaceful place to call home, and his desire is that his children soar on the wings of hope.

Sometimes being loved so much is scary. It comes with certain vulnerabilities. Receiving love is an act of trust.

We have a cat that refuses love because she is afraid to trust. We offer the same love to her as we do to all the other cats, but it probably doesn't look like we love her as much. We never pet her. She won't let us. She hisses and runs away. We gave her a special name, just like we did the others. Her name is Paisley.

We are like Paisley when we refuse to be God's treasure. We might know that he is watching over us, but that does not mean we have a relationship with him. However, God is always giving. Relationship happens when we receive and give love back to him in natural response.

The lesson from Paisley is to let God love you so that you don't miss out on the wonderful blessing of his joyful presence, and all the benefits from it.—k.m.

Divine Placement

Truly my soul finds rest in God; my salvation comes from him.
Truly he is my rock and my salvation;
he is my fortress, I will never be shaken.
—Psalm 62:1-2

My dog Winston, a miniature schnauzer, used to wait on the left side of the sofa on his towel while I was at work. I would say good-bye and leave, and he'd hop to his place and wait until I returned. He'd be sitting right there in his spot when I opened the door. He'd perk up as I walked in, and when I gave the word, he'd run to me for hugs and kisses. Now maybe he wasn't there *all* day, but I have a mental picture of him waiting patiently and quietly until I returned to give him food, exercise, and love. He trusted that I would return, and he trusted that I would meet all his needs.

Even when other dogs entered our family, that spot on the sofa remained Winston's. Excitement, visitors, and hyper moments did not move Winston from his place. The other dogs could not get him to budge. I had given him a "place" and that's where he waited to hear from me.

I've had many dogs, but none ever understood the concept of "place" like Winston. He knew if he waited for my word, his rewards would be great. He accepted that waiting in his place was a good thing.

Patience to wait in our "place" given by God is not a common attribute. We are nudged from our place by peer pressure and people who want company in whatever they are doing. We get in a hurry to move or experience instant gratification, when real love is just about to walk through the door.

When we feel the fast-moving stomach-tightening anxiety urging us to be moving instead of waiting, let us just be still. Let us wait. The real voice we wait for is that of our Master. Waiting is not always easy, but when we are waiting on God, we will always find a blessing meant just for us.
—d.o.

January 25
Smart Sheep

I am the good shepherd.
I know my own and my own know me.
—John 10:14

In John's gospel, Jesus says *I am* many times. "*I am* the good shepherd." "*I am* the truth." "*I am* the gate." "*I am* the resurrection." He is making a connection with the *Great I Am* in the Old Testament: "But Moses said to God, 'If I come to the Israelites and say to them, "The God of your ancestors has sent me to you," and they ask me, "What is his name?" what shall I say to them?' God said to Moses, 'I AM WHO I AM.' He said further, 'Thus you shall say to the Israelites, "I AM has sent me to you"'" (Exodus 3:13-14).

Jesus said he and his father are one. John's Gospel opens with a creation scene that rings with familiarity from Genesis 1:1: "In the beginning was the Word, and the Word was with God, and the Word was God." That Word is Jesus, who became flesh and dwelled among us. Fully human, fully divine. It's a mystery. It's a miracle. Do you realize what this means?

God has walked in your shoes.

What better shepherd could we possibly have than someone who knows his sheep that well?

Sometimes sheep are portrayed as dumb, but the point of the Good Shepherd message is to focus on the Shepherd. How could sheep be dumb for following Jesus? We are wise to keep our eyes on the Shepherd.

God never says, "I am what you perceive me to be," or "I am whatever makes sense to you . . . for today." No. God says, "I AM." What God is and who Jesus is are not concepts, but truth and being.

We know Jesus by the revelation of God. You hear a whisper in your heart say, *I am*, and you answer. The smallest heart-cry can call the Shepherd to your side.

The Good Shepherd knows you, and you know him. You know God. Do you realize what this means? You're walking in *God's* shoes!—k.m.

January 26
Is It Sin . . . If You Don't Get Caught?

"I have the right to do anything," you say—but not everything is beneficial.
"I have the right to do anything"—but I will not be mastered by anything.
—1 Corinthians 6:12

We have two dogs that have big, fluffy beds in the den where they are allowed to sleep, relax, and enjoy their chew toys. Since they also have free roam time on the farm, they get into things that aren't allowed in the house, much less on the furniture.

As long as someone is in the house with them, they are the picture of obedience. They go to their beds like good doggies. However, when we leave, they know they have the freedom to do as they like. There is no one to correct them or to see they are breaking a rule. When the temptation just becomes too great, they will sometimes inch their way onto the couch and take a nice long snooze. We know this because of the telltale shedding we find as evidence.

There are things that tempt us too. When no one's around we can get away with them. Sometimes we can even get away without getting caught. We eat something that's bad for us. We go somewhere we know in our hearts is not in our best interest. We keep company with someone who doesn't affect our lives in a positive way. Is it all right to do whatever we want as long as no one else gets hurt? What does it do to our souls when we do something that harms our bodies?

Each little negative thing we do adds up. It becomes a negativity account that destroys us. It might destroy us in increments and might not be a big deal to the rest of the world, but if it affects us negatively at all, it's not ultimately something we should be doing. We know what's right and good for us because it rings true inside us. We always recognize it as a "God thing."—d.o.

Secret Communion

Call to me and I will answer you,
and will tell you great and hidden things
that you have not known.
—Jeremiah 33:3

H ave you ever noticed how the animals seem to know so much that we don't? I trust our animals more than the weather channel to inform me that a storm is coming even before I can see a cloud in the sky. Sometimes I wonder who's really doing the caretaking. Our animals have profound instincts that are, perhaps, available to us, but often lost in the mundane and frantic existence we try to call life. They haven't forgotten how to pay attention. That's their secret. They don't fight sleep when they're sleepy; they don't fight hunger or thirst; they don't deny what they know. We have much to learn from these wordless wonders.

And they have secrets. Ever noticed that sneaky little feeling you get when you enter a room and your dog is looking at you innocently, but you know something is up? And there's the cat, sauntering into the room like nothing just happened. They're in cahoots, those two, but nobody's talking. Later you discover the loaf of bread you just bought, ripped open so that the two of them could partake of an unorthodox communion together.

Sometimes, unlike our furry friends, we are thirsty and don't even know it. Thirsty for God and for love, that is. So when you feel the urge to call to God, don't ignore it. Call, seek, respond to the urge inside that is haunting you like an angel song. God will answer. As promised, he will show you great and hidden things that he wants you to know, things that will make your life sweeter, your relationships strong and true, and your walk with the Lord rich and real.—k.m.

January 28
Cliff Climbers

They are the ones who will dwell on the heights, whose refuge will be the mountain fortress.
Their bread will be supplied, and water will not fail them.
—Isaiah 33:16

There was a time when the majestic bighorn sheep of the Rocky Mountains numbered over a million. Now they've dwindled to a fraction of those early numbers present in the newly discovered western frontier of the United States.

The males of the species crash violently into each other in head-to-head combat during mating season, their heavy circular horns fiercely defending or demanding position in the herd.

No matter the appearance of fierceness, these animals are still sheep. They live in perpetual danger. They are a food source for many, a trophy for some, and generally live in danger for the whole of their lives. Yet God created all sorts of protection for these very special creatures. First of all, they are colored to blend in with the rocky elevations, and it's almost impossible to spot a mountain sheep from a distance.

They can move up a cliff face using ledges as narrow as two inches for footholds, skimming cliffs at a speed of nearly fifteen miles per hour, bouncing from ledge to ledge covering spans as wide as twenty feet with one leap.

When it comes to food, they find scarce vegetation in cracks in the rocks and water collected in tiny streams and indentations in the craggy slopes. They use their hooves to scrape the spines off cactus, and consume the succulent moisture and nutrition inside.

Their lambs are born on some of the steepest inclines, allowing protection against any predator that might come to feast on easy prey.

In the arid, unforgiving summits of desert mountains, God provides them comfort and safety. He'll do that for us too. He will equip us with all we need to survive in the harsh climates of our lives. He'll always give us an escape route, while those who seek to destroy us are left behind on ledges below. What looks like unforgiving rocks is the provision by God for our safety.—d.o.

January 29
Love, Love, . . . and Love

Beloved, let us love one another, because love is from God;
everyone who loves is born of God and knows God.
Whoever does not love does not know God, for God is love.
—1 John 4:7-8

Sometimes it's just not easy to love one another. Sometimes we—and sometimes others—aren't very lovable. Moods and personalities clash, circumstances create tensions, and fear divides. But God commands us to love.

Love your family, the ones you know the best. This may be the greatest challenge to love, because it is with family that we are the most vulnerable. It may be easy to think God will love us, faults and all, because God is God, but our people, our loved ones, tend to strike back when we hurt them, or fail them, or just plain get on their nerves. We set high expectations on others and set ourselves up for anger and disappointment. Learn to love your family and loved ones for who they are. And love them even when they don't know how to love you back. Have compassion on them when they are down, and rejoice with them when they are happy.

And learn to love your wider circle, too: your neighbor, the people you go to church with, the people you work with, the nice lady at the pet groomer who always offers a smile and always takes such care of your baby. This love is about being kind and friendly, without ever being superficial. Don't keep the real thing locked in a safe at home when you leave. Love has different boundaries of respect in different situations, but love is still love.—k.m.

January 30
I Don't Like Spiders and Snakes

*Two of every kind of bird, of every kind of animal and of every kind of
creature that moves along the ground will come to you to be kept alive.*
—Genesis 6:20

I hate snakes. I don't even like the reptile house at the zoo. Growing up
in the swampy deltas of Louisiana, I was constantly in the presence of
snakes. Water moccasins were everywhere. Ground rattlers slithered out
of woodpiles. Copperheads and coral snakes were colorfully hidden in
leaves as we walked through the woods.

One day, as a little girl, I bent down to peer into a culvert where I loved
to catch crawfish, and as I tried to focus on the mud castles where the
crustaceans lived, what appeared to be a black stick turned into a sleeping
serpent just inches from my face. It was a cottonmouth, stretched and
cooling in the muddy water. I could hardly move. From my mouth flew
one of those silent screams where fear was greater than my body could
express.

Now, as an adult, I have come in contact with metaphoric snakes that
appear out of nowhere to tempt me, to attack me, or to distract me from
what God has prepared for me. It may be in the form of a negative attitude from a family member, financial difficulty, or insurmountable problems that make us want to give up. In those times, in the face-to-face
contact with serpents, we must call on faith to give us courage to face the
snake and deny its power over us—and sometimes, to simply give a silent
scream and back away.

Courage is never the absence of fear. Courage is going on in spite of
the fear. God provides us with armor to protect ourselves, even when we
walk in close contact with snakes we don't see until we are looking them
eye to eye. We must never overestimate the power of the snakes, or un-
derestimate the power of our God.—d.o.

Quacks Like a Duck

*Let the words of my mouth and the meditation of my
heart be acceptable to you, O LORD, my rock and my redeemer.*
—Psalm 19:14

Recently, we were staying at a beautiful resort on the bay in San Diego. Along the path between the bay and the lobby, there were all kinds of birds and one psychedelic parrot on the middle perch. He was quacking as we approached, and I wondered if the ducks felt honored or intimidated by the realistic impersonation.

As we stood in front of the magnificent bird, he took command of the conversation. He said hello several ways, with various accents apparently picked up from other visitors from around the country. He repeated some other phrases and then blew us a kiss.

Sometimes people are like parrots. We repeat what we've learned. This can be a good or bad thing. I had a Sunday school teacher who used to say, "Garbage in, garbage out!" meaning that what you feed your mind will come back out in your words and your life. When we join in gossip, we tend to repeat those stories like parrots, almost without thinking. If we don't think before we speak, we often trample the feelings or reputations of innocent people, often even people we love. When we repeat negative things, even about our own lives, we begin to believe our own fearful, faithless words and create our own rough times.

When we spend time with God, read his Word, and share in conversation with others with the same heart-set, our attitude stays in line and our words create love rather than discord. When we set our minds on good things, good things happen to our words (Colossians 3:1). Maybe it's not such a bad thing to be like a parrot; let's just make sure we repeat the best things.—k.m.

February 1
Turtle wisdom

For wisdom is better than jewels,
and all that you may desire cannot compare with her.
—Proverbs 8:11

When I was a child, I associated wisdom with the "wise old owl." Now, I think the turtle is wise too. There was a Galapagos land tortoise in the Australia Zoo named Harriet who was 175 years old when she died. They say that great wisdom comes with age. It stands to reason. I don't imagine a foolish turtle would live so long.

Wisdom is worth seeking. Do you think to pray for it? Ask God to give you wisdom. Wisdom is important enough that five books in the Bible are dedicated to it. The Wisdom literature includes Job, Psalms, Proverbs, Ecclesiastes, and Song of Solomon. The eighth Proverb is a beautiful poem giving a voice to wisdom, teaching that wisdom was there before creation. "Whoever finds me finds life and obtains favor from the LORD" (8:35). The author of the book of James says, "If any of you is lacking in wisdom, ask God, who gives to all generously and ungrudgingly, and it will be given you" (1:5). Another familiar saying from Proverbs presses an additional dimension: "The fear of the LORD is the beginning of wisdom" (9:10). *Fear* in this context means to respect the Lord, as the starting point for our learning wisdom.

Not everyone grows old and not all who grow old gain wisdom, I know, but isn't it tragic when those of us who are given good health, good fortune, and many blessings don't live life to the fullest? Wisdom is the way God guides us so that our lives can be lived well and be well worth living.

The wise old turtle appreciates life, and I daresay lives it fully as God intended turtles to live. Let's learn to be wise from Harriet.—k.m.

Hiss and Tell

This is what the LORD says to me: "As a lion growls, a great lion over its prey—and though a whole band of shepherds is called together against it, it is not frightened by their shouts or disturbed by their clamor— so the LORD Almighty will come down to do battle on Mount Zion and on its heights.
—Isaiah 31:4

A feral cat had kittens in a box in our basement. As I got near her, she hissed and intimidated me to leave her babies alone. Nothing could persuade her to leave them in the midst of my threat. Food did not tempt her. Loud noises and swift movements did not scare her. She was the provider and protector of those babies, and nothing would change that fact.

Hers was a love of super strength.

Have you ever felt you had no one to protect you that way? We become so focused on our fears and their strength to take us down, we forget about God's protection. No danger is so great, and no fear so frightening that our God is not stronger still. All the evil unleashed in the world at one time cannot shake his focus on us and our protection.

God cannot be frightened away or disturbed by the evil that comes our way. He is ever-present, and we are never alone. God sees us when we feel small, weak, feral, or invisible. He loves us when we think we are ugly and unlovable. And God hears all our prayers—even the silent ones.

So let the legions come against us. Let them try. We have protection created of pure Love itself that cannot be defeated, distracted, or destroyed. That is a love of super strength.—d.o.

February 3
Monkey Business

*Then our mouth was filled with laughter, and our tongue with shouts of joy;
then it was said among the nations, "The LORD has done great things for them."*
—Psalm 126:2

There's a little café in a wildlife park in Ethiopia where the monkeys sometimes come around begging for a bite of *Injera*, a pancake-like bread made out of *teff* flour. My daughter, Danielle, took an amazing photo of one of the little guys when she was there. He could win an Oscar for his sympathy-seeking performance. I'm sure he gathers quite a feast in the course of a day just for being cute. Monkeys are funny. They bring laughter to others and they seem full of humor themselves.

It's good to laugh. One of the Proverbs says laughter is good medicine. In Genesis, Abraham thought it was funny that a son was born to him when he was one hundred years old, so he named his son Isaac, which means laughter. Abraham's wife, Sarah, who was also very old, said, "God has brought laughter for me; everyone who hears will laugh with me" (Genesis 21:6). Laugh with joy. Laugh wholeheartedly. Laugh because life is just funny sometimes.

Sometimes in the midst of our sorrow there can be joy—even laughter—to help us through the tough times. It has been said that our sorrow is our joy in a different reflection. It has also been said that as deep as our sorrow has ever been is how high our joy can be.

We're all just a smile away from a good hearty laugh. I think God must have laughed when he made monkeys . . . and puppies and kittens . . . and aardvarks.—k.m.

February 4
Divining Rods

For we did not follow cleverly devised stories when we told you
about the coming of our Lord Jesus Christ in power,
but we were eyewitnesses of his majesty.
—2 Peter 1:16

Have you ever noticed how truthful an animal is? They are never convinced of a person's goodness unless it's authentic. My golden retriever, who loved everyone, had a few people he just plain didn't trust.

Now I, on the other hand, have been easily fooled. People who had success or money or fame could probably find their way into my trust because I admired their achievements. And, I have been hurt a lot in my life just because I wanted to be accepted and liked by people who turned out to be untrustworthy. We can be easily deceived; we buy into the fables of power and success, while the authentic truth eludes us.

When we ignore that little nagging voice of discernment in our rush to be part of a clique, we are often left feeling used. There really *are* people who seek to use us. There really *are* those who see our vulnerabilities and attach to them and suck out our joy. Once they've gotten what they want, they leave. And we are left hurting. But dogs use their built-in God-given divining rod of truth to determine trustworthiness.

We have that same rod.

God has given us an understanding of right, wrong, and truth. We are not created to be followers of the crowd. Once we get through the pain of being deceived, we have an opportunity to learn from that. If we listen to our hearts in all our dealings and relationships, we can be certain that God will lead us into the paths of his choosing and out of pain. We have a living example of the truthfulness in Christ.

And one of our greatest gifts in finding our truth-barometers is our pets, who have their own built in. They are usually better listeners to the authentic voice inside!—d.o.

True North

Then the LORD said to me: "You have been skirting this
hill country long enough. Head north."
—Deuteronomy 2:2-3

The earth has a magnetic force that points northward. People need a compass to show them true north, but many of the brilliant creatures in God's earthly kingdom full of magic and mystery somehow know when to head north and which direction that happens to be. Humpback whales, salmon, arctic terns, golden eagles, sea turtles, locusts, and, of course, the monarch butterfly, are among the species that gather to migrate north. They congregate and navigate their way home every year, driven by an unknown understanding and a life force. How do they find their way? Starlings orient themselves using the sun, while mallard ducks can find north by the stars at night. Loggerhead turtles sense the strength of the earth's magnetic field. Salmon use smell to find the exact stream where they were born. God told Israel to turn northward: "You have been skirting this hill country long enough." It was time to get on with it. It was time to be where God called them to be, to do what God called them to do. It was time to know the peace of an obedient heart in relationship with a loving God.

You are a child of God. Is your heart's compass pointing you the right direction? For every human being, there is a magnetic pull toward love, happiness, and home. Start walking. When you hear that whisper in your heart telling you to move a certain direction with your life, listen! It could be that the very thing you want so badly is the very thing that will change the world. At any rate, find your true "north," just like God's creatures.
—k.m.

February 6
The Bell Cow

Jesus went up on a mountainside and called to
him those he wanted, and they came to him.
—Mark 3:13

My grandfather, a Baptist preacher who made his living as a farmer, used to warn me about the "bell cow." In his cattle herd, he told me one cow would stand out as a loudmouth leader, so he'd put a bell around her neck. When he would call the cattle in for supper and milking, that old bell cow would answer back and lead the entire herd to the barn with her bellow and her bell clanging to and fro with every lumbering step. From time to time the loudmouth bell cow would fear a storm or an unseen worry and take it upon herself to lead the herd off in the wrong direction. And Pawpaw would find them stuck in a mud slew or across a downed fence because of that old bell cow.

In his church, he said, there were old bell cows too. There would be a person of credibility with some years in a church who'd just decide all of a sudden he or she knew better how to run things. They'd start ringing their bells of gossip and get a wave of distraction started, and before long, the church would be facing a split of some sort.

Have you ever followed a bell cow, caught up in a charismatic persuasive personality, missing the truth entirely? Have you ever ended up in the ditch when all you were doing was following someone you thought had the world by the tail, only to find they were just as lost as you were?

Every time we follow the "bell cow" instead of listening to God's voice, we'll end up far from the mountaintop. Distractions are not permanent, however, and at any moment we can turn our attention toward home, our barn, and get right back on course!—d.o.

Twelve Mountaintops

As the mountains surround Jerusalem,
so the LORD surrounds his people,
from this time on and forevermore.
—Psalm 125:2

Of all the mountains on planet earth, there are only twelve on which monarch butterflies find their homes in the winter. During this last stretch of winter on these isolated mountaintops just west of Mexico City, the monarchs reside and prepare for the long journey north, some to the United States and some to Canada. Three generations will pass during the great dispersion from the twelve mountains, and it is the great-grandchildren who will actually make new homes in many places across eastern North America.

This journey echoes the path of the ancient Hebrews. Twelve tribes of Israel scattered like the wind. Always searching for home and always getting ready to go again. For all of us, life is a perpetual journey. Every year is full of sameness and change, holding on and letting go as we all dance around the cycle of life.

And as we journey and meet those changes, it's important to remember God has promised to be with us all the way. The passage in Joshua 1:9 carries that promise with these words: "For the LORD your God is with you wherever you go."

It's hard to imagine a little butterfly making it all the way to the top of a mountain, but they do it all the time with the help of the wind. Maybe today you'll find yourself on a mountaintop, right here in the middle of winter, just like the monarch butterflies.

A monarch flies across a continent after leaving the mountaintop, with courage it doesn't even know it possesses. The monarch is just doing what monarch butterflies do, abiding where they abide, following the seasons and the wind that God set in motion long ago. God has provided for you, too, in this season. Trust. Do what you do and trust the wind—God's wind—to carry you to the next place in your journey, when the time is right.—k.m.

Light Chasing

Out in the open wisdom calls aloud, she raises her voice in the public square;
on top of the wall she cries out, at the city gate she makes her speech:
"How long will you who are simple love your simple ways?
How long will mockers delight in mockery and fools hate knowledge?"
—Proverbs 1:20-22

The kitten chased the moving beam of light back and forth from the tiny laser toy. Just as he pounced and caught the light, it moved again. Every time the little paws found the red light beam, he seemed so proud of himself. Then I'd move the light again, and away he'd go. He truly believed that he was capturing the elusive, playful light beam in his furry paws.

In the shadows, his mother yawned. She has played this game with him, too, using her tail to keep him occupied, gently swishing it back and forth as he tried to catch it. She uses the swishing tail game not only to keep her baby playing, but to teach him the survival skills of hunting. Her wisdom has come through experience and time. If her kitten pays attention and learns from her, he, too, will gain wisdom.

We are like kittens bouncing around, chasing light beams, believing we are capturing them. We are naive enough to believe that we are in control of everything in our world. We don't have the wisdom to examine the source of the lights dancing around us. We just reach out to the light, while wisdom waits for us to learn. We make mistakes when we impulsively move through life, but with each mistake we also learn how to survive. We learn that we are not in control of everything. *We learn.* Isn't that the point of this journey called life?

We will know wisdom when we have learned from the lesson of light chasing that the only true light is God's, caught for us and placed in our hearts to shine brightly in this dark world.—d.o.

Good Dogs

See, he is puffed up; his desires are not upright—
but the righteous will live by his faith.
—Habakkuk 2:4 NIV

When one of our dogs gets a "that-a-boy" or a "good-girl," they prance around the yard, step a little higher, noses in the air. They have doggie pride. It's the pride of love and self-giving—a serving heart. That kind of pride reminds me of the scripture verse above from Habakkuk. When your dog fetches a Frisbee, or comes when you call, or does his business outside instead of on the carpet in the back bedroom, he is pleased to please you, as though he didn't even know he could be so good. He's been good, "upright," you might say, because you've guided him, not because he knew how to please you on his own. He would have been perfectly happy to poop on the carpet, until you taught him to do otherwise. He has faith in your guidance. He has faith in you because he loves you. He doesn't know that he "owes" you. So, his "righteousness" is in being rightly related to his keeper—you.

We can learn from those "good dogs." On a profound level they can teach us something about a servant's heart, about pure motives and actions that are filled with gratitude. Love need not be mingled with self-centered pride. Real love is infused with faith. Your dog has a love-infused faith in you. And you, a love-infused faith in God. Our right relationship with God empowers us to love others with God's love, and all that right-relatedness is what righteousness is all about.

The miracle of God's love is made clear through the gift of Jesus. In love, he emptied himself in the ultimate sacrifice of self (Philippians 2:5-11).

Today, I will have faith in God to put pure, righteous love in my heart.
—k.m.

One Voice

Listen to what the LORD says: "Stand up, plead my case before the mountains;
let the hills hear what you have to say."
—Micah 6:1

The Great Pyrenees is a dog whose breed originated in the mountain regions of France as far back as 1800 B.C. They are often used to shepherd sheep. These dogs have a heavy double coat that enables them to be an effective deterrent to predators of sheep or goats.

Our family decided we needed a Pyrenees to help protect our farm from coyotes, so we located a rescue that had Great Pyrenees-collie mix puppies, where we picked out Jack, a little fluffy teddy bear. That small, cuddly stage lasted about a week. Pretty soon his feet were the size of feed buckets and his head was about the size of a garbage can lid. As we began to train him, we realized this big animal's feelings were easily hurt. He would literally become embarrassed at each correction, bury his big old head in his gigantic paws and cry. *Some guard dog,* we thought.

Then something happened. Instinct began to kick in, and this hairy beast began to run sentry around the outer edge of our farm, bellowing his baritone bass, intimidating coyotes, keeping them away from the farm with his powerful bark.

Jack's bark was his greatest weapon against the coyote packs. When his voice echoed across the valley, he sounded eight feet tall. When Jack was healing from hot spots and had to wear a bell collar, he seemed thrilled with the effect of his voice, magnified to huge megaphone proportions. Jack literally sang across the valley, enjoying the power amplified by the huge plastic collar.

As children of God, sometimes we are called to sit quietly waiting for God's instruction. But other times we are called to boldness, to use our voice to stand up for what we believe in and to make our beliefs known. Then our voice, like Jack's with the coyotes, can be used for good.—d.o.

February 11
Daisy the Wonder Dog

I believe; help my unbelief!
—Mark 9:24b

I met Daisy the three-legged Dalmatian long after the trauma that caused her handicap and nearly cost her life. For the first time, when I heard her story, I realized how cruel people can be, how apathetic. I met her after someone ran over her and left her. It was also clear she had been abused. A tight chain had been around her neck for so long that it was imbedded and infected. If my friend and cowriter Devon had not come along that road when she did, Daisy would have died. It was touch and go for many weeks. But she survived, and now she can run as fast on those three legs as the other dogs can. She's an amazing story. She's Daisy the Wonder Dog.

She's a bit edgy, as you can imagine. Her battle scars are not only physical. When we were first getting to know each other, she had to learn how to trust me. She was comfortable enough with me, but I quickly learned to be a little extra gentle with her so she wouldn't think I was going to hit her or punish her unfairly. Slowly she began to expect love rather than abuse from me.

She wants to believe in human kindness. When I pet her, she casts her big brown eyes up at me and makes the effort to wag her tail (which is not so easy when you are missing a hind leg), as if to say, "I believe in you, that you will be good to me. Help me even when I don't believe."

"I believe; help my unbelief." Those are the words spoken to Jesus in Mark's Gospel. Sometimes our faith and doubts live inside us at the same time, but if we love one another, faith will overcome in the end, with comfort, grace, and forgiveness. Daisy has helped my unbelief turn to faith, by her own growing faith in us.—k.m.

February 12
Run for the Hills

The Sovereign LORD is my strength; he makes my feet like the feet of a deer,
he enables me to tread on the heights.
—Habakkuk 3:19

Her gaze was still. She didn't move a hair as she stared at me. The beautiful deer paused mid-bite as I pulled slowly into the driveway. As she watched me, it was as if she was weighing whether I was something she could ignore, or a danger from whom she should escape. Without warning, she turned with white tail waving and headed across the gulch, her tiny feet appearing to barely touch the ground. She looked like she was flying!

She didn't cast a glance back at me, just moved with surefooted ease up the steep wooded hill across the pasture. She didn't miss a step. She didn't falter. She ran. She flew!

When the deer was created, its greatest gift of defense was the ability to outrun the enemy. The deer was not equipped to fight with teeth and brawn. The deer was equipped to get away.

Of course I had no intention of hurting the deer, but her instinct said *run*, and she did. We get instinctual warnings too. Have you ever felt that little tug inside you that says, *Turn and walk away. Run from this place or this person. Avoid this party. Don't take this job?*

When we are in tune with God's voice, we are equipped with the ability to discern the truth of our situation.

Have you ever felt unsure about something but done it anyway only to find your initial feelings were right on the money? When we ask God's guidance in all our decisions, business dealings, and relationships, God will guide us. It is up to us to listen. When necessary, it is up to us to run, fleet-footed up the mountain.—d.o.

I Beg Your Pardon, You Trampled My Rose Garden

Beloved, since God loved us so much, we also ought to love one another.
—1 John 4:11

One would think that love would be the most natural thing in the world to do. After all, we cannot live without it, and according to the Scripture, it is something God commands us to do, so it must be doable. Love, in other words, is one of life's nonnegotiables, not an option. Gotta have it, gotta give it, by God's design.

It is important to remember that love is not a mere emotion; it is an action. The writer of 1 John defines it clearly in chapter 3, verse 18, when he writes, "let us love, not in word or speech, but in truth and action."

Sometimes saying "I love you" with a hug and a smile is just enough; but other times love means spending the day at the bedside of a loved one in the hospital. Sometimes love means forgiving someone who may not even seem to deserve your forgiveness.

We are commanded to love no matter what. That's the way God loves us. It's unconditional. Do you ever wonder why it seems so much easier to love our pets unconditionally than people? If your best friend scratched up the furniture or chewed the heels off of your favorite shoes or trampled your rose garden, this person may not be your best friend for long! In a way, our friends do trample our rose gardens sometimes, with harsh words or careless actions. The important thing to remember is that we all make mistakes or act selfishly sometimes.

God's love invites us to love one another without question, through thick and thin, with words, actions, and respect.

Love, real love, for animals and for people, is not only possible, it is required. Today, let unconditional love begin with you.—k.m.

February 14
Bridges of Love

Love never fails.
—1 Corinthians 13:8a

Imet Jewel in a club in downtown Nashville. At his side was a beautiful black and white border collie he called Hussey. Jewel was homeless by definition. But as people passed him on the street, they waved and called the pair by name. For a homeless person, Jewel seemed right at home.

As Jewel began to tell me his story, he was served a bowl of chili by the waiter without his even ordering it. He told me that this club had "hired" him to watch over the place and keep out the riff-raff. For that, they let him sleep on the floor after closing, and he got his meals free.

He shared his poetry with me. Jewel was a gifted writer who created poetry from all he saw, but the other parts of his life, he couldn't figure out. He had an old van that served as a residence when the weather permitted. He had found Hussey when she was a puppy, and the two had become fast friends. Hussey was the only family Jewel had. She kept him warm in the winter and won the hearts of passersby on the streets. While he might have been a homeless person that no one cared to make eye contact with, it was Hussey who won people's attention and always brought in a buck or two here and there.

We as human beings need love. We hunger for it. You. Me. Jewel. All of us in society, the privileged and those considered "untouchables" of society *need* touch, affection, and attachment to another heart. All of us get our hearts broken and feel separated from the rest of the world sometimes. When God hears a heart break, he continuously sends bridges of love, to reconnect us to him.

If you look around today, can you see some of those bridges?—d.o.

February 15
If I were a Butterfly

He gives power to the faint, and strengthens the powerless . . .
but those who wait for the LORD shall renew their strength.
—Isaiah 40:29, 31

Somewhere today there is a monarch butterfly, sleeping deeply and dreaming of days to come. Soon it will be time for her to stir from her slumber and take flight. She will know when it is time to fly by the way the wind brushes her wings and whispers in her soul. She will know by the way the sun sends its warm rays to energize her.

For four months, she has been waiting, fragile as a tear and weary from a long flight. She flew longer than anyone thought possible. She rests so that she will have the strength to fly again. She is a fourth-generation monarch, the one called upon to fly the highest and the longest distances. The other monarchs live only six weeks, if they're lucky, but she will live eight months or more after she leaves the chrysalis. She and her companions look like a billion fragments of mosaic silk, diaphanous against the blue sky.

Sometimes we are like the monarch butterfly. We need rest, not just for our bodies, but for our souls. So, we wait in the safety of the arms of God, who created us for this day and every day that has gone before and every day to come.

Today, perhaps as you dream, you feel the quiet, lonely hush of knowing that you alone must spread your wings in response to the gentle breeze that will soon beckon you to move. Your walk with God is yours alone, and it is from the quiet times of waiting upon the Lord that you find strength for the rest of the journey.

Allow your soul to be still, and do not be afraid of what lies ahead. It's the season of believing. The winds of change are just around the corner, and you can be ready with hope renewed and the Spirit as your guide.
—k.m.

February 16
Grrrrrr!

Seek good, not evil, that you may live.
Then the LORD God Almighty will be with you, just as you say he is.
—Amos 5:14

Animals are like good and evil meters. Have you ever noticed that? Animals respond to innate goodness and innate evil.

I had a Great Dane named Sophie who was the biggest, goofiest dog in the world. She was a comedienne with feet the size of my hands. This dog got her head stuck in garbage pails, sat on a chair like a human with her legs crossed, and howled musically every time I sang. Sophie was just a big cuddle bug and loved everyone.

Then, one day we were out walking, and a maintenance man from our neighborhood association approached us. He always gave me a creepy feeling, as if he were watching me. My spirit kept warning me, but I ignored the feelings.

When the man got closer, Sophie pulled ahead of me and stood between him and me. Her hackles raised, a deep guttural growl began, and she turned into a wild woman! The man froze. I thought my "gentle giant" was going to have this man for lunch. A few weeks later, I was told he was arrested for breaking and entering some of the homes in the neighborhood.

People have built-in good and evil meters too. The Holy Spirit in us tells us about others, but also ourselves: where we belong or what places we should avoid, which might be harmful. He doesn't ever change those standards of the meter. He'll never order us to drop our integrity standards because business is business. He doesn't ever tell us to go into debt and not pay our bills to be closer to him. He does not ever tell us to be harsh to our children to make them better people. What he does tell us, that interior meter, is to seek good, always. And when we seek good, we find it.—d.o.

February 17
The Secret Code

I am the LORD your God.
—Leviticus 19

Sometimes when we come back home after a busy day, our dogs, cats, and horses look at us like they know something that we don't. I wonder what happened while we were away. It's just a funny feeling I get, but, of course, nobody's talking. I think they have a secret code—*Here they come, you guys, act normal.* During my daily prayer time, I always thank God for keeping us all safe and sound, and together, through all the crazy antics and codes, both seen and unseen.

Codes. We all live by them, really. Unspoken rules. Expectations. They are borne of tradition and history. They are galvanized within families and culture. Codes are not bad. We need them. Kindness is a code. Love is a code. It's a rule to live by, the secret to peace, happiness, and the fulfillment of your dreams.

We must know who made the code by which we live. God expected Israel to know why they should follow the holiness code, so he said it many times. "I am the LORD your God." This phrase runs poetically through Leviticus 19, like the chorus of a song. You can't get to the "how-to" of a good life until you get to the "why." We are created in the image of God, designed to be loved by God. There is a standard. A code that we cannot change. "This is what love is," God tells us, "because this is who I am."

Because we may not be used to it, at first, God's code may be confusing. Because unselfishness, kindness, compassion, and passionate care and concern for God's creation are not very . . . well, common or businesslike. But we can change the way we do business and life and live by God's code. *Act normal*; that is, *normal* by God's standard.—k.m.

February 18
May I Present to You This Beautiful Mouse?

There is a time for everything,
and a season for every activity under the heavens.
—Ecclesiastes 3:1a

We have two identical cats we like to refer to as The Schmengee Brothers, a fictional polka duo from a 1980s comedy show. This morning, one of the Schmengees was sitting at the back door with a field mouse that had met its little mouse doom in Schmengee's paws. Schmengee just sat there with his mouse, waiting for praise. Farm cats take their job of rodent hunting very seriously. They also are doing what instinct tells them to do. I feel sorry for the mouse, but both cat and mouse are simply living out the circle of life.

Life lessons through animals can almost always be found when we pay attention to moments like these. We have to broaden our scope and see the big picture. Our journey is filled with ebbs and flows and we live in a circle of life, too, that often can seem vicious. And it seems the tighter we hold on, the harder it is to hold on to anything.

The circle of life is something that everyone lives in; all share the same struggles. God isn't giving prizes to all the good people and punishing all the bad ones. He doesn't grant champagne wishes to the people who read their Bibles every day. People who are in God's hand are not promised they'll be better off with no more trials or cares in life. Quite the contrary! God's children are faced with hardships and hurts throughout their lives, but we live in the promise that we will never face the tough times alone. We have a comfort and a shield for those times. Every impossible pain we experience, every loss, and every broken heart refines our faith. How would we ever know we had faith if we were never given the chance to use it?

The circle of life begins with birth and ends with death with only a given number of days in between. Let us learn to open our hands and let life flow through them, experiencing more, loving more, and sharing more.—d.o.

February 19

Who Saw the Angel?

The donkey said to Balaam, "Am I not your own donkey, which you have ridden all your life to this day? Have I been in the habit of treating you this way?" And he said, "No."
—Numbers 22:30

The biblical book of Numbers contains one of the most hilarious and tragic stories in the Bible, about Balaam. Balaam was a foreign prophet-for-hire, a non-Israelite who had pledged to obey Israel's God.

One day, he saddled up his donkey and headed off down the road, thinking he was going exactly where the Lord was leading. Suddenly, there was a fierce angel standing in the way, sword in hand. Seeing it, the donkey froze and refused to go on. Balaam couldn't see anything, so he struck the donkey and threatened to kill her for making a fool of him. That's when God opened the donkey's mouth and allowed her to give the abuser a piece of her mind. She reminded Balaam the she had been a faithful donkey and did not deserve to be so mistreated. Finally, Balaam saw the angel, who pointed out to him that the donkey had saved his life.

Balaam thought he was on the right path, but when the Lord directed him another way, Balaam was the stubborn one, and he wound up reprimanded by his donkey. We can learn a lesson from Balaam, to listen to the Lord every step of the way. Sometimes he leads us down a path that will have many twists and turns as we go! But there is, perhaps, even a greater lesson to learn from Balaam. Be kind to your animals and by all means, listen to them. They may be smarter than you are, or better yet, they may see the angels all around us.—k.m.

February 20
Sing, Sweet Bird . . . Your Cage Is Open

Sing, Daughter Zion; shout aloud, Israel!
Be glad and rejoice with all your heart, Daughter Jerusalem!
—Zephaniah 3:14

Rescuing animals from dire situations calls for a special person. The work is difficult. Any animal taken from a neglected or abusive situation is not always loving and grateful. Sometimes they are downright mean, literally biting the hand that feeds them. Hurt manifests in a variety of ways before love can begin to heal it.

Among the manifestations are these:

"I hurt, so I must hurt you."

"I have been hurt, so I require extra care and over-the-top attention."

"I hurt, so I just want to be left alone."

Animals respond to pain in so many different ways that it becomes hard for people to help even if they really want to.

Some abused animals cower and are never quite able to trust again. Have you ever felt like that? Do you react to love and attention by withdrawing, putting up emotional walls, and becoming hard to reach? The ones who hurt the most seem to be the ones who push love away the hardest.

Are people trying to reach out to you right now, people you have held at bay with unreachable standards? Are you asking for perfection from people just because you have been hurt so deeply you feel you deserve more than what is humanly possible? God delivers us from our abusers, but what good is deliverance if nothing changes about us? If we choose to be imprisoned by our pasts, our gift of freedom is never realized. God wants us to be free to be loved again. Bring your hurt heart to him, so he can put love where hurt has too long resided.—d.o.

February 21
A Windy Day

It is the spirit that gives life.
—John 6:63

There is so much life around you every morning when you have animals to love. The dogs wake up exuberant—tails wagging and glad you're finally up. The cat may have given you a wake-up call with a gentle paw to the cheek. Outside the window there is activity all around, the quiet bustle of a winter day. Every morning is like the first morning, somehow. Every day has its own energy, its own breath, its own gift.

It's Spirit. Without it, we're a still life, a two-dimensional memory of moments past. It is the Spirit who animated the world on the first day of creation. It's the Spirit who will animate life today.

In Hebrew, the word for spirit is *ruach*. The *ruach* hovered over the face of the waters in Genesis chapter one. *Ruach* is also the word used for *wind* and *breath*. Every breath you take today is *ruach*, the Spirit of God giving you life.

Jesus compared the Spirit to the wind. "The wind blows where it chooses, and you hear the sound of it, but you do not know where it comes from or where it goes. So it is with everyone who is born of the Spirit" (John 3:8). Take joy in all the gift of this new day. The Spirit of God is blessing you with abundant life. There is no telling what the day will bring, but you can count on the promise that God's presence is *hovering* over, taking care of you every stretch of the way.—k.m.

February 22
The Comfort Rod

Whoever spares the rod hates their children, but the one who loves their children is careful to discipline them.
—Proverbs 13:24

Fancy wouldn't load in the trailer, which looked like a dark noisy cavern of danger to her. I had little experience with horses, so I deferred to the people who said they knew better. The sound of shouting and whips did nothing to make the frightened horse load in the trailer. You could see her try, but it was just so frightening. One trainer said, "If you don't make her load this time, she never will." She whipped until Fancy's eyes were ringed with white and the horse let out a horrible scream, dropping down on her knees.

It was clear that chasing fear by adding more was excruciating for Fancy. I grabbed the whip from the trainer and helped Fancy back to her stall, where I brushed her until she stopped shaking.

The following week, I took Fancy back to the trailer. This time I got in the trailer first with some sweet feed and some sweet-smelling hay. Then, moving around her, I used a gentle hand, nudging her toward the feed. I helped her put one foot on the trailer, then another. Slowly, she moved to the hay, and we quietly closed the door behind her. The horse was in the trailer: no trauma, no fear . . . just dinner and a gentle voice.

I love passages in Scripture that talk about the good, gentle Shepherd who uses his rod and staff to rescue the lost lamb. The words of Psalm 23 say, "Your rod and your staff, they comfort me." The psalm doesn't say, "Your rod and staff beat me, and through that, I'll become a better person." I heard a preacher say once that instead of a disciplinary rod, he used a fishing rod. Every time his children would do something good, he would take them fishing!

Let us use comfort and kindness to create the world we want all around us. When we correct with kindness, we get kindness in return. Isn't that what we want in the first place?—d.o.

February 23
Fearless Faith

Do not fear, for I am with you, do not be afraid, for I am your God; I will strengthen you,
I will help you, I will uphold you with my victorious right hand.
—Isaiah 41:10

Lily is a sweet black dog who came to live with us when we agreed to board her big brother, Jack the horse. The two are inseparable, so we gave her the first stall on the right. We made her a cozy home with a doggie igloo and plenty of straw, which she prefers over the blanket.

Lily is old and wise. She can only hobble around because she has stiff joints, and her eyes are milky with cataracts, but she gets where she wants to go. She rarely comes up to the house with the other dogs.

One day, there was a severe weather warning, though the sky was perfectly sunny. With hardly a cloud in the sky, Lily came up to the house and found shelter in the hay bales we had stacked under the carport. She had not seen the weather channel, but she had gotten the message somehow that it was time to take cover.

An hour or so later, a strong wind arrived so suddenly and with such force that we barely made it to the basement. My son heard the thunderous roar first and yelled that we should take cover. Hail the size of golf balls began to slash the window screens. We were not in the basement for even sixty seconds and it was over. A tornado had twisted through, leaving a trail of damage. We immediately checked on the animals, and there was Lily, safe and dry, peeking out from the house of hay.

I thought of the Isaiah verse encouraging us not to fear, and realized that Lily had exemplified fearless faith in action. She must have heard that still small voice guide her to a safe place, and God was surely with her. She was not even trembling after the storm, but looked quite calm and content.

Today, listen closely for God's guiding voice in all of your circumstances. Lily's fearless faith is available to all of us, all the time.—k.m.

February 24
Whale Song

The second angel sounded his trumpet, and something like a huge mountain, all ablaze, was thrown into the sea. A third of the sea turned into blood, a third of the living creatures in the sea died, and a third of the ships were destroyed.
—Revelation 8:8-9

A recent story told of a gray whale that had become ensnared in a man-made spider web of fishing nets and mooring ropes. She tried her best to swim, but every movement caught her more tightly in the nets. Her struggles weakened her to such a state that her future seemed dismal. Then a fisherman spotted her and called an environmental group, who quickly responded.

The only way they could help the gray whale was to dive into the water with knives to try and free the poor girl, cutting strand by strand before she drowned. The clock for her was ticking loudly. And the danger for the divers was dire because even an unintentional swish of the powerful tail would kill a human being.

Those there weighed the consequences, but the decision was made after they saw her eyes. They said, I need help or I will die. The team furiously began to free her. One rope, one net at a time, they fell away. As the last one dropped, the whale seemed to joyfully swim in circles. She swam back to each one of the divers and looked them in the eye, nuzzled them, and seemed to thank them before she joined the migration that awaited her. The divers cried.

Our lives are also mired with traps of human creation—sometimes we even create our own nets. Our pasts wrap around us as we struggle to breathe. But we have a Father-diver who frees our spirit, allowing us the freedom of the life force of the whale!—d.o.

February 25
Cats of Thousands

Let your "Yes" be yes and your "No" be no.
—James 5:12

One of the best things about having a thirty-acre farm is plenty of space for our animal friends. We're not the kind of family who easily says no to cute kittens and puppies or to adult animals in need of rescue.

One day, a friend told me she had rescued a black cat from a drainage ditch. She couldn't keep it, so she asked me if I would please take it. "Sure!" I said, "I have a thirty-acre farm!" We already had four happy outdoor cats that often slept in the barn. One more would hardly make a big difference. Soon after we said yes to the drainage-ditch cat, we rescued four more. By cat number thirteen, we finally learned to say no.

The math doesn't even equal a cat per acre, but about ten of these cats *really* want to see what's going on in the house. They wait behind the storm glass, looking like the cast of a Broadway musical, and at the first crack of an open door, they dash in. And once hidden, they can't be found. Needless to say, herding them takes a lot of time. They'll make you late. They'll hide until you're gone. And if they can't get in the house, they'll try and stow away in your car.

One thing our animals have taught us is how to keep our word. When you say yes to them, they'll hold you to it. "You're going to love me," they demand, and soon through every frustration, scratched-up chair, or computer key ripped off your laptop, you find your heart melting when they curl up beside you purring affectionately.

You might say they gave us the repeat opportunity to show consistency, love, and a kept word—a Christ-like nature.—k.m.

February 26
Wisdom Scars

Your love, LORD, reaches to the heavens, your faithfulness to the skies.
—Psalm 36:5

His name was Earl, a tiny gray kitten born feral in my friend's barn. Earl spent the next several weeks comfortably snuggled in the front pocket of my overalls. As he got older, he got in a fight with a neighbor cat that got the best of him with a swat to the ear. It abscessed and Earl Kitty let me take care of the dressings each night. It healed, but the ear always hung lower, tilted, like a fedora.

When we moved to the farm, Earl was so disconcerted he disappeared into the night. We searched, but Earl was gone.

Years passed, and we saw nothing of Earl. I kept feeling that he was out there somewhere, afraid, watching from afar.

Then one day, I saw a flash of gray run into the storage shed. I followed the flash and saw a gray tail swishing behind an old barrel. I walked around it to find a big-headed gray cat, hissing with a loud warning to stay away. His eyes were sea-foam green. He was wild as he could be, but on his ear was the tell-tale scar.

Survival in the wild had turned Earl into an almost unrecognizable shadow of his former self, but love eventually lured him back home.

We become scarred and torn when the wild world perverts our souls with sins unmentionable in order to survive. We don't even look like ourselves anymore. But love reaches back and our memories of it begin to restore us. It turns out love misses us when we are gone.—d.o.

Cliff Hangers

The badgers are a people without power, yet they make their homes in the rocks.
—Proverbs 30:26

There is a rodent native to Israel called the rock badger. In the Old Testament, it was called the *shaphan,* but many English translations use the word *coney.*

The "badger" the biblical writer spoke of lived in the mountainous region of Israel, where they could stay dry during the winter rains. The writer wants us to learn from these animals. They are frail and afraid, but they know what to do about their dilemma—hide in a safe place! They hide in the clefts of the rocks, away from anything that can harm them. The writer of Proverbs 30 encourages us to run to the rock like they do, and God is that rock, our refuge and strength.

How do you make God your refuge? When you are afraid, alone, or your heart is breaking, pray. Call on the Gentle Shepherd, and he will cover you, protect you from the rain. And if you are in such a dark place that your prayers feel empty or Scripture's precious pages don't speak, call a friend or a church, and reach out for encouragement from others who know the Lord.

Having God as your refuge during hard times can begin during the good times. Life with God is a way of being and knowing, a heart-set of faith, an understanding carved out of relationship with him. You call on the people you trust, but that trust is established day in, day out, one coffee date at a time. The same is true with God. We need to "make our home" in the rock of his presence.

Knowing where to run and hide is the secret to the little biblical animal's survival. It's ours too.—k.m.

The Seeing Eye Cow

You will be ever hearing but never understanding;
you will be ever seeing but never perceiving.
—Matthew 13:14b

The animal rescue farm needed help desperately for its many animals with special needs. While the drought sent hay and feed prices for animals soaring, farms were being forced to cut back on everything.

The rescue had taken in a blind pony from a man who was going to take him to the slaughterhouse. Not knowing how he would fare at the rescue farm, they gave the sightless fur ball his own paddock. He learned his parameters quickly. He adapted right away, but it was soon apparent that a horse, even a blind one, is a herd animal. The little blind pony was lonely. Even though well fed and cared for, his heart was broken, so he began to fade away from life. He was blind, but he knew that *survival* is far different from *living*. Life requires connection to another living being.

A strange partnership formed when a crippled calf came to the rescue farm. No one could have imagined that he would become the answer to a prayer. Put in the paddock with the blind pony, the calf limped over to share sniffs and greetings. As the calf grew, the bond between equine and bovine became strong and solid. The blind pony now had his very own seeing eye cow.

Our souls see each other without sight, without hearing, and without preconceived notions of what "should be." This comes as a gift from God to ease our loneliness. When our souls see each other as we are and they reach out for love, a safe environment and a forgiving place in the world is created—a shared spiritual paddock.—d.o.

February 29
Herding Cats

For the Lord disciplines those whom he loves,
and chastises every child whom he accepts.
—Hebrews 12:6

Josie was the courageous survivor of a flood so devastating that houses were floating down highways and hotel lobbies were capsized ships. Josie runs like a greyhound, with expressive brown eyes full of sadness and gratitude. She has an intensity about her that is not quite desperate, but not quite settled.

Since the flood, she now lives, works, and plays as if she's found paradise on our farm as she chases turkeys, sings with the train, and helps feed the horses. She herds everything: the cars, the children, and most effectively, the cats. She especially likes to herd cats when we are watching. At first, we thought she was chasing them for recreation, like a normal dog, but once I noticed her pattern and the way she would look back at us for approval during the chase, I realized her herding gifts. One day, I watched her get seven of our cats, one by one, all onto the same table, where they sat hissing down at her with obedient disdain. It was an amazing feat.

Josie does not dislike our cats. They're *her* cats now. She loves them. She feels responsible for them and guides them with authority. Josie's authority sometimes reminds me of how it is with God. In order to take care of us, sometimes it is necessary for God to guide us with the authority of conviction—even chastening. We might feel a prick in our heart about harsh words we've said or a poor choice we've made or for not taking care of our body. God through his Holy Spirit reminds us, and he invites us (herds us) to his feast of love and peace and joyous living at his table. At first, we may misunderstand and try to get away, until we realize that we are being guided by grace and we are shepherded through God's love.—k.m.

Howling Your Heart Out

Praise him with the clash of cymbals,
praise him with resounding cymbals.
—Psalm 150:5 NIV

Our dog Josie can't sing. She tries, but it sounds more like sustained screeching. The first time she hit the barnyard cabaret, we thought she was hurt, but as we rushed to her, there she was with her companion canines, Jack and Jessie, nose upward, trying to howl at the train. Jack has a beautiful baritone voice. Jessie has a sweet country-girl voice. Veronique knows her vocal limitations and chooses to simply watch or sometimes bark along like a rhythm section. Josie, however, is blissfully oblivious to the concept that singing is supposed to sound song-like. She sings in dissonant harmony with the other dogs.

I imagine our praises swirling around heaven blessing the Lord are in dissonant harmony with the host of angels. How could we not be a cacophony of noise and clatter? What must the song of the human race sound like to heaven?

Probably a lot like clashing cymbals. Religious differences, cultural differences, personality differences . . . what a crazy choir.

Some days I can hardly get my song to rise. I feel pulled by the undertow of stress, culture, and confusion. There are days when my heart simply doesn't sing. But, I sing anyway. That's what I learned from Josie.

We can trust that, as we all give it all we've got, living in his grace and learning to love one another as God loves, then God will turn our collective song into a truly beautiful song of praise that will reflect his glory on earth as it is in heaven.

What's stopping you today from dreaming big, from singing loud and long for the sheer joy of it? There's a crescendo echoing up the mountain. Want to join the chorus?—k.m.

The Kindness of Strangers

For God will bring every deed into judgment,
including every hidden thing, whether it is good or evil.
—Ecclesiastes 12:14

I have a friend, an executive with a deep love for animals, who, every day on his way to work, drove by a dog, noticing the creature and its environment. This particular dog was chained outside the owner's home with no dog house in sight. As the weather got hot, my friend started for work earlier each morning, giving himself enough time to leave a big bowl of water and food anonymously for the dog.

Each time, the dog looked up at him with a grateful glance as he drank the water as if he were in a desert and this a once-in-a-lifetime rain. This ritual was repeated daily, and the dog began to wait in happy anticipation for his new friend. Another anonymous present one night was a big dog house. Then he added a portable dog kennel with a cover. With every new gift, the time he spent with the dog created a bond.

So, one evening when he saw a car in the driveway, he stopped and knocked on the door. The owner of the dog turned out to be a nice person who had just taken on more than he was ready for with a dog. He wasn't mean. He was overworked and underpaid, and his circuits were just completely overloaded when it came to his life, and his dog's care was just a reflection of that overload. As he spoke with my friend, he began looking relieved at the prospect of his dog going to a new home.

Instead of instantly criticizing the young man for his poor care of the dog, my friend spoke of his own growing love and attachment to the animal. Change did not happen because of judgment but because of love, the only true motivation for good.

All the good works in the world don't pave our way into heaven. All our bad deeds don't keep us out. To God, every heart and motivation is transparent, and he compassionately deals with all he sees.—d.o.

March 3
Lost and Crowned

When I look at your heavens, the work of your fingers, the moon and the stars
that you have established; what are human beings that you are
mindful of them, mortals that you care for them?
Yet you have made them a little lower than God, and
crowned them with glory and honor.
—Psalm 8:3-5

The psalmist writes that we are crowned with glory and honor: you, me, and all human beings. In Psalm 8, the psalmist does not specify which human beings are crowned with glory and honor; he doesn't declare this distinction only for Israel or the righteous. Human beings are simply part of the work of God's hands. We are crowned with glory and honor because God made us so.

To say we are crowned is to say we are granted royal status, and what that looks like is dominion over the works of God's hands. *Dominion* is a tricky word. The Hebrew poet who was so inspired to write these words must have been caught up in a moment of awe and wonder.

The idea of "dominion over" might make us think that animals were created only for our pleasure and service. We can rest assured that the psalmist was speaking from a place of both our service and that of the creatures being a humble task. The animals and, in fact, the earth are a gift, as are our caretaking responsibilities. In the second chapter of the book of Zechariah, for example, the Lord is going to measure Jerusalem, and it will be immeasurable because of the multitude of people and animals in it. What a blessing!

Jesus taught us what our crown really means—we wear the crown of a servant, just like he did. One who rules in God's kingdom is called to rule with love and righteousness, empathy, and compassion. It is only through Christ that we obtain the crown God intended.—k.m.

Compassionate Wisdom

The wise have eyes in their heads, while the fool walks in the darkness;
but I came to realize that the same fate overtakes them both.
—Ecclesiastes 2:14

The pit bull barked incessantly behind a chain-link fence, waiting for his master to return. Days later, he was still waiting. A medical volunteer working in the flooded region kept passing the dog and couldn't get him out of her mind. Finally, she stopped to get a closer look, and saw diesel fuel and burns on the dog's emaciated body. She also found him to be a sweet dog, not a vicious bully as his barking suggested.

As the volunteer began investigating, she discovered that none of the neighbors knew whom the dog belonged to. They all said he had just been there waiting for days. No one had fed or watered him, thinking that someone else would.

As the volunteer continued looking in the area and out in the bayou, she saw the bottom of a capsized boat that had floated to the surface. Authorities joined the volunteer and found the body of the dog's owner underneath it. Based on what they found, they determined that the man had been trying to get to safety or help other people get to safety when the gas tank on his small boat exploded. The man had drowned, and his dog swam through the burning fuel to the bank. His canine friend had continued to bark faithfully, trying to get someone to help his master.

It is up to us to be compassionate when disaster strikes. We are called to reach out to a brother or sister or creature in need, as part of the same family, God's family. We are called to give our time, our money, and our kindness wherever we find need. None of us are islands immune to pain, and sooner or later, we will all need someone's help.

That is who God made us to be: helpers. We are called. We are the answer.—d.o.

March 5
Religious Reasons

Religion that is pure and undefiled before God, the Father,
is this: to care for orphans and widows in their distress.
—James 1:27

Tyrone, our cat, is old. He's outlived each of his nine lives and looks like a caricature of himself now. His teeth are gone, he sneezes all the time, and even though he sometimes has trouble jumping up onto the cat table, he can still dash through the kitchen door just before it closes if he really wants to be inside. He goes straight to the refrigerator and waits for someone to open it. He's a walking lesson in resilience and attitude. He's not exactly rude; he simply doesn't care what anyone thinks.

He has his own private nurse: Josie the dog. She seems to know when Tyrone is hurting. She massages him gently, using her teeth and muzzle. It almost seems as though Tyrone is telling her, "Now a little to the left . . . great . . . now could you get that shoulder blade?" She even cleans his ears. Tyrone is soaking wet by the time she is finished, but he seems to feel better.

Josie is a perfect example of the lesson James presents to us in chapter one. Religion, he says, is about helping those in need.

People get hung up on the idea of religion sometimes. James reassures us that *religion* is not a bad word. Religion that is pure and undefiled is something the world needs. It must emanate from the heart and show in our actions, especially toward those who often are forgotten by the world.

When we allow our actions, even our giving ones, to come under God's holy scrutiny, we end up with motives that are pure, with actions divinely guided, and with wisdom to know how to help those in need. When we keep our lives constantly before God through prayer, time in the Word, and worship, we learn to live by the Spirit. And natural fruits of the Spirit result in goodness, mercy, and good deeds.—k.m.

March 6
The Horse's Ax

Does the ax raise itself above the person who swings it, or the saw boast against the one who uses it? As if a rod were to wield the person who lifts it up, or a club brandish the one who is not wood!
—Isaiah 10:15

I watched the muscles rippling on the sweat-glistening thoroughbred as he victoriously crossed the finish line. As the crowd went wild with winning tickets clutched closely and losing tickets littering the floor of the stands in piles, people congratulated the high stakeholders as they gleefully went to collect their money.

The jockey was soon interviewed by the press as to how he did it. The owners of the horse were lauded for knowing a winner when they see one. The trainer got credit too. The sponsors of the race highlighted the underwriting for the event. Everyone danced around, pinning medals on themselves as the winning pony, the real hero of the race, was walked past the crowd to be cooled down and bedded for the night. Yes, everyone was part of training and recognizing the horse's greatness, but just as "the ax" should not be forgotten by the one who chops with it, the horse shouldn't be forgotten by the one who rides.

Pride pops up in some odd places, even when we don't realize it as we praise the outcome of our talents rather than the Source that made it possible. Our talents are a gift from God; we are his conduits, not his peacocks. When we give God the glory for our glories, we place first things first. We lift God up, and God helps us put things in perspective—giving praise to God and to those things that deserve praise, rather than focusing on ourselves.

Does this mean that we should never accept praise, be awarded or lauded for our accomplishments? Of course not! But we must always know the source of our strength. We are here to shine like stars. We are here to do great things. God created each of us to be his heart on this earth. What a brilliant chance to become all we are to be!—d.o.

The Alligator and the Heron

Let the peace of Christ rule in your hearts.
—Colossians 3:15

On a recent trip to Florida, my daughter Danielle caught a photo op. Her talent lies not only in how she snaps the camera but also in the story she sees through the lens. She spotted a heron standing peacefully in the swamp. As she lifted her camera and aimed, she noticed movement in the water just behind the great bird. There, lurking and waiting, was an alligator. The bird seemed at peace, perhaps oblivious, perhaps confident, but at peace nonetheless. She snapped the picture and watched for a while until the bird moved on and the alligator missed his chance for dinner.

Maybe the alligator wasn't hungry.

Maybe the alligator had heron last night.

Maybe God wanted the heron to live another day.

There are some things we do know. Dangers lurk. The world is like those swampy waters where people, circumstances, and temptations threaten our peaceful walk with the Lord every day. There are many days when we have no idea how close we actually come to the alligators that wait to snatch away our joy or even our lives.

Whenever I have those close calls, I, too, tend to speculate on the reasons I came through unscathed:

Somebody must be praying.

God's Word must be taking root in my life.

Grace.

I am reminded by that crazy bird of a lesson life has taught me, though: watch where you're standing! Stand with God.—k.m.

Green Leaf in Drought

*True, he struck the rock, and water gushed out, streams flowed abundantly,
but can he also give us bread? Can he supply meat for his people?*
—Psalm 78:20

The cattle in the fields were so thirsty, they were dying. The drought had lasted so long that rivers, streams, ponds, and private lakes were too dry to quench the land. Without water, nothing survives.

Then from everywhere in the country resources poured in—water, hay, and help stopped a full-blown disaster from happening.

We are often faced with drought: droughts of money, droughts of time, and droughts of love. We can feel just as desperate and alone as farmers watching cattle die. And as the debtors come calling, as you become stretched too thin, as you face another night alone, it is very tempting to sit in the middle of the floor and wrap yourself in a big, extravagant pity party. We believe we are in a totally hopeless place with no way out.

But, stop! God knows every need you have ever had, and he hears your prayer now. God has you in his hands. Just as water from the rock was given to the children of Israel, God will provide for you. When the world tries to convince you of drought, trust in God's ability to care for you. God might fulfill our needs by taking away something, but he will never remove something without providing amply for you.

God might help differently than we expect, but he will always help. Do you trust God enough to let him love you? Today, fall into God's arms and drink from the overflowing stream that will never ever run dry!—d.o.

I Feel Good . . . and Everything Else

Man became a living being.
—Genesis 2:7

I am surprised when people say animals don't have human emotions. Clearly, they do. Actually, it would be more accurate to say they have emotions in common with humans. We are not the only species with souls. According to Genesis 2:7, God breathed into the people and they became living beings, or souls. The Hebrew word for soul is *nephesh*. This word first appears in the Bible in Genesis 1:20 in reference to the living creatures. The *nephesh* is the life force of a being.

God's life force breathes through all creatures. Saint Francis gave us a beautiful hymn expressing this in his Canticle of the Sun, which praises God's creation and creatures who are wholly in service to him

When the psalmist says, "Bless the LORD, O my *soul*, and all that is within me, bless his holy name" (Psalm 103:1), he is expressing wholeness of being. The Hebrews did not separate body and soul the way Plato and the Greeks did or the way we do.

We associate the soul with emotions. Life is about feeling. What would a family gathering be without the joyous hellos and tearful good-byes? How sad would it be to get no overzealous greeting from the dogs when you got home at the end of the day? How boring life would be if the cats didn't act ticked that it took you so long to get home to feed them.

Some warn about our being overemotional, and others try to separate the emotion from spirituality. But God's first commandment was to love with all the *heart*. It is uncomfortable to deal with sorrow, guilt, anger, and humiliation, but beings with souls experience them all, and we need compassion and understanding to help us through these emotions.

The world would be a better place if people would develop a love for the emotional-spiritual gifts we are given from God, and to be patient with one another on the dark days when we are as fussy as schnauzers or as ornery as a tomcat.—k.m.

A Good Day for a Miracle!

Crowds gathered also from the towns around Jerusalem, bringing their
sick and those tormented by impure spirits, and all of them were healed.
—Acts 5:16

"Don't buy her, she's crazy," they said of the beautiful young mare in the pasture. I had always wanted a black and white horse, and though she was a bit high strung and untrained, there was something that called out to me from this beautifully fine-chiseled horse. Her ears had a cute little hook to them and her fast, stomping feet were tiny and well formed.

Often horses that are high strung are deemed impossible to train. I don't agree that a horse can be impossible to train. Most high-strung horses are just frightened. A frightened horse can be cured with patient, kind teaching. You can't make horses do something they don't want to do. But you can definitely make them so trusting of you that they'll stop running away from what (in another context) might frighten them.

A horse resists pain, scary situations, and the unfamiliar. But a horse responds to kindness, a gentle voice, and a nonchallenging approach. The black-and-white horse became one of my best friends. She slowly felt safe enough to follow me anywhere I went, trusting I would not lead her into danger.

I was moved to tears when a young hyperactive and highly functioning autistic child who had been brought to the barn was paired with my hyperactive and highly functioning horse. When the child approached her, both became calm, quiet, and manageable. The child, who could not focus on any one activity, focused. The horse that could not stand still, stood for an hour while this youngster brushed her.

There is always hope in healing when God is at work. God works miracles with our imperfections. God even works miracles with what the world considers a fault. God finds all of us a fertile ground for miracles!
—d.o.

March 11
If You Can't Eat 'Em, Join 'Em

The wolf shall live with the lamb.
—Isaiah 11:6

Abby was the only girl in a litter of six sheltie puppies. She had a calm disposition, as nonthreatening as a dog could be, which is why I was surprised one day to find her holding a baby rabbit in her mouth. She had found a nest, and I got the impression that she had already had her main course and was now on dessert. When she saw me, she froze with the newborn dangling from either side of her muzzle. Time stood still as we both realized what she had done. She gulped down the baby bunny as though conscience and belly couldn't quite get in sync, and looked at me helplessly.

Later that evening, we were sitting on the floor talking when Abby walked into the room.

"Abby, you ate the rabbit!" we said in a sad how-could-you-do-such-a-thing voice.

Abby's countenance dropped, her wagging tail drooped, and without missing a step, she did a U-turn and walked right back out of the room, dejected and repentant.

A few weeks later, another bunny family was born in Abby's domain. She didn't touch a single one.

The following spring, we bought a pet rabbit. Our yard was secure, so when he was big enough, we let him out to play. One day I saw something go across the yard. The rabbit ran from right to left. Abby was close behind, barking playfully. Then, back from the left came Abby, the rabbit close behind her. They were playing chase! Abby went through a transformation. Her natural taste for bunnies changed because of her love and respect for the people she loved. Now she loved the bunny like a friend, instead of like dinner.

That's how it works for us, too, when God convicts us. God changes the desires within us, and through God's grace we love enough to want to change.—k.m.

The Beagle and the Cross

For the message of the cross is foolishness to those who are perishing,
but to us who are being saved it is the power of God.
—1 Corinthians 1:18

Some things just don't make sense to the world. It's hard to understand in medical, black-and-white terms how holding a purring cat will lower your blood pressure. And it seems odd that rare hairless puppies in Mexico, when held against aching joints, can help reduce the pain and swelling of rheumatoid arthritis. The supernatural gifts between humans and animals have long been storied, but actual scientific causation and effect are hard to explain.

One morning while on the air with a radio show, I received a call from a distraught mother whose son had lost his beloved beagle. Her son was prone to seizures, and this dog was able to sense oncoming ones. The dog wasn't a trained seizure dog—he just had a gift he shared with the boy he loved.

Seeing an open door, the beagle had taken off in a chase of things unseen. The boy was inconsolable. An announcement on the radio led to the return of the boy's canine buddy, and all was well. And when the child called joyously to thank us for helping with the return of his dog, I heard such relief in his voice.

Important, life-altering realities can be difficult to explain. How do you explain the life-saving power of the cross to someone who interprets its value only through intelligence? When you know how a life can be changed through the gift of Jesus Christ, it is impossible to keep that message to yourself. When we see someone struggling, even if they don't realize they are drowning, we still wish to throw them a lifeline.

The basis of Christ's love isn't primarily found in logic or empirical, verifiable data. It's found in testimony. Our testimonies are the lifelines we throw to those around us who are sinking.—d.o.

Cock-a-doodle Praise

Yes, Lord; you know that I love you.
—John 21:15

Not far from my bedroom window is our chicken coop. It's a nice piece of chicken real estate. In the coop, we have a rooster with no sense of time. He crows whenever for whatever reason—morning, noon, or night.

When he crows, I think of the story of Peter in John's Gospel. He had promised Jesus he would always love him and stand by him, no matter what. Jesus knew better, of course, and told Peter just before all hell broke loose and heaven broke in that Peter would deny him three times before the cock crowed. You would think that with such a warning from such a source, Peter would have set his resolve to stay true, but in the midst of the frantic disaster that ensued, he lost his nerve and determination. When he was asked, "Weren't you one of his disciples?" brave Peter responded no three times. And that infamous screeching cry of the rooster filled the dark night.

Jesus spent forty days with Peter and the others after his resurrection. He was not a ghost, not a memory, not a dream. It was Jesus, walking around in eternal life here on earth. Jesus gave Peter another chance to keep his word. For the three times Peter had said no, three times after the resurrection, he got to say yes to Jesus. "I love you, Lord," he repeated. And this time, he meant it with his whole life.

Now whenever our rooster crows, I think of this story. We make mistakes. Sometimes we've made mistakes in the past that seem unimaginable now, and we can't undo them. But God can. He makes all things new. When we let God tell our story, it has a resurrected plot. Now whenever our rooster crows—morning, noon, or night—I literally pause for a brief moment and tell the Lord that I love him.—k.m.

The Winner's Circle

Watch out that you do not lose what we have worked for,
but that you may be rewarded fully.
—2 John 1:8

Fancy, my beautiful black-and-white spotted saddle horse, was used to winning. She pranced into the show ring with a bouncing head and a lilting gait, almost dancing in time to the organ music. She became used to getting her name called, being ushered into the winner's circle, and having the blue ribbon attached to her bridle for her winner's gait around the ring. She worked very hard and expected her full reward.

She so expected her reward that once when she was not announced as winner, she tried to walk from her spot to get her ribbon anyway. It was impossible to get her to understand that the prize was not hers.

Sometimes we struggle in the same way as Fancy. When we work hard to be our best, we might believe we deserve the prize, but we do not always get what we believe we are entitled to. However, when we follow God's will, the full reward is a gift we allow ourselves to receive.

How many times have you heard, "Well, I'm not perfect. I'm only human"? God made our unique human forms and celebrated his accomplishment. Then, he went even further to show us how to live and flourish within the limit of that humanity, showing by his very example. Jesus Christ was God Incarnate in a body made of flesh and blood. He walked on this earth to feel what we feel, to see, taste, and touch what we touch. He was fully human and fully divine. He was created in God's image, just as we are. He is living proof that we can strive for the top prize in all we do. We can expect to win. Our reward is not some blue ribbon, some accolade to hang on the wall, or even streets of gold. Our reward is the gift of eternal life in the constant connected presence of God himself. You are entitled. There are enough God-ribbons for all of us.—d.o.

March 15
Lions

The righteous are as bold as a lion.
—Proverbs 28:1

L ions are easy to love, as long as you don't run into them in the wild. They have characteristics we admire: they are majestic, bold, courageous, and strong. But they can also be cruel. Lions show up frequently in the Bible, both Old Testament and New. Sometimes they are like C. S. Lewis's Aslan, and sometimes they appear like Satan.

Isn't it ironic? We have Jesus as the Lion of the Tribe of Judah (Revelation 5:5), and the devil roaming around like a roaring lion seeking whom he may devour (1 Peter 5:8).

Is it any wonder the devil would roam around as a roaring lion? He's a copycat. The devil is the character who wanted to be God, who was eaten up with jealousy and pride to the point of his own destruction. He never seems to realize he can't win the war, and if he does realize it, that knowledge surely doesn't stop him from trying to win a few battles.

Sometimes we pay attention to the wrong lion and become intimidated by the wrong roar. You see, Jesus roars with authority, righteousness, and judgment. The devil, on the other hand, roars with deception, anger, and fear, to try and convince us he is mightier than our king.

Jesus never coerces us with fear—the truth is, Jesus doesn't coerce us at all; he simply loves, he simply gives, he simply invites, he simply guides in a way that requires no forceful persuasion. When you fall, or when you hit rock bottom, Jesus waits with grace and healing right where you land.

Satan, on the other hand, comes looking for a feast of trouble that he expects you to cook up. "Resist the devil," the Bible says, "and he will flee from you" (James 4:7). To resist the devil, we have guidance from the book of James: draw near to God, submit to God, and stay fervent in prayer. And, with these tools, we are confident to know that because he is always by our side, we can call upon our Lion of the Tribe of Judah at any moment for help.—k.m.

To Follow the Crowd or to Lead the Masses?

Do not follow the crowd in doing wrong.
When you give testimony in a lawsuit,
do not pervert justice by siding with the crowd.
—Exodus 23:2

Did you know that counties all across our great, civilized American countryside support cruel dog fighting and cock fighting? And in Spain, a bullfighter savagely kills a bull with a sword, the crowd cheering as the beast eventually falls to his knees. Around U.S. racetracks, greyhounds are raced while the losing dogs are shot behind the track. Table tennis balls are put in the nostrils of race horses to suffocate the competition or to claim insurance money if the horse has an off season. It's all justified if the animal wins or they bring financial reward, right?

Crowds have often gathered to entertain themselves at the expense of animals. When we allow others to perpetuate harm on God's creatures, justifying it by not participating ourselves but doing nothing to stop it, we are as bad as the participants. We are called to do the right thing, by ourselves and by God's creatures, not just to look the other way.

We are called to set an example, to be leaders in all we do. People of faith are even referred to in the Bible as "a peculiar people." Maybe standing up for what is right is peculiar in this world of crowds of lowest-common-denominator behavior.

One woman—Jane Goodall—made history at the age of twenty-six as one of the first people to take the risk and enter the wilds of Tanzania to study primates. Her research still benefits the environment of all living creatures today.

One man, Albert Schweitzer—pastor, theological leader, concert organist, surgeon—founded an important African hospital and became an animal rights activist, a supporter of civil rights, and a flag-waver against nuclear arms. In 1952 he won the Nobel Peace Prize for his commitment to all creatures' rights.

One person can make a difference, and these two examples prove that we can speak up against the status quo as we seek a better world. It matters that we stand up against the crowd for what is right. And it *matters* that, in doing so, we stand out as "a peculiar people"!—d.o.

March 17
The Gift of Beauty

Esther . . . was fair and beautiful.
—Esther 2:7

Niki was our tricolored collie, born in North Carolina around the same time as my second child. Niki knew she was beautiful. She was unusual for a collie, like an exotic Lassie with her black coat, white mane, and sable accents. Her fur was long and sleek, her eyes expressive and wise. She was the perfect dog for small children because she was so gentle and patient.

Since summers in the South can get awfully hot for a long-haired breed, one year someone suggested that I get Niki shaved. I had never heard of shaving a Lassie-dog. They wouldn't look very collie-like, now would they? Hollywood might not renew her contract! Still, Niki wouldn't know the difference, and she would be so much more comfortable.

So I had her shaved. Boy, was she skinny under that thick coat! She looked like a greyhound with a really big nose. We laughed playfully at her, but she did not find it amusing. She seemed embarrassed. Niki was absolutely miserable for the rest of the summer. She was not herself, no longer outgoing and playful, no longer confident. I imagined this would be how a lion would feel if you shaved off its mane. She stayed inside during that summer, and I vowed never to shave her again.

One person commented that Niki was vain, but that wasn't true. She didn't have the sin of pride. Niki's story reminds me of the story of Esther in the Scriptures: Esther knew of her own astounding beauty and used it to save her people. Rachel, Ruth, Mary . . . all lovely, or so the stories go.

When someone is beautiful and does not know it, that's tragic. Every person I've met has a distinct beauty. Celebrate your beauty today. Cherish this gift. Celebrate who God made you to be.—k.m.

Monkeys and Gold

Once every three years the merchant ships came bringing
gold, silver, ivory, apes, and monkeys.
—1 Kings 10:22b NKJV

The ancient kings of the Bible were always comparing their wealth. A king's power was often signified by how much gold he had in his coffers. King Solomon had not only gold, silver, and ivory, but apes and monkeys—which he considered treasures!

Some believe that since monkeys and apes were not indigenous to the area, they would be considered an extremely rare, expensive treasure befitting a king. Solomon might have simply enjoyed them as pets. Or perhaps he was creating a zoo for the people of his kingdom.

But the fact that they are listed in his great riches along with horses and mules shows the great value King Solomon placed on his animals.

Have you thought about the ways our animals are treasures to us? They give us unconditional love and remind us that we are worth loving. When the world says we are not enough, our pets treat us as if we are all they need. It's as if God sent us animals to reinforce how much we are treasured by *him*. We need entertainment. We need to laugh. We need to be unconditionally loved. The bond between animals and humans has existed since the beginning because God ultimately knew that we all needed a world full of shared treasures.—d.o.

March 19
Fussy Little Bird

Feed my sheep.
—John 21:17

I remember the day I caught sight of my first hummingbird suspended in midair at the edge of our carport.

Up to that point in my life, I had experienced significant sorrow. Since the time I was a child, people asked me why I was so sad. For me, life was sad. But life can be joyous, too, and that was something I had forgotten until this particular day, when the hummingbird showed up with its song of joy, a foreshadowing of days to come. They say the hummingbird represents joy, and I responded to that joy so much that I hung a hummingbird feeder on the porch to invite more joy.

I saw one or two hummingbirds spread out over time. I tried putting more sugar in the feeder. I bought more of the red nectar. Then one day, a pastor friend of mine with a whole yard full of hummingbirds told me you have to keep the feeders clean. He cleans his daily, he said, and these fascinating, persnickety creatures are there all the time.

I didn't think much more about it that day, but got busy with other things, until one afternoon in the springtime, I was sitting on the front porch when a hummingbird breezed in. She paused at the dirty, buggy feeder but didn't drink. Then she flew right over to the porch swing, fussed at me, and stormed off. Naturally, I stopped what I was doing and cleaned the feeder, refilling it with fresh nectar. She promptly came back and brought friends.

The story of the hummingbirds makes me think about the Christian witness. Remember when Jesus told Peter to feed his sheep? Peter had to get a clean heart first before he could be a shepherd, a tender of the sheep. A dirty heart or dirty feeder won't do. Allow the cleansing tears and the Holy Spirit to wash your soul through and through. The Lord wants to cleanse away haunting memories, disappointments, and the sorrow of a broken heart. What is your hummingbird that helps you cry your tears but also helps you embrace God's joy?—k.m.

March 20
The Loser Club

The lion perishes for lack of prey, and the cubs of the lioness are scattered.
—Job 4:11

Have you ever felt like you just couldn't do anything right? Have you ever felt like everything in the world was coming against you?

The story of Job's suffering is made even more terrible when he is given this proverb from his so-called friend Eliphaz. This "friend" of Job's used proverbial sayings of negativity to point out to Job that all the horrible things happening to him were born out of Job's own wickedness. And to rub it in, Eliphaz told Job that the reason he was speaking out was for Job's own good. How sad it is, that people who call themselves friends are often the ones who hurt us the most.

The old lion might just be hungry because he can't run fast enough to catch a gazelle anymore. The lioness's cubs might be scattered because they find mates in another pride. The reason for the good and bad in life might be answered with the thought . . . life happens. It is how we deal with life and life's circumstances that come our way that is the testament to our love of God—or our lack of faith.

If you are facing the negative attitudes of your "friends," maybe it's time to spend a little less time in the counsel of the negative and spend some one-on-one time in relationship with God. God has not branded any of us with a big *L* for loser on our foreheads. He's written his name on our hearts, and that very act of grace has made us all winners!—d.o.

March 21
Luna Light

Those who are wise shall shine like the brightness of the sky,
and those who lead many to righteousness,
like the stars forever and ever.
—Daniel 12:3

The luna moth that only flies at night appeared on our farm, and I suspect we have that black walnut tree on our property to thank for their presence. The luna moths appear near the tree, laying their eggs on the bottom of the leaves. The moths are pale green, and are also known as the "giant silkworm moths." They have eyespots on their hind wings, long tails, and when the light hits, then they seem to glow. They are silky visions in the graceful moonlight.

Sometimes I like to picture Jesus and his disciples sitting on the shore of the Sea of Galilee under the night sky. I imagine Jesus loved stargazing. The ancient Hebrews believed that their loved ones who died numbered among the stars in the heavens. This is what Daniel believed when he wrote, "Those who are wise shall shine like the brightness of the sky, and those who lead many to righteousness, like the stars forever and ever" (Daniel 12:3). I imagine Jesus smiling as the disciples talked about loved ones they had lost, and the stars reminding them of their presence.

Jesus and the luna moths know things we easily forget. They remind us of those things that shine in our darkness.

Ironically, the luna moth emerges from its cocoon on a *morning* two weeks from its pupation. It has no mouth. It does not eat. It lives for one week, and then dies. So the luna moth spends longer getting born than being alive.

The days are not ours to keep; they are gifts. There is a way, even in the responsibilities of life, to have a quiet soul, to cherish this side of eternity and all the reminders that glow in the night sky.—k.m.

Just the Way You Are

Before I formed you in the womb I knew you.
—Jeremiah 1:5a

One day, I was reading the listing of animals up for rescue and adoption, and I found several "puppy mill accidents" looking for homes. Among them were the most adorable poodles, apricot in color, warm and fuzzy. Because of puppy mill inbreeding, they had been born without eyes.

Also on the list were tiny dogs born without front legs. These teacup Chihuahuas were adapting to little nubs to support the front of their bodies. Watching the videos of the little pups, I realized they were walking on their hind legs, learning to balance and deal with what they had. They weren't bothered at all by having what the world considers imperfect bodies.

Years ago, I read a story about a puppy in a shelter that was born with several abnormalities. The shelter was about to euthanize him, but the attendant, who had been fighting to save the little guy, felt something in his heart that said he'd be a perfect pet for someone. So he prayed for that perfect someone to come along. Later that day, a shy little boy came to the shelter. Suddenly he lit up! He spotted the puppy without front legs and made a beeline to him.

"Mom, he's just like me!" he exclaimed as he reached out to the dog, revealing arms that had no hands.

That puppy was God's gift created with a special boy in mind. He was perfect in all his imperfections, just as the little boy was. We have all been formed by God with unique callings, unique gifts. When we look in the mirror and see faults, God sees beauty. He made you to be exactly who you are. Every curve, every bulge, every bony knee, every gnarled inch of us is something that God calls beautiful and has a purpose for—God makes all things beautiful in his time.—d.o.

If I were My Dog

*Thus says the LORD of hosts: Render true judgments, show kindness
and mercy to one another.*
—Zechariah 7:9

Did you ever play the "Which Animal Would You Be?" game as a child? You know, you would say, "If I could be any animal, I'd be a bird, so I could fly," or, "I'd be a dolphin, so I could swim the ocean and fend off the sharks," or how about this one: "I'd be my dog so I could be treated the way I treat him"?

It's the Golden Rule: do to others what you would have them do to you. When Jesus taught this principle in Matthew 7:12, he was, as he noted himself, simply teaching the Law and the Prophets. And I do mean *simply*. Jesus was great at taking what people had overcomplicated and making it accessible.

Fairness, mercy, and kindness to one another have been God's requirement all along. Jesus wasn't revealing new concepts antiquating the Old Testament and ushering in the New. Rather, the New Testament begins with Jesus letting the children of God know that they had missed the point of their own teaching.

The Golden Rule seems perfectly clear, yet we sometimes find ways to misconstrue even this beautiful law. You see, though we are all alike, we are all unique. Each of us has a story and a personality with intricate nuances, and those differences affect our relational perspectives. What you would have done to you is not always what I would have done to me. Jesus was speaking from a servant's heart. In order to do unto others as Jesus meant it, we have to seek to understand the "other" better than ourselves, to show tolerance in the areas in which they are different from us. We have to put ourselves in their shoes, and then meet them there with love.

God has followed his own rule, understanding exactly what we need through Jesus. And then he fulfilled that need. God took on our nature so that now we can take on his.—k.m.

March 24
Instinctual Faith

That day when evening came, he said to his disciples,
"Let us go over to the other side."
—Mark 4:35

Animals are equipped with hearing far more sensitive than we have. A quake at sea, though far below the range of human hearing, can be heard by animals. After the tsunami hit the coast of Thailand in 2004, killing thousands of people, accounts surfaced of animals acting strangely the morning before, perhaps because they knew something was amiss. They had an instinctual urge to run away from the sound to higher ground.

When Jesus asked his disciples to cross the Sea of Galilee, their natural and learned instincts told them to be afraid. Though the lake is only eight miles wide, they knew that storms are likely, so night travel on the Sea of Galilee would be very dangerous.

As Jesus slept, the men worried. When they felt that they wouldn't survive the storm, they shook Jesus awake in panic. "Do you still have no faith?" he said as he calmed the waters.

Even after Jesus has asked us to trust him, and he's in the boat with us, we become afraid. We question his will for our lives. We balk at his requests. We don't trust that he will do exactly what he promises.

If Jesus said to you, "Let's cross the sea together tonight," what would you say? Would you remind him of the dangers and say no? Would you step into the boat, but panic halfway through the journey? If Jesus said, "I know the dangers of this journey I'm asking you to make, but I'll be there with you all the way," would you go?

When instincts fail us, Jesus stands in the gap. Faith is not something we are born with. Faith is a gift that we have to use to even know we've got it. We are never guaranteed a life without trials, but in those trials, our faith grows. And in that faith, in crossing the stormy water with Jesus, is where our relationship with Christ truly begins.—d.o.

Wow, I Love This Place!

Let us go with you, for we have heard that God is with you.
—Zechariah 8:23b

We named our farm Big Sky Heaven Blue as a statement of gratitude. You enter through a rickety wooden gate that frames either side of a cattle guard, which, incidentally, does not intimidate the horses in any way whatsoever. My son painted a sign on a crooked old piece of plywood, so the fence is emblazoned with the name of our farm and a few fluffy clouds to boot, just to show how heavenly we think this place is.

Our dogs seem to think so too. We have fostered a dog or two, and when these new kids on the block show up, Josie, Jessie, and Veronique give the grand tour. "These are our horses! Those are our millions of cats, and we have chickens over there!" They are loved and cared for, and they feel secure in knowing that this place is theirs as much as ours. They're the best kind of show-offs, wanting to share what they have with everyone.

God's people are supposed to shine just as brightly about our loving, merciful God. When we know we are loved, when we walk in holiness and happiness because the Holy Spirit is guiding us every day, and when we love others with God's love, the excitement is irresistible. Judgment or criticism of the world will never win people over—but love and grace will. Jesus said, "And I, when I am lifted up from the earth, will draw all people to myself" (John 12:32).

Sometimes we act like we want to keep our faith to ourselves. Maybe we're afraid to be bold and share the good news. Perhaps we have forgotten what good news it is! But don't worry if you're not the door-to-door witnessing type. Just live and move and have your being in him, and his light will do the rest.—k.m.

A Hard Fish to Swallow

It has given me great joy to find some of your children
walking in the truth, just as the Father commanded us.
—2 John 1:4

One morning I was walking along the river walk, and I saw a water bird burst to the surface with a fish in her mouth. She gulped, and her long skinny neck revealed a moving lump as the fish continued to swim against the current of her swallow. She kept struggling, diving under the water and then up again, her head lifted to the sky, struggling to get her breakfast down her throat. She had to eat, but what a difficult thing to swallow!

Truth can sometimes feel a lot like swallowing a big fish in one bite. It's what we thrive on, but sometimes it hits us right in the face, and though we need it to live, it's hard to get down. We have to face truth about ourselves and about the families we grew up in, and we have to accept the truth about situations that are just not going to get better.

Walking in the truth, as mentioned in 2 John, is the same thing. When we seek truth in our relationship with God, we are seeking authenticity. We seek *answers* from God, so we are *seeking* God. That communication is what relationship is all about.

But when his word is sometimes too big for us to take in all at once, God allows us to break it down bit by bit, until we get the nourishment we need to live. Many people use a fast-food approach to the truth, allowing a few PowerPoint messages and a cool pastor to spoon-feed highlights, but that method is not a real relationship. When you put in the time and effort for real relationship with God, the result is pure, everlasting love that fills the empty spaces and offers slices of truth to bring us closer to God at every turn.—d.o.

March 27

Do You Still Love Me?

Love . . . bears all things, believes all things,
hopes all things, endures all things.
—1 Corinthians 13:4-7

Our kitty kingdom is a constant source of fascination. I love watching the dynamics among them, the personality types, the social order, and the peculiar behaviors.

Anna is a white kitty with a crooked tail and crossed eyes. Her mama's name is Turtledove, and she's a short-haired tortoiseshell, who is actually smaller than Anna. Turtledove and Anna stay close to one another. The mama kitty socializes with the other cats, but Anna, for some reason, doesn't, although she was not a feral. But while she doesn't interact with other cats, she and her mama have a special affinity for one another.

We have another mother-and-child pair with a tender relationship that has remained sweet and affectionate all along. Schmingy 1 was a twin boy and their mama, O'Keefe, loved them both equally, grooming and cleaning them right into their adulthood. When Schmingy 2 disappeared, Keefer gave all the more love to Schmingy 1.

These familial pairs remind me of the blessed union between parent and child. Sometimes the world tugs at the parent-child relationship, trying to wedge a distance between them, but we must keep the faith for our children and pray for them diligently every day. Likewise, we must love and honor our parents and pray for them.

Families are a place where our hearts are tested on a regular basis. Is your love true? Are you a kind person, patient, forgiving? Home is the cradle where tolerance is nurtured into the hope that heals the world.

In some situations, it may seem impossible to heal, forgive, and forget, but by God's grace, there is a way. Jesus' message of love is about reconciliation. If he can fix the relationship between perfect God and broken mankind—and he already has—then he can give us renewed faith in one another.—k.m.

March 28
Gossip Hounds

*Because you disheartened the righteous with your lies, when I had
brought them no grief, and because you encouraged the wicked
not to turn from their evil ways and so save their lives. . . .*
—Ezekiel 13:22

I wonder if dogs hang out at the groomer's and gossip about other dogs
while they sit under the hair dryers. Do cats tell lies about the other
cats to get ahead?

People, on the other hand, love a good scandal. I once told a friend to
stop gossiping, and she replied, "I don't gossip! Everything I say is true!"
Have you ever been the victim of some of that so-called true gossip? It
hurts, doesn't it?

At no time is a negative story for a person's own good. When we spread
negativity, we breed negativity. When I was the victim of a jealous person's whispers, I chose to ignore it, thinking that time would prove my
integrity. Unfortunately, a false witness can be very effective in destroying
a person's reputation if this person carefully chooses who, where, and
how the stories are spread. I lost a job because of it.

In the Bible, good people were attacked with lies for not participating
in the demonic ways of the crowd. Nowadays, our good names can be
tarnished when we don't go partying with coworkers or accept some
under-the-table income. This is the way gossip works. Crowds gather
around the proverbial water cooler to share the scoop. If we don't participate, we are no longer part of the crowd. We are outcasts because we refuse to participate.

But we are *never* to fall prey to the peer pressure of liars. God asks us to
be better than the world. We might have no recourse against liars, but
God promises to deliver his people out of the hands of the wicked. The
first step—always—against a false word is to say no, standing strong with
the integrity God asks of us.—d.o.

I Love You. Take Me for Granted

*So whenever you give alms, do not sound a trumpet
before you, as the hypocrites do in the synagogues and in the streets,
so that they may be praised by others.*
—Matthew 6:2a

We all want to be appreciated, and it makes us feel good when someone we have blessed or helped says thank you. No doubt, many of us would do good things for others even if we were not thanked. On the other hand, a sliver of darkness can slip into our hearts and almost without noticing, we can develop certain expectations that, when not met, lead to resentment.

Some people will thank you profusely for your love and kindness, but gratitude is a gift, not a privilege. Some people, especially family, take for granted that you're supposed to love them, and we have to remind ourselves again and again that recognition isn't the reason we love.

Veronique is a spoiled princess puppy from a royal collie heritage who constantly takes my love for granted. But really she isn't ungrateful, she just settled into our relationship. Her love runs deep, and I feel all the more loved and appreciated by her somehow because she is so secure in my love. She trusts me.

That's the key. Sometimes what feels like being taken for granted simply means you have a bond of trust with another, a sacred thing we should celebrate! Gratitude, then, happens as an exchange, a knowing confidence. Appreciation is expressed in the joy of the relationship.

If I get right down to it, all of our animals expect good treatment without expressed gratitude because we love them so much. The cats are downright rude about it sometimes, and the pony, Geronimo, is a tease. Love is not something you have to fight for or earn, it is not something that can be coerced. It is a gift, the truest gift, the pure reflection of God, and we give it knowing that God always sees, even if the recipient doesn't.—k.m.

The Dolphin Circle Dance

Sing to the LORD a new song, his praise from the ends of the earth,
you who go down to the sea, and all that is in it,
you islands, and all who live in them.
—Isaiah 42:10

I have always been drawn to dolphins. Visiting marine parks was such a joy as I watched trainers work with dolphins who seemed so playful and knowing. On every beach trip with my family, I would stare at the horizon in hopes of dorsal fins waving from a distance—never to find a single one. As an adult, I joined a group of friends on rented Jet Skis and set out into a gulf cove one afternoon, not expecting to have my first real encounter with a dolphin. Yet as we all buzzed off in different directions, out of the water bounced a big beautiful dolphin who looked me right in the eye. As I circled this dolphin two of his friends joined us leaping and playing around me. There was a rhythm and a joy that moved between us, a dance where only we heard the music. I was not a stranger invading their space, but a new friend they invited to their party.

A similar thing happened as a group of us headed to some gulf islands off the coast of Florida to do some shelling. As we slowed to enter the no-wake zone a pair of dolphins began loping alongside, hopping up to catch a glimpse as they surfaced and sank in synchronized harmony. In all the times I've tried to see a dolphin in the wild, I never have. But when I have simply enjoyed the moment, taking in the water, the peace, and the sunshine, dolphins have appeared over and over. Maybe they are drawn to the joy.

Sometimes we try so hard to find what we are looking for that we miss the opportunities swimming all around us. God's way defies logic in that he beckons us to be still, to wait, to give way to the quiet. In those silent moments, when peace and joy are palpable, we draw more peace and more joy to us.

Maybe your search for something has been so intense that you have become discouraged. You have been watching the horizon for someone you wish would appear or waiting for a job to materialize or money to show up in the mailbox. Today, spend time with God in praise, gratitude, and joy and see if the metaphoric dolphins begin dancing around your boat.—d.o.

Home Is where the Freedom Is

If the Son makes you free, you will be free indeed.
—John 8:36

Our pony cannot be contained. I think he takes his horse suit off when we're not watching, and underneath he's really a skinny little monkey. His lips are his opposable thumbs. He'll use them to unlock the stall door of his big buddy, Tucker, so he can come out to play with him. He can find the vulnerable place in the most secure fencing.

Geronimo, though he refuses to be fenced in, likes knowing where home is. He usually only escapes from barnyard to backyard, and the only damage done is to our fruit trees.

We can live without the pear trees. The real problems arise when Geronimo makes his way into the neighborhood. Then he is in danger, and he endangers others. He may feel free, but what he has really done is enslave himself to a situation that could cost him his life. Without even knowing it, he's limited his own choices. Once the sun goes down and the other horses are being nurtured and cared for, Geronimo wants his food, his water, his stall, and his hugs, but he's gotten himself stuck in a situation without them.

Sometimes we're like that pony. We don't even know why we do certain things, and often don't even realize that we've done wrong until someone else gets hurt or until we are wounded by our own choices. The good news is that our God is loving and compassionate. He knows that we're like "a calf untrained" and he brings us back so that we can be restored (Jeremiah 31:18).

The Holy Spirit guides us and teaches us what sin is and how it can quickly bind us. With a little tug on the heart, a reminder through his word, or even the gentle words of a godly friend, we are set free to love, and be loved, wholeheartedly.—k.m.

April 1
Cross Breeds

God chose what is foolish in the world to shame the wise;
God chose what is weak in the world to shame the strong.
—1 Corinthians 1:27

A powerful theme that prevails throughout the Bible, beginning to end, is that God's ways are higher than ours, his thoughts beyond what we can comprehend, try as we may.

It is specifically the message of the cross that Paul calls foolish—foolish to the world, that is. God chose to save the world through the cross.

This is our Christian story. Do you ever wonder how the gift of the cross applies to all creation? I know Jesus died to redeem humankind. How does my knowing this bless my dogs, cats, and horses, the elephants in Africa, the luna moth, and the bears in the Smoky Mountains?

It matters to all of creation when we accept the gift of grace given at the cross. Every day that I live freely in the light of God's forgiveness and love is a day that I have more love to give. The Apostle Paul said in Philippians that he wanted to know Christ in his suffering, to identify with the cross by laying down his life for the sake of love. This Jesus kind of love is in action when we take care of an elderly dog, nurse a wounded cat, or give money to help prevent the extinction of a precious species. Love is in action when we help teach others how to take care of animals.

The New Testament is full of imagery of animals worshiping around the throne with the people in heaven. It's a mystery, but every time we give thanks for the saving work of the cross in our lives, we participate in the beautiful redemption story for *all* creation.

Today as you walk with the Lord, take time to consider how your faithful relationship with him reaches beyond your personal redemption and connects with God's plan for the world. What you give your thoughts and life to matters, not just for yourself and your happiness, but in God's grand scheme of things! Pay special attention to the mystery of Jesus' redemptive work on the cross, and let him lead to a deeper understanding of what it means to the world that *you* received personal salvation. It's not for you alone, but for everyone. Your personal choice to receive the "foolish wisdom" of the cross is one of the greatest gifts you can give to the world.—k.m.

April 2
The Swimming Dachshund

The LORD . . . lays the beams of his upper chambers on their waters.
He makes the clouds his chariot and rides on the wings of the wind.
—Psalm 104:2-3

The world is full of beach people and mountain people, motoring road people and trail people. But one of the most fascinating groups I've encountered is lake people. Lake people have a culture all their own.

I accepted an invitation to join some lake people who weekly leave their condos to get on their houseboats and troll linked together across the lake to their favorite spot.

One of the boaters owned a dachshund, a dog bred for digging into holes and ridding farms of rats and moles. Dachshunds are not "lake people." However, this little wiener dog, with his short little legs and long body, wanted to join his canine buddies already enjoying a nice swim.

He barked in anticipation as his owners affixed a small, wiener-dog life jacket on him. He wasn't the diver the other dogs were, so the owners gave him lift-off, tossing him out into the water with his friends. His great big ears became wings as he took flight, looking more like a buoy than a dog. He hit the water and began churning those little legs with such joy, his fun-loving buddies chiming right in. One exuberant Labrador kept bringing him back to the boat in his mouth—I think the pint-sized hound enjoyed flying as much as he did swimming!

When we feel ill-equipped for life, God has ways of equipping us. When faced with a responsibility, we feel like we have legs like a dachshund when we need to swim. God can equip us for all our dreams. He wants us to fly! He wants us to swim! He wants us to splash around in our hope in him today.—d.o.

April 3
Chicken Run

We know that all things work together for good for those
who love God, who are called according to his purpose.
—Romans 8:28

When we get ourselves into situations, it's easy to forget that even through our mistakes, our Heavenly Father is lovingly teaching and guiding. "All things" include my mistakes, bad attitudes, resentments, anger, and temptations.

One of our cats has ample opportunity to learn from his mistakes. Curiosity has not killed him, but he's sure gotten himself into some pickles. His name is Yoda. Yoda was fascinated with the chickens when we first got them. The chickens can stay inside the shed or roam freely and safely in the fenced-in hen yard. The outdoor area provides great entertainment for several of the cats, but they usually watch from outside the fence. Yoda, however, decided he needed a closer look one day. He waited patiently until feeding time, and when we opened the shed door, he zipped in. We foolishly thought the chickens might be in danger, but we soon realized that poor Yoda was the one being chased by four hens and a rooster! He couldn't find his way out, and there was no catching him in all the commotion. We had to finesse the shed door in such a way that he could dash out without releasing any of the chickens. Yoda has never tried to get into the chicken house again. Neither have the other cats.

We make mistakes sometimes, but even through the trials we bring upon ourselves, we can learn the power of God's forgiveness, compassion for others who struggle, and the importance of walking in obedience to God. He only wants what is good for us. Understanding the promise of "all things" leads to a perfect heart.—k.m.

Elephant Tears

Oh, that my head were a spring of water and my eyes a fountain of tears!
I would weep day and night for the slain of my people.
—Jeremiah 9:1

The mother elephant saw her baby take its last breath. Her sorrowful wail could be heard round the world as the herd circled and joined in a choir of tears. Though scientists have long tried to dismiss animal emotion as anthropomorphic, our hearts tell us otherwise. Why would an elephant sob with real tears when distraught at a circus? Why would a herd circle a body and take turns carrying the bones of their fellow animal to a special place where other elephants are buried, covering the body with earth and returning year after year to solemnly observe the spot? Why would a group of elephants surround a store in Uganda where the feet of their friends were being sold as ottomans, and shovel the building so full of earth that the feet became buried?

Emotion is a part of the living being. We are told to "be positive" and are pumped full of antidepressants so we can minimize our ups and downs, but the Bible tells us that Jesus wept, not that he got over it and put on a more positive attitude. He wept over the loss of his friend. He cried for the suffering in the world.

When we have sorrow, we have every right to feel it. So what if we need to circle our loss and bury it, returning each year to remember? We are as much our pain as we are our joys. Elephants' tears are contrasted by their displays of joy. They trumpet loudly, running in fun-loving circles, showing loving affection for each other. They feel happiness and sadness, and it's a beautiful thing. Life was never meant to be one long emotion of nothingness. We were given peaks *and* valleys, and a Savior who walks with us through both.—d.o.

April 5
Cat in a Cool Blue Pond

Blessed are those who hunger and thirst for righteousness,
for they will be filled.
—Matthew 5:6

Some of the most hilarious creatures I've ever met live in a tiny man-made pond in Carmi, Illinois. Catfish. Great, big, friendly catfish. They eat Purina catfish kibble, and they'll practically jump up onto the pier to get it. They dance and swirl and poke their crazy whiskers out of the water to look around when they hear you coming.

I had not realized how tame catfish can be or how funny they are. I don't know how many there are, but I named twelve of them after the minor prophets: Hosea, Joel, Amos, Obadiah . . . Obadiah is all banged up, with scars on his head. He must be the tough fish on the block; either that, or the worst fighter. If you ride around the pond in the paddleboat, leaving a trail of the kibble, those fish, Obadiah in the lead, will follow you around the whole pond like a pod of dolphins.

These fish are hungry all the time, and that's what they remind me to be—hungry all the time for God's Word and the good things it teaches. When I read Paul's words that I should pray without ceasing, I think of that kibble those fish nibble on constantly.

Throughout my day, I have opportunities to "hunger and thirst for righteousness," to make the loving choice when someone hurts me, or to reject fears that try to overtake me. Sometimes, I lose my way, but I hunger to draw near to God again and find forgiveness and grace.

Once, I heard a preacher say that the child of God is content, but never satisfied. We are content in knowing God has put us in the pond and provided all we need; yet we are always to want more. Let us hunger for more of God, all the time.—k.m.

April 6
Is Today a Full Moon?

Why do the wicked live on, growing old and increasing in power?
—Job 21:7

The wolf pack is a beautiful example of power working for the betterment of the group. The alpha male protects his pack by hunting and keeping other alphas away from his breeding female. The female, also a strong hunter, raises her pups. Younger wolves are prevented from breeding by the older wolves—nature's method of birth control. Too many pups means more mouths to feed. Eventually, the younger wolves set out on their own to form a new pack.

But we aren't wolves. In the journey of human survival, we can all, theoretically, not only survive, but succeed. Society provides room at the top for anyone who works hard, right? But we see people with ruthless tactics zoom up the corporate ladder while the salt-of-the-earth salesman struggles to keep bread on his table. We can find logic in nature with individuals of a wolf pack working together, but in the civilized world of everyday business, it just plain hurts when evil comes against us.

The truth is, we might not make a million dollars or live in the biggest house in town. People who have no moral scruples might pass us by on the highway to success, but God doesn't bless good people with riches and bad people with poverty. He blesses his children with the desires of their hearts. God wants to bless us until we are overflowing with his joy, not just participating in survival. Let God fight your battles instead of seeking revenge on those who have hurt you. Let God direct your path. When God is the desire of your heart, you have already received your greatest blessing!—d.o.

April 7
Catmongers

Whoever does not love does not know God,
for God is love.
—1 John 4:8

I grew up with the idea that if you were a dog lover, you had to be a cat hater. We were in no uncertain terms dog lovers, so in our minds, "cat people" were selfish and arrogant. Then one day I learned a great lesson about my presumptions.

I was visiting a friend in San Francisco when I met Honey, the first cat I ever liked. As we sat talking one day, Honey climbed up onto the couch, sat beside me for a few minutes, and then eased over onto my lap and started "making biscuits." I had never seen a cat do that. In fact, I don't think I had ever even held a cat. Honey was a tabby, pretty as could be. She gently earned my trust, and she gave me a true gift: she somehow melted an icy place in my heart. In that moment, that loving kitty helped me let go of a judgmental attitude I didn't even know I had. She and I bonded for the rest of that trip, and I became a cat lover from then on.

Jesus taught us to love one another, and he loves without condition. Whether you're a dog or a cat, a mix or an exotic breed, God loves you the same. We are called to love that way, too—with compassion extended to all of creation.

I'm so glad I met Honey. I have had many cats since then, so I guess I'm a "cat person" now. What a joy!—k.m.

April 8
Bee Good, Honey

In that day the LORD will whistle for flies from the Nile delta in Egypt
and for bees from the land of Assyria. They will all come and
settle in the steep ravines and in the crevices in the rocks,
on all the thornbushes and at all the water holes.
—Isaiah 7:18-19

I was just a little girl when Mr. Antley brought us some homegrown honey. The honey was pure and shined like clear amber around a big waxy piece of honeycomb in the jar. Never before had I seen honey with its own honeycomb. They don't put those in the little squeezy bears at the grocery store.

Beekeeping was Mr. Antley's hobby. The bees didn't sting him, which I couldn't even fathom. It seemed that every time I walked across the yard's sweet clover, my bare feet got at least one good sting. But he would wear his helmet and talk to his bees, and they just buzzed on, as if they knew he was taking care of them.

Recently, I heard a beekeeper on a public radio station sharing the fate of the world's vegetation without bees. Did you know that without bees all our vegetation would die and the animal kingdom shortly after that? We are dependent on those tiny creatures for our very existence, and most of us don't even know it.

The show was meant to encourage more people to keep hives in their backyards, but I took it to heart at an even deeper level. God has made all of us so interconnected with one another that even a tiny buzzing bee is necessary for life as we know it.

We are the keepers of this planet. Can we plant something without overusing harmful pesticides? Can we volunteer to clean up an area or stop erosion? Can we lift our voices against that which is destroying our world one tiny insect at a time? With every act of kindness we offer to the earth—a gift from God—we agree with Scripture that "the earth is the LORD's" (Psalm 24:1).—d.o.

April 9
Stinky Smells and All

Thanks be to God for his indescribable gift!
—2 Corinthians 9:15

*L*ove is a gift. Animals seem to know this better than people. Isn't it refreshing how uncomplicated pet love is? They either like you or they don't, and if they love you, you know it. When Josie, Jesse, and Veronique greet me at the end of the driveway every day when I come home, I think, "God must love us so much to have brought us together." They make me smile; I make their tails wag.

Love is not man-made. We don't manufacture it; God does. God loves every one of us, even when we feel unlovable. Paul wrote in Romans 5:8 that God proved his love for us by sending Christ to die for us while we were still sinners. Jesus said there's no greater love than to lay down your life for another. That's what love does. It gives all.

God's love is accessible. We can give love because God gives it to all of us. We have access by faith to the great love that created all the beauty around us. We have access through prayer to the peace of mind and soul that comes with knowing that the One who loves us most knows our every circumstance.

Love more than you need. Animal people do this so well, especially those who do animal rescue. They are gifted at knowing how to love the animals unselfishly. They make sacrifices of money and time, get scratched and kicked, and deal with stinky smells, all in the name of love; yet they don't think of it as sacrifice. It's a Jesus-attitude.

Wouldn't the world be a better place if we could look at people with all their quirks and peculiarities and find them as fascinating and worthy of love as we find the animals? Let's get in on the gift of loving today.
—k.m.

April 10
Just Love

Do horses run on the rocky crags? Does one plow the sea with oxen?
But you have turned justice into poison and the fruit of righteousness into bitterness.
—Amos 6:12

An amazing veterinary clinic in town helped pets at about half the cost of any animal clinic in the area. The clinic recognized the growing homeless population in a shantytown near the river and saw that it also had a growing population of pets. Animals were dropped as strays and became part of this unsanctioned community. So, doctors, assistants, and animal volunteers loaded up supplies and vaccinations and headed to the tent city. Free of charge, they cared for as many animal needs as they could.

A reporter covered the story, and instead of inspiring support, the veterinary clinic was served papers to immediately cease their work for the homeless people's pets. The city named liability, health hazards, and potential malpractice threats as the reason for the shutdown.

The thinly veiled truth behind the excuses was that people in power didn't want the people or their pets in the vicinity of their city. These people of influence sought justice and got it. Or did they?

Justice for Christians is not about giving people what they deserve or what they've earned. We are called to have the heart of Christ. We are to give and forgive when the gift is not asked for, expected, or deserved. We are not called to be "fair" in life. We are called to love. We are the Living Testament of grace and kindness. As it says in Philippians, we are to shine like lights in the world. One person at a time, one sweet act of loving-kindness at a time, we can turn rocky soil into fertile ground where God can grow.—d.o.

April 11
Capturing Beauty

There is nothing outside a person that by going in can defile,
but the things that come out are what defile.
—Mark 7:15

A friend told me about a method of catching moths and butterflies to collect and preserve as though she was telling me about a sordid past. These living works of art can be turned into something akin to ceramic figurines. She said you have to catch the young ones whose colors are more vibrant and put a drop of formaldehyde on the head so that they will die quickly and still be beautiful. She told me about all this with remorse, and I was inspired by the way she cared. She is a person who has grown in love. She has learned the value and sanctity of life. She knows that the smallest acts of kindness and grace make us better people and that the smallest acts of cruelty make us worse. But formaldehyde dropping is no small act to the butterflies and moths.

Life is life. Life is precious.

Life is not ours to question or take away, yet we have the power of life and death in our hands every day. Jesus put it a little differently. He said we have the power of life and death in our *hearts*.

God made the world beautiful. He included fascinating surprises. He gave us resources and the means to be good stewards of them. It's God's world, not ours. We are called to love it, without question. You could say:

Love is love. Love is precious.

Love is not ours to question or take away.

God's art is all around us, connected, alive, and all an expression of his creative love. Maybe it's easier to observe the exquisite details of a butterfly when she is not fluttering around, but to be graced with a moment of living art in motion is worth so much more than the shadow of life trapped by misused power.—k.m.

April 12
Angry Little Dog, Big Loving God

And there I will meet with you, and I will speak with you from above the mercy seat,
from between the two cherubim which are on the ark of the Testimony, of all things
which I will give you in commandment to the children of Israel.
—Exodus 25:22 NKJV

My life had started out with such promise and I was in the midst of plans to be a missionary. Then, without warning, several horrible things happened: a sexual assault, a loss of innocence, and the exercising of my right to choose as a result left me feeling abandoned by God. Bad things were *not* supposed to happen to good girls. I was nineteen years old at the time, and I believed that my promise had been stolen from me. I threw away my foundation and began storing anger deep within, hardening myself so that nothing could hurt me again. I was convinced that a God who let his precious child be so hurt was not the God for me.

So, God sent a little dog into my life. An aggressive little dog that no one wanted to be around was caged in the back of a shelter where I volunteered. His days were up, and he was about to be euthanized when something made me open his cage. His growls ceased and he jumped into my arms, licking my face, and letting me know that he was not all bad. I took him home that day, and he began to love me back into the belief that I was worth loving. When I stopped accepting God's love, God just sent love to me another way.

No matter who we are, we will eventually come in contact with pain. God is not in the pain, but he is in the healing. Forces whisper to us every day, saying that we are not worthy. The lies pick at our self-esteem and convince us that God is not there for us. But, God was. God is. And God will always be. *That* is our promise, and nothing, no one, can take it away from us!—d.o.

April 13
Still Life

So teach us to count our days that we may gain a wise heart.
—Psalm 90:12

B uck was a roly-poly puppy, the chubbiest one in the litter. Rambunctious and adorable, he stole our hearts the minute we saw him. He and his siblings were nipping and growling ferociously, tumbling around in a humane society pen when we walked into the pet store. We were sure that we were meant to adopt this little fellow who left his playmates to come over and lick us wildly. The humane society representative grilled us well before allowing us to sign the adoption papers, but Buck was already a member of the family.

As Buck grew, we made guesses about his breed. We decided that his markings indicated Doberman, and his coloring pointed to chocolate lab. His eyes were an intense light hazel. He could've probably run the length of a football field in record time, but he never seemed restless living in a suburban home with a yard that would fit between the goalposts. He learned not to jump up on visitors, but it took everything within him not to give visitors a big ole Buck hug when they came in the door.

One day Buck was lethargic, not himself. A visit to the vet brought the diagnosis of cancer. He would need to have his spleen removed, and if he lived, he would either have seven to ten more months, or he would live out his healthy life span for several more years. The surgery was expensive and risky, and it would be hard on Buck.

Buck had walked with our family through some tough times, so we decided to walk with Buck through his. The surgery went well. The chemo worked.

God values life, and teaches us to value life too. Buck lived exactly seven months after his surgery, and we treasured every day we had with him. His life was surely worth saving.—k.m.

April 14
Power Seeds

As he was scattering the seed, some fell along the path,
and the birds came and ate it up.
—Matthew 13:4

One year, we planted grass seed at the farm. The horses and the birds took advantage of the process to scavenge as much seed as they could from the buckets and the parched, hard ground.

It's so hard to be the planter. In the moment, I never think about the fact that horses just want to fill their hungry bellies. They don't care if they knock you down in the process because they want what they want when they want it. They don't intentionally want to harm me, they are just following their nature. Because they are *horses*.

Birds are dependent on nature to provide, so they look at my distribution of seeds as provision. Because they are *birds*.

We often go into the world with our buckets of seeds, thinking the way will be easy because the calling is from God. Nothing could be further from the truth. God's calling is sometimes filled with needy, hungry scavengers, rocks, and harsh conditions. In our anger and frustration, we can stomp over to God and give back his big old bucket of seeds because things don't go as we planned. Or, we can keep planting.

Horses will be horses. Birds will be birds. Rocks will be rocks, and people will be people. We cannot control the outcome of the seeds. But God is working on the "one" seed. We have no idea which one is "the one"; we are just called to plant. God does the rest. Don't focus on the outcome *you* see. Focus on the outcome *God* sees. Allow God to "plant" the miracle he has planned through you today!—d.o.

April 15
Dodge Frog

The river shall swarm with frogs.
—Exodus 8:3

I love the way the humidity on a balmy evening in the South brings out the frogs. They're everywhere on our neighborhood streets. The pavement must feel good, like a warm, wet, unsinkable lily pad. In our family, we watch closely as we drive home and swerve the right direction, so they don't jump right into the tire's path. We developed a game we call "Dodge Frog." Thankfully, our street is not busy.

Sometimes we see so many frogs that they could rival the biblical plagues. They hide in the grass, in the mud, on the carport, and any place a water hose has been. They jump at just the right moments to scare you to death, and the dogs will chase a hopping toad all around the barn, sniffing at the lumpy curiosities.

It may seem like too much trouble to watch out for the frogs the way we do, but they are living creatures who bring us the gift of laughter when they startle us and make *us* jump. It hurt my heart one day to hear someone joking about trying to run over the frogs, just for fun. Love cares about all creatures.

Frogs represent cleansing to some people, because they seek out the cleansing rain and the puddle-baths left by a downpour. There are many life lessons we can learn from frogs, from cleansing to amphibious adaptability, but my favorite is the lesson I take from our neighborhood frog-swarm: the power of a multitude. It reminds me of the story from Exodus, where the frogs are troublemakers because there are so many. They served God in their own unique froggy way to frustrate Pharaoh's plans to keep Israel in bondage. For Egypt, it was a plague when a gazillion frogs obeyed God's command and hopped onto the scene, but for Israel, it was a blessing because Pharaoh got the point that as long as Israel was held in bondage, the frogs would multiply. I guess it's a good lesson that if enough of us hop around together for the Lord, we can set the devil running!

Today, we can "hop around together" by calling our prayer partners and praying together or by going to church and worshiping together in one accord or by working in unity to help spread the good news of the gospel. Spend time today appreciating your brothers and sisters in the Lord.
—k.m.

April 16
Goody Two-whiskers

In fact, everyone who wants to live a godly life
in Christ Jesus will be persecuted.
—2 Timothy 3:12

We have two cats on the farm, Monkey-face and Patty. Monkey-face has always done the right thing. She never "goes" outside the litter box, and she doesn't claw the furniture or mark territory. She tries to please us because she understands the privileges of following house rules.

Patty is the total opposite of Monkey-face. She rushes into the house, immediately sharpens her claws on the wingback chair, and "goes" anywhere BUT the litter box. She has been given the same opportunities as Monkey-face, but she has chosen to willfully stick to outdoor cat behavior. So Patty has to live outdoors. Her unwillingness to change has dictated her circumstances.

Have you ever been called a goody two-shoes? *Prude, pious,* and *holier-than-thou* are common ways to insult people who try to be their very best. Rule-followers are often ridiculed, and rebels are lauded. Social expectations leave us all feeling that to be loved and accepted, we must lower our standards and go with the flow.

The rules God gives us are to be kind and love each other. Don't get jealous over other people's stuff. Be loyal, decent, gentle, and not overindulgent in things that are harmful. The rules aren't there because God simply wants to give us a bunch of rules. He wants us to live in the lush provision of love he has for us. All we have to really do is agree to be loved and love back. Then all the other rules fall into place.

The point of following the rules is not to get special goodies from God. We follow the rules because that's what love does. The natural results of God's rules of love are the fruits of the spirit—such as patience, kindness, and self-control. Love is the *only* way we will ever fully enjoy the lives we are given.—d.o.

April 17
Cliché, Pussy Cat!

For while we were still weak, at the right time Christ died for the ungodly.
—Romans 5:6

Have you ever heard the phrase, "You've made your bed, now you have to lie in it?" It's cliché for the consequences of bad or foolish behavior. Fair? Maybe. Kind? No. If Scripture is clear about anything, it is that God is all about helping us through our mistakes and poor choices.

If animals could talk, I don't imagine they would bother with such a vindictive sentiment, either. Just think of all the predicaments cats get themselves into. And think of all the places they make their beds! A cat will make a bed out of anything. They'll sleep in the sink, on a washcloth, under a car, or in a motor, a basket, a shoe, a guitar case, on a laptop . . . shall I go on? We should let the cats rewrite the cliché for us. How about this: "I've made my bed; now would you please help me out of it?" Now *that's* grace.

The Old Testament is full of story after story about God mending messes. God is faithful; Israel is not. God keeps his promises; Israel does not. Israel makes her bed in the enemy camp; God rescues her.

The New Testament is where grace enters the picture. Jesus died for us *while we were yet sinners.* Jesus pulls us out from our bed under the car before backing out of the driveway.

If Jesus were rescripting that old cliché, he might say, "You made your bed, but don't worry, I lay in it for you." And so he did. He lay in a tomb, but not for long. He rose to new life and lives his story through us now.
—k.m.

April 18
Slow Rain

Ahab had said to Obadiah, "Go through the land to all the springs and valleys.
Maybe we can find some grass to keep the horses and mules alive so
we will not have to kill any of our animals."
—1 Kings 18:5

I found a riveting picture in the newspaper this week of a cow carcass drying in the parching sun of south Texas during a tremendously long drought. Thirst and dehydration are terrible murderers. They have no mercy. They know no compassion. They move swiftly and deftly, taking their victims down, one by one. The only hope is rain.

Even after a drought, torrential downpours don't satisfy as much as soft gentle rains with a steady flow. Steady and constant allows the land to drink in the moisture, unlike the downpours, which cause fast and furious floodwaters, flowing downhill or downstream before much can be absorbed.

God sees us when we are in a drought. He agonizes when we search to quench our thirsty spirits. Sometimes we are drawn into a flash flood and get turned on to Jesus in one explosive salvation moment. Then we leave the oasis of that experience, and it's back into the desert again where we remember the water, but the oasis is miles away. Many of us try to live from one oasis to another, one desert to another.

There is so much more than the oasis for all of us. We need a steady flow of God's Word, God's love, and fellowship with others, not long stretches of desert interrupted by quickly ending flash floods. The water God offers will never run dry. Our walk does not end at the altar, it begins . . . one drop of living water at a time.—d.o.

April 19
Fine Feathered Feast

Love your enemies and pray for those who persecute you.
—Matthew 5:44

Clementine and Charlie Brown left indelible impressions on my childhood. She was a slow moving basset hound, and he was a spunky little brown dachshund. Together, they would waddle side by side across the three yards between my friend's house and mine. Every day, those two characters would do their rounds up and down our street. They were right there when we played ball or flew kites or set off sparklers on the Fourth of July.

One year, my dad built a cage to protect the two yellow chicks the Easter bunny brought me. The two dogs managed to finesse their way into the cage and, with an unexpected burst of agility, the two amigos caught my chicks and ate them for breakfast. I found a tiny feather or two near the scene of the crime and saw the guilty pair licking their chops and lingering nearby in case we had left any more treats running around.

I was heartbroken by what happened, but I also knew that it wasn't exactly the dogs' fault. My young heart somehow knew that it would serve no good purpose to hate them. Hatred begets hatred, and if we choose that path, even in the small things, we put darkness into the world. I wanted to be a conductor of love. Love begets love.

God's presence brings the sweetness of understanding, and he helps us find solutions that bring peace, not division. He can give us the gift of forgiveness for those who make mistakes that harm us—or our Easter chicks. There is never an excuse not to love, because God will always make a way.

The next Easter, my parents gave me a cute bunny. Dad built a nice tall cage with a sturdy latch, and my bunny lived for a very long time. I guess Clementine and Charlie Brown went back to their kibble.—k.m.

April 20
It's Just a Chicken

Jesus looked at them and said, "With man this is impossible,
but with God all things are possible."
—Matthew 19:26

Going into a henhouse and finding a little warm pile of eggs is like Easter every morning. But one morning, I looked out my window as usual and saw something terrible—an open henhouse door.

I ran outside and saw a motionless pile of white in front of our collie, who was nudging the white hen with her nose in between insistent barks, as if trying to resurrect her. The hen's eyes were blinking up at me. She was scared. She was in shock. But she was alive.

Picking her up, I spotted a gaping neck wound that would certainly be fatal. I ran into the kitchen where Kim was fixing coffee.

"Call the vet," I yelled.

The doctor listened to the details and paused. Then she laughed. "I haven't worked on a chicken since vet school but . . . this is just a chicken. Most people would call that dinner."

We were appalled. This was not *just* a chicken! This was *our* chicken, our best laying hen!

As Kim hung up the phone, I felt determination. I heard the voice of my little chicken-raising grandma in my head. "Bring me some thread and a needle," I said.

Kim assisted as I stitched the hen's neck back together with green thread and an iodine wash. We kept her in a cage and treated her with antibiotic cream and iodine three times a day. On day three, she squawked, stood up, and revealed a warm, freshly minted brown egg as thank you.

Sometimes in life we end up in predicaments that seem hopeless and the world chalks us up as "not worth the effort." In God's eyes we are never "just" a chicken, and we are always worth the effort. He has just the right remedy for the wounds of our mistakes. Our mistakes might show, like the green thread that laced together our hen's neck, but they only serve as a reminder that God did not give up on us.—d.o.

April 21
The Communion Tree

For you shall go out in joy . . . and all the trees of the field shall clap their hands.
—Isaiah 55:12

The dogwood tree just outside our front door blooms for one week of spring in a pure blaze of white-blossom glory. It always seems to bloom the week of Easter, no matter which week it falls on, which is appropriate because of the folk legend that Jesus was crucified on the wood from a dogwood tree. The legend says that the dogwood never again grew big enough to make a cross after Calvary. The four-pointed blossom forms a cross, with tints of red on the edges signifying the blood of Christ shed for us. Dogwood is like a communion tree, blooming in remembrance of Jesus.

I have covered our dogwood with birdhouses and feeders, creating a communion of another kind. Some days, it looks like a Christmas tree full of bright-colored birds. Mingled among them are little gray birds, brown ones, and speckled ones, some hopping from branch to feeder, while others dance around the ground picking up the seeds the other birds spill. I've noticed that the little birds fare better because they feast while the cardinals and blue jays fight.

Three of our cats love to stalk the tree. O'Keefe, Paddy, and Yoda make a playground of it. When our dog Josie stands guard, the cats watch the bird parade from the front porch.

It's a tree where tensions, sharing, cooperation, and God's provision play out all through the day, just like in the cacophony of the human race. Friends, scoundrels, and defenders comprise the human race, but we can choose how we interact. We wake up to a world full of challenges and blessings with the red-tinged reminders of Jesus' sacrifice every day. God knows our unique predicaments and has made a way for forgiveness and love to be our highest purpose. Let's live today in remembrance of him.
—k.m.

April 22
Holy Cow

His disciples answered, "Where could we get enough bread
in this remote place to feed such a crowd?"
—Matthew 15:33

Springtime was when all the farm babies began to appear like gifts in the night. My grandpa always knew exactly how many head of cattle he owned. To me, it always looked like a gazillion—just a big bunch of animals that all looked alike.

One day when I was seven years old, my grandfather told me to pick a good calf. I picked a sweet, white-faced Hereford with gentle brown eyes and a cute, cow-licked red body. He bawled to his cow-mama and she nudged him to her udders where he suckled contentedly. I loved meeting the new calves each season.

"You picked a good one," he said. "We'll get him fed and fattened, and in the fall we'll take him to the slaughterhouse, and that's the beef our family will eat for the next year," he said.

"Eat him?" I was mortified. "You didn't tell me I was picking a calf to eat! Let me pick again! I would rather eat her . . ." I pointed to an old red cow that looked like leather over bones, chewing her cud.

"You are old enough to know where food comes from. Any animal on a farm is raised for a purpose, and we are to be grateful for their gift and sacrifice. So, we take care of them the best we can," he explained.

I would never look at a grocery store's plastic wrapped meats and not realize the gift of life it was. Food magically appears and we throw away approximately half the food we are supplied each year, some ninety-six billion pounds of edible food that could feed our starving world. As Christians who are called to "feed my sheep," we must understand where our food comes from and how we can be better stewards. I don't believe that we should all become vegetarian, but I do believe that in the miracle of God's provision, we should appreciate, share, and never waste what has been given, always making sure that we reach out to stop hunger in every way we can.—d.o.

April 23
Levitical Cat

Create in me a clean heart, O God, and put a new and right spirit within me.
—Psalm 51:10

Scruffy as he may be, our old cat, Tyrone, is as finicky as they come. One day, he patiently taught me the proper and acceptable way to serve his dinner. I plopped his small dollop of soft food on the plate he had used earlier, but some of the food crumbs from breakfast had hardened on it. He tried to go with it, but just couldn't, so he quietly sat by the plate and waited. With only a look, he put me in my place. So I got a new paper plate, put the fresh food on it, and he went back to his meal.

If Tyrone were an Old Testament character, he would be a priest. And priests need clean vessels. The priests in ancient Israel taught the people about insisting on purity. Every bowl, every candle had to be purified and holy. And once a year, the high priest would enter the Holy of Holies to offer a cleansing sacrifice for the people. God wanted the people themselves to be clean vessels too.

God hasn't changed. He still wants us to be clean. It's okay to be finicky when it comes to living a holy life. Jesus made a way for us to be clean. He reconciled us to God; he washed everything that was tainted with yesterday's crumbs. Just like Tyrone's insistence upon a clean plate, we can insist upon a clean lifestyle, knowing that we are empowered by the Holy Spirit. Whenever we are tempted to make choices that are unloving or unhealthy, his Spirit reminds us that we are made for something much, much better.—k.m.

April 24
Odd Bedfellows

A friend loves at all times, and a brother is born for a time of adversity.
—Proverbs 17:17

Our friends moved to a condominium, and with their children out of the house, there just wasn't room in their lives for the family dog, so we took him in. When the new dog arrived, we realized he was far into his senior years and had many ailments. He began to wander and get lost in the woods. He wandered so far one night that we didn't find him for two days, and when we did, he was too weak to walk back to the house.

Since he didn't integrate well with our other dogs or cats, we created a soft home of sawdust with an igloo and a nice dog bed in a horse stall. The Old Man seemed comforted by the boundaries, which must have resembled the privacy fence around the place where he grew up. He had a "runabout" each day, but only supervised ones.

We also had a wild, unsocial rescue cat named Squirt who kept her sour personality on full-tilt bad at all times.

One night, I was feeding the Old Man when Squirt strolled out of the igloo in his stall and began to eat with the Old Man. I was shocked. This unlikely pair appeared to be . . . friends! I later discovered that they cuddled up and slept together, this lonely old dog and the cat whose fear made enemies of all. Each brought the other comfort.

The last two years of the Old Man's life were not lonely because of an odd sweet friendship. Some of the best friendships can be born from life's hardest times, and even the hardest hearts soften when love takes root.
—d.o.

The Brief and Meaningful Life of Moses the Kitten

What God has made clean, you must not call profane.
—Acts 10:15

Moses was a spunky orange-and-white kitten who was born ready to take on the world. By the time he was weaned, his personality was bright and mischievous, playful and funny. He had the making of a great leader. Our dog Jack recognized the potential of this tiny mountain of a kitten and decided to claim him as his protégé. That big white dog would carry Moses around carefully like a mama cat. But one day, Jack played a little too rough. A lifeless form lay at Jack's feet. He nudged him in disbelief. Moses was gone.

After Moses died, Jack went into a depression. It took a lot of love before he came around. When he finally did, he became all the more determined to protect all the other cats and animals on the farm. He had acknowledged his mistake, grieved, and with his big sad eyes he seemed to communicate to us that this kind of thing would never happen again.

Jack has the kind of courage about his mistakes that we all need.

We are transformed for the better when we admit our mistakes and bring them to God in all honesty. God does not want us to grovel or carry guilt around, but wants us to receive his love and forgiveness wholeheartedly, no turning back. His plan of redemption is for a clean heart. To be sanctified, says Dennis Kinlaw in *The Mind of Christ*, does not mean we never make a mistake. Rather, it means that we are sensitized to error. We don't get bogged down, calling ourselves failures when God has cleansed us. More and more our will becomes aligned with God's will as we learn to walk in obedience.—k.m.

April 26
Free Horses

Suppose one of you wants to build a tower. Won't you first sit down and estimate the cost to see if you have enough money to complete it?
—Luke 14:28

"The cheapest expense in owning a horse is the money you pay to buy it," someone told me once. I had no idea what that person meant because, at the time, my full-time job was going well, and I could afford the luxury of my habit. I would often refer to a new horse as a "bargain."

Then the unforeseen happened. I lost my largest business account, and with it, my horse-keeping budget. I experienced the weight of the heaping expenses after the purchase when I could not pay for them. The horseshoes, vet bills, stable care, and the boarding bill escalated.

The horses began to suffer because of the circumstances of my financial life. The horse trainer with whom I boarded asked me for full payment, or he would have to sell my horses for the boarding bill. I asked for one week, in which I sold seven horses. As the last horse was driven away, I sat down and cried. Then I handed the barn owner the cash he was owed.

Never again did I breed a horse just to have a baby in the spring, or say yes to a free horse without knowing that I would be able to care for the animal for the rest of his life.

We always need to look down the road to see the potential blessings and problems in all our yeses. Saying good-bye to an animal you have loved is harder than saying good-bye before you grow to love it. And the concept applies to all the things we agree to without considering the reality of time and financial constraints, as well as the emotion they will require day in and day out. Being a good Christian does not mean always saying yes. It does mean seeking wisdom in each opportunity as it comes, choosing only those God has designed for you. Always listen for God's voice before saying yes . . . or no.—d.o.

April 27
Reflections

The earth is the LORD's and all that is in it, the world, and those who live in it.
—Psalm 24:1

Theologian-scientist John Polkinghorne said, "At present, too much theological thinking is very human-centered." We humans tend to think the world revolves around us. So who is redemption for? Is that an outlandish question?

The Bible says God saves people and animals. Psalm 36:6 says, "You save humans and animals alike, O LORD." No, animals are not recited the four spiritual laws and asked to say a sinner's prayer, but God loves them and desires that they have a good life. The final book of the Bible even paints a picture of every creature *in heaven and on earth* worshiping around the throne of God. Perhaps that is what he is "saving" them for.

What would it look like to have our theological thinking be more inclusive of other species? Jesus said he is the Way, the Truth, and the Life. Everything about this world hinges on his mission that all be reconciled to God and that creation be set right.

There is, no doubt, a unique role that we humans play in God's plan. We are set apart in order to participate with God in the bringing of his kingdom on earth. Our unique humanness that is designed in God's image must be for the purpose of fulfilling God's plans not only for us as individuals, and us as a species, but for the rest of universal creation.

Do you ever wonder if the animals "see through a glass darkly" (1 Corinthians 13:12 KJV)? Maybe it's not such an outlandish question after all, to wonder if the animals catch glimpses of God. They certainly seem to be full of gratitude. Ever watched your dog or cat or horse take in the sunrise? We are wise to recognize that they, too, are part of God's divine plan.—k.m.

April 28
In Defense of Cats

This day I call the heavens and the earth as witnesses against you that I
have set before you life and death, blessings and curses.
Now choose life, so that you and your children may live.
—Deuteronomy 30:19

Man's best friend might be a dog in the cliché, but I have been completely satisfied to curl up with a kitty's little purr motor lowering my blood pressure and stress.

Cats must have chosen the wrong public relations firm in ancient days compared to dogs. Cats are portrayed as villains, witches, and spirit suckers, while dogs rescue people from abandoned wells. How unfair is that? When the topic of pets arises, it doesn't take long for groups of people to draw the line between the dog people and the cat people. I was always *on* the line, because both are God's gift to me.

In our world of pigeonholing and judgments, we categorize everything. People, places, and pets become just another way to say you aren't in the crowd of coolness. Society is always moving the bar around so that no one can reach it. We always find new ways to create "us" and "them": black or white, fat or skinny, boxers or briefs, dogs or cats. Comparisons and competition create feelings of being a loser. Those classifications and criticisms can make us pull away from life and fall short of God's glory for us.

God created individual spirits in all creation—humans, dogs, cats, and even woolly worms. God didn't make any junk. He made beauty in all things for us to love and enjoy. Cats are God's reminder that we are independent creatures, free from the herd instinct to follow the crowd. We are never to fall prey to the criticisms meant to pull us away from life. We are called to learn from cats—choosing life every single time, and an animal that's modeled the phrase "nine lives" should certainly be able to show us how!—d.o.

April 29
Hi, Lily

You are precious in my sight, and honored, and I love you.
—Isaiah 43:4

When Isaiah the prophet delivered these words to the children of Israel, he had already reminded them that God created them, redeemed them, called them by name, and delivered them. God wants his people to know that his love reaches beyond Israel's tribe to all people. He did not redeem Israel merely for Israel's sake, but so that they could be a part of his plan to bless all creation.

God speaks this passage to people, not a person, but we make no mistake by taking it personally. One life makes a difference to the whole, while the rest of the family menagerie is precious to God too. "Consider the sparrow," Jesus said. He was teaching us that to God, even a tiny bird is important.

When someone, person or animal, does not know they are special, it affects the way they perceive the world and the way they treat others. I guess that's why God made such a point of telling us we are special.

We have a sweet girl who came to live at the farm, a black dog named Lily, who did not, at first, know that she was precious to us as our honored guest. She is gentle and old, and her eyes are expressive and kind. Lily would not come up to the carport with the other dogs at dinner time, or seek the usual pats on the head. We thought perhaps she was not bonding with *us*, but in time we realized she wanted our kind attention as much as the other dogs did.

I often think about how people feel awkward, alone, or afraid sometimes, like Lily, and how others often misinterpret their actions as rude or ignore them completely. Some are less able than others to accept love. Trust must be earned. When I look to God's Word for understanding, I am reminded that the very best we can do is embrace God's very best for us, and then reflect his love with gentle patience. The more of us who know how loved we really are, the better we will be able to remind others that they are loved too.—k.m.

April 30
Footprints on the Pink Couch

Your path led through the sea, your way through the mighty waters,
though your footprints were not seen.
—Psalm 77:19

The pink-and-white striped couch became the focal point of my new den as soon as it arrived—a perfect replica of a picture I had pulled from a decorating magazine and copied color by color. I had saved for every piece of furniture, each rug, and every framed print. Though I was renting, it felt like my first home. I stood back and surveyed the room, holding the picture up to make sure I had successfully duplicated all the elements of the professional decorators.

A gentle rain fell that night, washing the outside patio clean and turning the leaves a more vibrant green. I put a leash on my dog for a walk, and upon returning, he ran through the house with joyful abandon. Then, I saw the new pink and white sofa, a line of muddy footprints running up the seat cushions, over the back, and down again in schnauzer speed-racer style.

I rented a steam cleaner, unaware that steam would create a browning effect on the sofa fabric, so the tiny footprints became larger and larger ugly brown stains. No matter how I tried, the remnants of paw prints remained. Friends offered advice, such as "Get rid of that dog," but I decided that love for my puppy was much more important, invested in a washable slipcover, and enjoyed watching Winston curl up on the couch. The only one who knew about the footprints was me. My life was picture perfect again, and underneath it all, the unseen footprints represented faithful love to me.

God is like that for me. I can't explain tangibly how God shows, proves, and expresses his love to me every day, but I know that he is present. His path cannot be erased. When the world tries to wash away God's love for us, it just gets bigger. God's path is a good path, picture perfect . . . keep following.—d.o.

May 1
Dare to Trust

Jesus said to them, "Come and have breakfast."
Now none of the disciples dared to ask him, "Who are you?"
because they knew it was the Lord.
—John 21:12

My collie, Veronique, has very small eyes and a nose that catches every smell, making up for her lack of peripheral vision. People always ask me if she's blind. I tell them, "No, she just can't see." I've watched her befuddlement when we come home and pour out of the car as she tries to discern who is who.

I suppose that's how it was with the disciples when they encountered their risen Lord for the first time after the first Easter. They knew they weren't seeing a ghost. It really was Jesus, and beyond what their eyes could see, they trusted what their hearts *knew*.

I love how the gospel writer and disciple John writes that when they saw Jesus after his resurrection they didn't *dare* ask their Lord who he was. I'm sure Jesus would have understood. They could have asked, "Lord, is that you? Can it be?" But they didn't *dare*.

This was their chance to show the Lord, their savior and friend, that they finally got it. They had not recognized him at first out walking on the water, they had argued with him about the plan, the death he must suffer, they had slept through his agony in the garden of Gethsemane; but now, in this last chapter of John's book, they finally figure out that they can trust what their hearts know, even when they can hardly believe their own eyes. Perhaps they didn't dare question because they wanted the Lord to know they got it and that they were finally taking him at his word, and that's worth everything.

It makes me feel happy when Veronique recognizes me because I know she trusts that recognition of someone who loves her and will take care of her. She seems so relieved when I come home, like that means everything is going to be okay. And so it is.—k.m.

May 2
In a Real Mess

But the Israelites said to the LORD, "We have sinned.
Do with us whatever you think best, but please rescue us now."
—Judges 10:15

Geronimo is a pony with a curious heart. He always has to be on the other side of the fence. Neighbors and police officers have called on numerous occasions when Geronimo has taken leave to enjoy bites of budding gardens or holiday floral decorations.

Now, wire of any kind, especially loose fence wire, can be lethal to a horse. Caught in a wire loop, a horse will pull back with fear and force until they've cut through tendon and bone. The more afraid they are, the harder they pull.

One night, I noticed Geronimo standing close to the fence away from the feed buckets. I figured he was just investigating, but an hour later, he was standing in the exact same spot—the same position. I heard him whinny, but he never moved. When I walked up to him, I realized that he had worked two legs into a complete tangle of wires. He was half in and half out of the fence. I don't know how long he had been there, just standing, waiting, depending on his humans to get him out. With a few wire-cutting snips, he wiggled free and ran to his food bucket as if nothing had happened.

We get into awful situations of our own making, and when we're immobilized by the muck and mire, we call on God to help. Knowing we've caused the tangle we're in, we still wait for God to snip our snares. We make bargains with God until we feel free and rescued, but then we continue with the same behavior until the next time. And the cycle repeats: we sin, God rescues us, and we go back to the food bucket. You would think we would avoid the pitfalls, but God's love is always forgiving and rescuing even when we fall into the same trap, time after time after time.

I'm so glad that God loves first, rescues second, and judges last, but how can we break the cycle? We can ask God to do with us what he thinks is best, and he will answer. If we're willing, God will save us and will change our lives, so we don't have to fall into the same snares over and over.—d.o.

May 3
Pretty in Pink

For God alone my soul waits in silence, for my hope is from him.
—Psalm 62:5

In September of 2010, two wildlife photographers were chasing wildebeests around Kenya when they discovered a pink hippopotamus. She was like a rose petal in the middle of a chubby gray conglomeration, with delicate charcoal freckles dotting the otherwise strawberry ice cream skin of her face and back.

The sighting of this rare creature was no surprise to native Kenyans who were familiar with the banks of the Mara River where she was photographed. I would feel pretty lucky if I saw a pink hippopotamus—unless, of course, I was standing too close, as hippos are prone to attack. But to scientists, her pink skin is no mystery. She has a condition called leucism that causes her skin to produce less pigment.

We tend to set our expectations on what we deem normal, though we've seen tons of happy surprises, God-wrought surprises in the universe. God did, after all, make lightning bugs and hummingbirds, ibexes and leafy sea dragons. He used the unfaithful children of Israel to prove what faithfulness is; he defied the laws of medicine when he healed the sick and gave sight to the blind; he rearranged the laws of nature when he walked on water and disappeared from a mobbing crowd as though he had been beamed up; and he used death to prove the power of life.

Nice, predictable, normal life is simply out of the question in God's world. Gray hippos may be all we see now, but, like the Kenyans, we shouldn't be surprised by pink ones. When we open our hearts and minds to the possibilities of God's power and faithfulness, he opens our eyes to see those pink hippos milling around every corner.—k.m.

May 4
A Bunny's Tale

What I feared has come upon me; what I dreaded has happened to me.
—Job 3:25

Adam was one of our bunnies, bought on Easter from a roadside farmer stand. We didn't know a lot about rabbits, but we understood that keeping them cool and dry was important, so we housed him in the shed with our chickens, where we thought he would be well protected from predators.

Dogs love to chase rabbits. Our dogs found a way to open the door to the chicken house and knock over the rabbit cage, causing a horrible commotion. We ran to see Jack, our Great Pyrenees, chasing Adam down. Adam had gotten free from his cage and was hopping like mad to escape the jaws of the behemoth. Jack closed the gap, wrapped his big furry paws around the bunny, lay down, and rested his huge head over the trembling rabbit. He held Adam soft and secure until we could get to the rabbit and take him into the house.

After examining the rabbit, we found not a scratch on him, but his heart was beating like a drum solo. An hour later, he died without warning. After reading about the weakness of a rabbit's heart and how fear can cause heart attacks, we realized that fear had claimed his life.

Danger, real or imagined, can create incredible fear in us. And like in our bunny Adam, when fear is allowed to bloom, it only attracts more fear, paralyzing us from living fully and doing what God calls us to do. The enemy uses fear to keep us from moving, sap our strength, cause our downfall, and debilitate our spirit. Today, let us draw God closer than fear and allow peace to grow within us, calming our wildly beating heart.
—d.o.

May 5
The Ibex and the King

He made my feet like the feet of deer, and set me secure on the heights.
—2 Samuel 22:34; Psalm 18:33

The Nubian ibex lives on the rocky desert shores of the Dead Sea. With their curled horns, they stand proudly on high places, and these cloven-hoofed mountain goats can glide across the steepest rockiest mountain, their strange ponytail beards whipping in the wind.

Jesus must have seen a lot of ibexes when he walked around Israel. He spent some serious time on those desert shores and in those mountains, perhaps enjoying his creation through them. He knew all about them: how they live in separate herds, male and female, coming together only once a year to mate. He may have watched the young with the mamas, who guide and protect them until they are old enough to brave the cliffs on their own. They must have reminded him of these beautiful verses from the Torah that he cherished so much.

Jesus also knew that the ibex faces many dangers seeking the high places. They may reach the heights where eagles soar, but the golden eagle, in particular, is not such a good host. It will attack a young ibex for food, so the mama ibex must teach her babies to be swift and agile very early on.

In our continuous climb toward righteousness, toward the life Jesus has given us, Satan will follow, and he will attack. The closer we get, the more intense those attacks will become. He knows how we love the heights of life in our Creator, how those times of rest or excitement in Jesus can inspire and strengthen us, so Satan will do whatever he can to destroy us.

Don't give up on the climb. One step after the other, continue to draw nearer to your source of life. Be strengthened by the heights and be encouraged under attack.—k.m.

Prayer with Your Best Friend

Then I heard every creature in heaven and on earth and under the earth
and on the sea, and all that is in them, saying: "To him who sits on
the throne and to the Lamb be praise and honor and
glory and power, for ever and ever!"
—Revelation 5:13

Dogabon is an odd cat who keeps to herself and enjoys sleeping on the front porch on a small stump. She bends over the stump like it's an altar every day, closing her eyes as if she's in prayer. It makes me wonder if animals actually *do* pray. Do we as humankind have the singular opportunity to commune daily with God in beautiful relationship? If that is so, how do we use this most awesome privilege?

People ask me all the time how to pray, but I have never heard anyone ask how to have a conversation with their best friend. God wants that kind of conversation. He doesn't have limitations or requirements on our prayer time. He doesn't give us more stars if we wake up and give him two hours on our knees, and he doesn't give us fewer stars if we sing praise songs as we brush the horses and muck the stalls. God just wants us to want him.

Some people like praying with a fishing pole in their hands. Some like to pray on the morning walk with the dog. God is not so much concerned about the where and when; he's more concerned that we just do it—that we run to our prayer stump each day to tell our God that we love him.

I want to be freer in my prayer. Revelation says that every creature will praise him, every knee shall bow, and the whole world will sing passionate praises to our God. As you pray today, join with the Revelation creatures' enthusiasm for our King, the Lamb of God.—d.o.

A Friend So Grackle

God's love has been poured into our hearts through the Holy Spirit that has been given to us.
—Romans 5:5

The Nubian ibex can live up to twenty years, partly thanks to the grackles who peck for parasites and any other critters that could be harmfully hiding in their hides. These black birds flock around the mountain climbers, sometimes fighting over which grackle can feast on the bugs of which goat. It's the grackle law. No grackle is stuck without an ibex, and no ibex is without a grackle.

It's a good thing the grackle and the ibex don't overthink the issue, because they seem like an unlikely pair. They just follow a natural instinct and everybody is loved and cared for. People, though, are always looking for a reason, a motivation, or a payback. But don't you sometimes wish we could simply take care of one another without overthinking it? Love for the sake of love. Love for the sake of another.

Not often do we find a friend who will love us, bugs and all, or especially think our bugs are a blessing. All kinds of parasites in our lives—addictions, moodiness, money issues, or a past full of mistakes—can alienate others just when we need people the most. Without God, our natural instinct is to judge, but judgment never healed a soul. Only love does, and that's what God calls us to do. When we walk close to the Lord and allow his love to be first in our hearts—*poured into our hearts*—his kind of love and kindness becomes natural instinct.

If you have one friend in this world, someone who gives you a hand or a paw to hold, who likes you, bad moods, bugs, and all, you are truly blessed. But whether you do or not, ask God to make you the kind of friend who can love in spite of the parasites in others' lives.—k.m.

May 8
Cicadas on the Halfshell

All the men of Judah answered the men of Israel, "We did this because the
king is closely related to us. Why are you angry about it?
Have we eaten any of the king's provisions?
Have we taken anything for ourselves?"
—2 Samuel 19:42

The great cicada invasion of our area occurs in the spring of every thirteenth year. The noise is deafening until they breed and pile up dead, their progeny lying underground to incubate for the next thirteen years. They are little harmless monsters to many, but for dogs and chickens, cicada year is a jubilee year. They love the crunch and nibble of cicadas!

I found a dried cicada, took it down to the chicken yard, and watched one fat hen run off with it in her beak, the other hens chasing her around the chicken yard in a frenzy. The lucky one swallowed her steal in two gulps and made all the other hens cackle with jealousy.

When people gather with conflicting expectations, relationships fall apart over what's mine and what's yours. Think about the selfishness we see when families war over an inheritance. Everyone feels entitled to more, more, more, and familial bond is torn apart, just like that little cicada. The legacy of entitlement breeds children who take all, regardless of others' needs, but a legacy of Christ-centeredness begins by deciding to love more than demanding fairness or self-fulfillment.

Jesus has taught us that love is kind, but it is seldom fair. We can share in Jesus' inheritance when we care less about *being* right, and more about *doing* right. When God intervenes, lifeless hulks of relationship live again. No family is a lost cause in God's kingdom. All of us are his children, and he can teach all of us to stop taking for ourselves and live for each other.
—d.o.

May 9
The Blame Game

No one who conceals transgressions will prosper,
but one who confesses and forsakes them will obtain mercy.
—Proverbs 28:13

Imagine a man who had a rough day at the office. Feeling justified in his bad mood, he fights his way home through heavy traffic, rehashing the events of the day in his mind so by the time he arrives, he is fuming all the more. His wife is waiting with dinner and lots on her mind that she needs to discuss from her own challenging day, but he has no patience for her and abruptly snaps that he just wants to eat in peace.

Soon, little Johnny comes running loudly through the room, ready to show her the new picture he colored, but in his excitement, he accidentally knocks over the cup of milk. Mom loses her temper and reprimands him with a sharp edge. Johnny runs crying to his room in frustration, where the family dog sleeps peacefully on a beanbag chair. He wakes up with a wag of the tail to see his boy, but is greeted with a harsh whack on the nose with a plastic baseball bat. No one bothers to pay attention to the yelp.

Blame passes quickly from one person to another. You don't even have to say out loud, "I blame so and so." It just spills over with presumed entitlement that you deserve better, and it makes you forget how to behave. Blame doesn't stop to think. And worst of all, by definition, it doesn't take any responsibility.

Patterns of blame create cycles of pain. At any place in the blame chain, someone must act differently. We have been given God's nature to use in tough situations. We can choose to do as Jesus did and break the cycle of blame even, and especially, when someone might "deserve" it. One thing is for sure, the poor dog will be much happier when everyone takes responsibility for love and kindness.—k.m.

Make My Presence Known

Their young thrive and grow strong in the wilds;
they leave and do not return.
—Job 39:4

A feral cat may not ever be tamed. I have tamed many, but I've "lost" just as many back to the wild. Even after accepting a bottle, warm baths, and sleeping in my lap, something pulled one particular wild kitten of ours back to her birthplace. This kitty's beautiful rust, gray, and white-coated body recoiled from advancers, and her amber eyes held fright in every glance. When it was time for her to be spayed, we managed to capture her with oven mitts, amazing our vet. She said that in all her years of working on ferals, this one was *the* wildest. The cat's apprehension was her ultimate defense against all that might hurt her.

For years, she roamed the outskirts of the farm, keeping to the brambles that shielded her from coyotes. She survived floods and all manner of dangers. We could call to her, and even though she wouldn't come near, she would make herself known. If she was hungry, she would meow in an unbelievable cry, loud enough for us to hear her inside the house. No amount of our love or care for her could overshadow her fear. But when she needed something, she always made her presence known.

God hears those lonely cries in the dark when we need him, and he never makes us come to him. He doesn't even require us to meet him halfway. God will come all the way, make all the moves, beat down the walls of our own personal hells, if need be. If we are afraid of church, he will meet us in a barn. He will care for us even when we scratch and bite and fight against him. Thankfully, our salvation is not dependent on our perfection. Our perfection is dependent on his salvation.—d.o.

May 11
Mysteries in Dreamtime

We look not at what can be seen but at what cannot be seen;
for what can be seen is temporary, but what cannot be seen is eternal.
—2 Corinthians 4:18

The color blue reminds me of things eternal, perhaps because the sky is blue and seems endless, so I imagine heaven is in it or beyond it somehow. God's eternal nature is the first thing I think about when I see a blue dragonfly. They are somehow reminders that God's world is full of eternal blue accents that speak of a world beyond ours.

Dragonflies come in practically every color of the rainbow. It was in Louisiana where I first saw one in blue. It was a steamy day just before summer, and I was walking by a small pond. The cicadas and frogs chorused louder as the heat of the day began to fade into evening, and out over that pond those blue dragonflies went chasing after the skeeters. Then the birds went chasing after the dragonflies. I went to get a closer look, and I found that the dragonflies had bright blue eyes.

I imagined that God gave them those crazy blue eyes so they could see forever, just like the endless sky went on forever or the big, blue ocean seemed to, especially to my young mind.

To this day, the dragonflies (properly called blue-eyed darners) remind me that I still don't understand a lot about this world. But even though I don't "get" everything, I have a God who can see past the sky, and one day he'll explain everything to me. And this thought, this fact, gives me hope today.—k.m.

May 12
Please Release Me, Let Me Go

I will walk about in freedom,
for I have sought out your precepts.
—Psalm 119:45

Fishing was one of my very first leisure activities. My parents would wrap up my infant carrier in an orange life jacket, place me between them in the bottom of the boat, and fish in the bayous of Louisiana. The sun would shine through the cypress in small yellow ribbons, and I would rock peacefully to the rhythm of that small aluminum boat as the water gently hit the sides. To this day, that boat is the happy place I go to in my mind. It's in my blood, I guess.

When I got a little older, my father was adamant about letting the young fish go back to grow up. He would show me how to gently let them off the hook, and give them a little shake to get them swimming again as I let them go. My favorites were the sun perch, so beautiful as they surfaced and the sun hit the orange of the scales just below the gills. It was never the catch I brought home that brought me the greatest joy. It was in the catch I let go. I did find it interesting that some of the biggest fights came from the smallest fish.

We are small fish who fight big battles. And sometimes we lose sight of the reason we are fighting, so we just create opposition. God pulls and we resist, not realizing our Father just wants us near him so that he can appreciate *us*, as his beautiful creations, then let us gently go.

The next time I feel God pulling me closer, I want to resist less, allowing him to delight in me and transform my heart, while I radiate in the joy of being in God's happy place.—d.o.

May 13
The Power of Prayer

For I will restore health to you, and your wounds I will heal, says the LORD.
—Jeremiah 30:17

I have been in prayer with a group of sisters and brothers in Christ where someone has prayed for a sick or lost or wounded animal. These kinds of prayers often provoke snickers. I suppose it is only innocent concern that praying for an animal like one would pray for a person could be irreverent. Yet, our pets are family, they are precious to us. Many people love their pets with a heart full of joy and commitment and treasure them as gifts from God. So why wouldn't we pray for our pets? Would it be wrong for a farmer to pray that his crops will be healthy so he can make a living and care for his family?

I learned the importance of praying for our furry loved ones from my mother when I was a child. I had trained my collie, Shane, to avoid the danger of the road. Our driveway entered on the slope of a hill where cars tended to pick up speed and zoom by. My girl was always obedient, but one day, a car came out of nowhere and hit her. I was terrified and devastated. My Dad and I rushed her to the vet, and Mom went to her prayer place, knelt, and began to weep, asking for God's help for Shane.

As the vet examined her, I braced myself for the worst. She wasn't bleeding, but there might be internal injuries. She was a brave girl through it all. After lots of prayer and crying, I wanted to give the vet a big hug when he told me Shane would be okay.

After God healed my Shane, we lived on with gratitude and grace. He used my sweet dog to remind my family that he cares about the same things we care about. God wants his creation to be healthy, and he delights in our trust in him to heal us when we're not.—k.m.

May 14

Mean Party in the Sky

The greedy stir up conflict, but those who trust in the LORD will prosper.
—Proverbs 28:25

Have you ever fed seagulls? One shows up and begs for a bite of whatever you are eating, and before he can scoop up the goody you've thrown, out of nowhere come twelve more squawking birds, trying to steal something for themselves. They aren't laboring to feed their young or share with others. They are just greedy opportunists trying to snatch whatever someone else is getting.

Fights begin, loud shrieking back and forth between birds, and the hope of a gentle feeding of a lone bird is over. Seagulls espouse an "if you have it, that means I don't have it, therefore I must take it from you" philosophy.

We have forgotten the commandment not to covet, while wrapping ourselves whole-heartedly around the "look out for number one" slogan. Jesus never exemplified this mentality. He never said to go after what other people have if you expect to get ahead in life. He never said go for the gold, especially when that means standing on the heads of those who already have the gold. Jesus said that there's enough gold for everyone in his kingdom. We can have as much of God as we want and life to the fullest in him.

Conflicts and jealousies arise in the church family over ridiculous things like who gets to sing the solo, who chooses the carpet color, and who gets to read the announcements. Greed, selfishness, or seagull behavior is the very behavior that can send a nonbelieving visitor screaming back to the world shouting, "Hypocrites!"

When we focus on lifting God up, trusting him to provide, all will be drawn to him. God wants to prosper us, all of us, in his love and his light. Prosperity in God's kingdom means more love. Love is the currency of heaven. We all get to be number one in God's world, if God remains number one in ours.—d.o.

Cheese, Please!

We speak God's wisdom, secret and hidden,
which God decreed before the ages for our glory.
—1 Corinthians 2:7

I sometimes pray that I will have the tenacity to search out the things of God with the same vigor our dogs have when they hear a rustle and go after it, or our cats when they catch a movement out of the corner of an eye and chase it down. We need to chase God down. In Genesis 32, Jacob actually wrestles with God's angel, demanding a blessing. Our little Jesse is like that. She, more than any of the other dogs, gets so excited about a piece of yellow cheese that she will jump, beg, sit, or dance the Charleston to get it. She won't give up. We shouldn't either.

God shows us a mystery, revealed in Christ. Jesus is the mystery, the door through which God's kingdom is unlocked and unleashed, the one through whom God has taken away the sins of the world. He is the living Word, through whom we become God's living message too (2 Corinthians 3:3). "These things," Paul says in 1 Corinthians 2:10, "God has revealed to us through the Spirit."

And Jesus tells us to search out that mystery: "Ask, and it will be given you; search, and you will find" (Matthew 7:7). Ask. Maybe faith is not about having all the answers; it's about asking the questions—not cynically, but with a true hunger to know. God welcomes our searching, without judgment. It's how we learn.

So what do we search for: what is our "cheese"? The Bible says our reward is God himself, whose precious presence brings peace to our souls. God's mystery answers your heart's cry now, yet unfolds more and more. Some days you might feel like you're the only one who gets it or as if you don't understand anything, but be like a schnauzer digging after a mole. Stay on it—the rewards will be great!—k.m.

Lost in a Storm

*When neither sun nor stars appeared for many days
and the storm continued raging, we finally gave up all hope of being saved.*
—Acts 27:20

In 2004, a tsunami rocked the Indian Ocean, leaving a seaside paradise destroyed and some 170,000 dead. I can't even imagine the ravaging devastation after the deep ocean flooded the shoreline towns. The destruction was so bad that elephants were unchained from tourist rides and circus tricks to lift heavy debris and look for bodies. Hope was nowhere in sight.

After the quake, an orphaned baby hippo was found huddled with other refugee animals and taken to a wildlife preserve. The little hippo ran squealing to a giant old tortoise, who began to hiss and snap at the youngster, but he just wouldn't give up. He must have thought that rude 130-year-old turtle was his mama, because he curled up next to her and swam with her, and soon they became friends. The story of this unusual pair hit the news. Among the stories of death and destruction, people found hope in the strong bond between the orphan and the old, hard-shelled reptile. I believe our world is filled with events, some caused naturally and others caused by humanity. Some occurrences are good and some are bad. But God is always in the rescues, the hopeful stories, and the reaching out by humanity to others in need. A natural disaster is rife with anguish, but in those same desperate moments, miracles abound. People from different parts of the world think of someone other than themselves, rushing to give time and money to end the suffering. In the valleys of disaster, God hears our cries and paints pictures of hope all around us.

When we get caught up in our own disasters, family struggles, the threat of financial ruin, and all the significant pain that we experience as individuals, we can know that we have a God of hope who always carries a miracle in his heart for us. There are no orphans in God's kingdom, only children of God. If you feel like the storm will never pass, remember who your father is. God is always there, behind the clouds, ready to send you the perfect rescue or comfort when you need it.—d.o.

Growling for Grace

A new heart I will give you, and a new spirit I will put within you;
and I will remove from your body the heart of stone and give you a heart of flesh.
—Ezekiel 36:26

E ver hear phrases like, "You can't teach an old dog new tricks"? Well, you can! Our animals, young and old, learn lots of new tricks. There's another phrase often said about some people: "He will never change." Wrong again! People change.

God wants to help us change for the better, and he does that by giving us a change of heart. He goes to great lengths in the Bible to tell us that he is patient with us if we're slow learners. People are not born with hearts of stone; there's a reason they harden. Sometimes they make poor choices, and sometimes they lack discipline. As a result of these choices, people carry around blame or anger with themselves, which looks like harshness on the outside. Sometimes we simply don't know any better.

A heart of stone is a broken heart in disguise. On the outside, people see depression and anger, but on the inside there is hopelessness, despair, and fear. We've rescued some furry babies who had broken hearts. They growled at us, snapped at the other dogs, and needed lots of TLC. They learned, though, and they responded to kindness.

Jesus heals broken hearts when we accept his love and grace. Trust him to soften you through and through.—k.m.

May 18
Someone Else's Dream

Finally all the trees said to the thornbush, "Come and be our king."
—Judges 9:14

Have you ever bought into someone else's dream? My joyous hobby of loving horses became a competitive business almost overnight. Soon, I was breeding horses for better traits and entering competitions that made me a nervous wreck. I tried to keep up with the Joneses of the horse competition world, but all I did was wear myself out.

Even worse, the former joy of brushing my old horse in the afternoon turned into show preparation and training time for all the new horses. I had to stop trail riding so that I could attend more shows. All of a sudden, the love I had for my horses was replaced with stress, anxiety, and nervousness.

Pictures and blue ribbons were not worth the price I paid with my peace. For some people, horse competitions might be exactly what God made them for, but not me—I'd asked the thorn bush to be my goal and my king.

We will do whatever it takes to get what we think we want. We get it, but then we wake up with thorns to pick out and bills to pay. But even when we've spent so much time seeking the wrong things, we will find relief in our hearts when we fall into God's arms and allow him to guide us.

Even if we are in over our heads, God honors the choice to let go of the burdens we place on ourselves when trying to live up to other people's expectations. God makes good the mistakes we've made trying to be something we are not the second we release the thorn bush and give him the reins.—d.o.

May 19
How God Saved the Sheep

And I heard a loud voice from the throne saying, "See, the home of God is among mortals.
He will dwell with them; . . . they will be his peoples."
—Revelation 21:3

The children of Israel were always messing up. They made new resolutions every morning and then broke them by sundown. They were no better than anyone else, and God never said he chose them because they were better. So why did God choose them?

Why would God play favorites with the human race?

Perhaps God's method was similar to the way we chose our animals. Ever pick a puppy out of a litter, knowing that, with its eyes riveted on yours, it was telling you it wanted to be yours?

That's how it all began with Abraham—he recognized the voice of the true and living God. It had been a while since anyone had heard that voice, as though the whole human race stepped into a soundproof booth for years. During that time, God's heart was grieved. He kept talking, loving, and reaching out, but no one heard. I wonder what made Abraham hear that day what no one had heard for so long. Was it the shape of the clouds or the beauty of the sunset? Was it a ripple on the water or a warm feeling in his heart? Maybe he saw an eagle flying or a wild donkey drinking from a wadi in the desert, and had a thought of God. Whatever it was, he responded. He believed, and that counted for everything. One word of faith uttered, and God promised him the world. *That* is the answer to "why Israel?" God only needed one person to respond to him, and God could work with that, one life at a time.

God chose Israel to show the world the power of his grace. Abraham chose God, so God chose Abraham, delighted to pour his magnificent love on someone who wanted it. God wants to choose everyone and release his provision and protection onto his people.—k.m.

May 20
The Bug Collector

For the creation waits in eager expectation for the children of God to be revealed.
—Romans 8:19

For my elementary 4-H club, I didn't have space to raise a sheep, a goat, or a heifer for my project. My project needed to be something that could be catalogued and recorded in a journal daily. No farm animals were allowed in our 1970s-era subdivision, so I chose projects that fit into city life: sewing and bugs.

I made an apron, which bored me to tears. But entomology, the collection and study of insects, proved to be exciting and full of lessons. My mother was not thrilled to find everything from beetles to cockroaches dried and pinned sacrificially to boards around my room. Exoskeletons rested in jars, crickets ate raw potato, and catalpa worms chilled in the refrigerator. Everywhere you looked was a garish collecting area for my project.

As my collection grew, I began to see the delicate detail and purpose in all these interesting creatures. Spiders, though not insects, were in the collection for their beautiful bodies and artistic design. Their webs were a work of art. Cicadas sang songs. Crickets and grasshoppers played their legs as instruments. The wings of dragonflies were stained glass windows, and ants were the contractors and architects of a dream world.

I was given no trophy for my season of work in the bug field, but I was rewarded with a knowledge that everything created by God has a purpose, an intentional design, and a unique beauty. When we look through a microscope even at the very smallest of life-forms, we can see pattern, design, and art in every single one. The deeper I look into God, the more of him I find in everything, in every creature, in every one of us.—d.o.

May 21
Oh where, Oh where Has My Polar Bear Gone?

The righteous know the needs of their animals, but the mercy of the wicked is cruel.
—Proverbs 12:10

Time doesn't heal all wounds.

Many animals are near extinction, not because of natural process, but because the human species has rooted them out, hunted them away, depleted them for medical research, or committed such abuse and neglect that they destroyed the very ones they were here to protect.

Tigers, wild apes, polar bears, rhinos, and pandas, to name a few, are species on the brink of extinction. Other species, such as the Asiatic lion, are already extinct in certain areas. No more lions roam in Israel. No more of certain Brazilian macaws swing and chatter in the wild. And Australian gastric brooding frogs, funny little creatures that scientists used for research to cure stomach issues in humans, don't bob and bounce in puddles anymore. Urban development or other such "progress" causes these God-designed creatures to disappear. The dusky seaside sparrow of Florida is gone. The world has seen its last Columbia Basin pygmy rabbit, as well as the unique katydids that were only found in the San Francisco Bay.

These extinctions are not God's doing. The ecosystem God developed doesn't match the results we see today. We have a commission from the Holy One to love and protect these animals and to respect their existence, just as surely as we have a commission to help humans who suffer. Our care for our animals speaks a lot about our character, as Scripture says.

We are called to pay attention. Read about endangered animals. Maybe God will lead you to give a love offering to help them. Maybe God will give you a platform to help educate people or to change policies that protect them.

God can give us wisdom to know what to do. What we can all do today, right now, is pray. Time doesn't heal all wounds, but God can, and we are enlisted to help.—k.m.

May 22

A Change of "Dreamery"

And afterward, I will pour out my Spirit on all people.
Your sons and daughters will prophesy,
your old men will dream dreams,
your young men will see visions.
—Joel 2:28

There was a young man we know who followed in his famous father's footsteps as a singer/songwriter. The shadow cast was a long one, and comparisons flew, cruel and constant. The young man shared his father's legacy, but he deserved to shine in his own light.

So, at an animal shelter celebrity event, instead of taking pictures with fans, he cleaned animal cages, walked dogs, and volunteered himself into a whirlwind. He left with a dog that day and renewed his vision and his dreams—the ones God put within him, the dreams God never forgot. He's turned his life toward a whole new direction, with the music as the complement instead of the focus.

The new shadow is one *he* casts, because he is fulfilling God's plan for his life. He is quite an inspiration, making me look at all the things I do because I *should*. What do you do because someone told you that's what you should do?

We get so saturated in being who we feel we are supposed to be that we overlook what God has planned. We cannot find peace and fulfillment in the visions people have for us. God's dream for us might be bigger than what the world sees for us, bigger than what our family sees, and even bigger than what we see for ourselves. When we ask God to fulfill his plan for us, and he breathes his spirit into our being, we begin to realize the miracle of allowing God to work in us. Suddenly our age doesn't matter, or our gender, our financial situation, or even our physical limitations. God is our only limit to the dream.—d.o.

May 23
Picasso's Tears

Am I a God near by, says the LORD, and not a God far off?
Who can hide in secret places so that I cannot see them? says the LORD.
—Jeremiah 23:23-24

Picasso is a Maltese from North Carolina. He has no manners because he is blissfully spoiled. Cuteness has paid off for this silky white bundle of fur with a little black nose and dark, expressive eyes. He minds only one person on this earth, his human dad, a retired businessman with a mischievous playful nature much like his dog's. Picasso's human mom is the reason Picasso was adopted into the family. Plagued with anxiety and a broken heart carried over from an abusive and sorrowful childhood, this beautiful, classy lady loved God's handiwork that she saw in the Maltese.

One day, when she was at home alone with Picasso, she had a stroke and passed away. Picasso was with her for hours, out of his mind with fear. He knew she was not okay. Picasso was her last companion in life and in death, the only one who was with her at the end. If ever a family has wished dogs could talk, it was hers. How fast did she go? Did she suffer at all? Did she cry for help? Please, dear God, tell us she went instantly, that nothing could have been done if someone had been there.

But, Picasso wasn't the only one with his mom when she died. God saw her suffering and knew exactly how to comfort her with an animal she loved and cherished. She didn't die alone.

Now, spoiled as ever, Picasso is calmer, as though he shares the burden of his mom's passing. Now, he somehow represents her. Her clothing, jewelry, car, and even her photo have finality about them, but Picasso is alive, with memories, with love, with bad habits that she helped instill in him.

Picasso lives in Florida now with his dad. Neither one has the words to say what their hearts hold inside for their lost loved one, but they both know that God cared for the one they loved, and that God never abandoned her, but comforted her to the end.—k.m.

May 24
Bad Dog, No Biscuit

Therefore, since we have these promises, dear friends,
let us purify ourselves from everything that contaminates
body and spirit, perfecting holiness out of reverence for God.
—2 Corinthians 7:1

My Great Dane puppy dragged me down the street; she ate a table as she began to get her adult teeth, and I found myself to be a lost ball in high weeds in regard to dog training. Dog treats were not enough to get her to heel, roll over, or even just sit. She was a big overgrown mass of muscle and did not understand my commands, whether soft or loud.

I called on a professional trainer to help me, and the first thing he did was take away all the dog treats. He said, "When you train them to work for a biscuit, you aren't training them at all. You teach them that the reason they are to do a behavior is for a reward."

His advice sounded like pure hooey. What dog would do what you needed him to do without a treat? But in her first lesson, my Dane was doing everything the trainer asked without a treat of any kind. She looked up at him adoringly and moved on the leash without so much as a tug. Her favorite reward was love, as it turned out.

We, as untrained puppies in God's world, might start out following God's rules and laws because we see some exciting reward in it for us. We seek to find favor or financial reward or even streets of gold when we die. We say *yes!* to Jesus because we want to avoid the fear-filled stories of a burning hell. But God wants us to love and follow him because we *love* him.

When the reward we seek is Jesus, then the desire of our heart will always be fulfilled, as he perfects us in a beautiful love relationship giving all of himself for all of us. Today, enjoy living and loving in the reward of simply . . . Jesus.—d.o.

May 25
Blue Skies of Another Feather

Look at the birds of the air . . .
—Matthew 6:26

In Brazil, flocks of deep blue cross the sky, their wings ringed with gold and their cheeks brushed with it. The hyacinth macaw is the world's largest parrot, and only about 6,500 now live in the wild—an improvement compared to twenty years ago when there were half as many. At one time, these macaws were abundant, but thousands were illegally captured and sold as pets, mostly on the international black market, where one bird alone could bring in twelve thousand dollars. Others were destroyed by deforestation, and many more by locals harvesting the macaws to make feathered souvenirs for tourists. Tragically, four other blue macaws related to the hyacinth did not share their brothers' surge and are now extinct.

We always hear that one person can make a difference, if they care enough to take action, and that is exactly why the hyacinth is not extinct. A twenty-seven-year-old biology student, Nelva Guedes, was on tour in the Pantanal, where most of the hyacinths live, when a flock of indigo beauty flew over. As she watched them in amazement, her professor said these birds would be extinct in her lifetime. In that very moment, she made a decision. She changed the plans she had made for her future. She was now on a mission to prevent the extinction of the macaw.

Nelva started the Hyacinth Macaw Project and gained the support of the World Wildlife Fund (WWF) and some others. She has dedicated her life and talent to the hyacinth's survival in the wild, not just to saving a few hundred in captivity, but training them to live as God intended.

Despite the plans she had for herself, this young woman was willing to literally "look at the birds of the air" and follow God's plan instead. God knew that with her talent and vision, she could do something to make a better world, so he sent the birds across her path and she paid attention.

Whether you're in the middle of planning a career, making a life-change, or even just changing what you do with your free time, be sure not to miss what God has for you. Look up and around you—what skills and passions has he placed in your heart to do great things?—k.m.

May 26
Shades of Black

To him who is able to keep you from stumbling and to present
you before his glorious presence without fault and with great joy. . . .
—Jude 1:24

Black Dog Syndrome is a term that describes how the last dog to be adopted from a shelter is always a black one. All sorts of reasons are given for this phenomenon. Black dogs don't photograph well, so they look like blobs on Internet sites for rescue groups. The dogs from scary movies or who are used to frighten people are usually black. Hunters who breed for better retrieving dogs will have huge litters of black puppies and take them to shelters when they don't pass muster. So, shelters are full of black dogs that don't have homes, won't get homes, and will be euthanized by the thousands.

Sometimes the biggest crime that black dogs commit is being too ordinary. Since shelters get more black dogs than anything else, they simply don't stand out when people look for a new pet to adopt. They are part of a big crowd of sameness, so they are transparent or invisible. Winston Churchill even called his depression a "black dog."

Humanity has a way of judging everything. TV competitions, reality shows, and even ministry events with evaluation sheets can make us feel that we never measure up. We often fall into the *transparent ordinary* category. We often feel like black dogs in a society that really prefers spots.

God judges so differently from the world. His judgment begins and ends with love and grace. Isn't it rich to know that God never ever sees a blob of alikeness in his creation? To him, we all stand out as his incredible handiwork, just like each big, beautiful black dog he made. One day, we will walk into eternity, and Jesus himself will present us before God, without fault and with great joy. That's what judgment looks like in God's presence. Today, live surrounded by love and the affirmation that we are never ordinary black dogs to God, even if the world says we are.—d.o.

May 27
The Color of Life

All things came into being through him, and without him not one thing came into being.
What has come into being in him was life, and the life was the light of all people.
—John 1:3-4

All God's creatures make things to fit their needs. Birds make nests, beavers build dams, and foxes make dens. Humans make musical instruments and skylines, cathedrals and religious icons. We have such potential for tapping into divine inspiration and participating in the constant remaking of the world in a positive way.

Sometimes, though, I feel like my world has gone the color of technology, a noncolor, really. We can't escape the need to adapt and create, but my animals keep me reminded that a hug can still soothe and that nothing can replace a great big lick on the face and a muddy paw on your clean shirt. That's the real stuff, the heart stuff. It's the stuff of *life*.

I think our pets bring us Jesus' light, just like we bring Jesus' light to others. Created by God, instead of by a member of God's creation, they remind us of what matters in life. They are alive with needs, temperaments, smells, and gratitude.

So many lives are lived through computer screens and cell phones now, but you can't earn a pet's love by networking. It's a relationship of organic proportions, costly, and worth so much. Our pets colorize the steel and gray world.

I suspect that God wants us to look at people as well as pets to remind ourselves that his creation—more than our creations—is important. He calls us to get muddy paws on our clean shirts from people, too, especially the ones we love. People's "muddy paws" might be a bad mood or an irresponsible moment, but we need to work it out so we can grow together. Remember that our lives together are the light of God's creation, and the living deserve more of our attention than the interesting things we've made.—k.m.

May 28
Fish Bandit

Finally, brothers and sisters, rejoice! Strive for full restoration, encourage one another,
be of one mind, live in peace. And the God of love and peace will be with you.
—2 Corinthians 13:11

A friend invited me to her Japanese garden with waterfalls and some of the largest, most brightly colored koi that I've ever seen. The tranquil water was inviting, and the ten fish were mesmerizing. We left to make tea, and upon returning, we realized one of the fish was missing. We looked around the pond, checking for dogs or cats that might have gotten into the fenced backyard. We didn't find the fish or the predator.

The next day, another fish was missing. For the next week, one fish each day would disappear. She questioned the neighbors' children and the gardener across the street. With only one fish left, she was looking out her back window when a very large blue heron swooped into her suburban backyard, which is nowhere near a large body of water, and flew away with the last fish in its beak. Mystery solved!

We make plans. We save for them. We carry them out. Then, out of nowhere, something we didn't even know to plan for destroys our carefully penned blueprints. We get downsized from a job, marriages get hit with financial struggle or health disability, and children disappoint us. We end up with our spirits like an empty pond, not even knowing who the thief is.

What do we do when our plans are gobbled up by a thief we cannot see? We ask God for his. God restores the years the locusts ate away, and he restores dreams that we've forgotten we had. The dream gobbler wants us to give up, but God wants us to give in to his love, his forgiveness, and his provision. God is waiting to fill your pond with big dreams, and he never runs out of fish!—d.o.

Family of a Multitude

Then you, together with the Levites and the aliens who reside among you, shall celebrate
with all the bounty that the LORD your God has given to you and to your house.
—Deuteronomy 26:11

There are lots of stray people in this world. People who have no family anymore, or who never did, or people who feel alienated from their families. Although sometimes, I think you hear more complaints from people who have families!

Our families are a blessing that disguises itself as a curse, it seems, or maybe we're just imperfect people often refusing to work together, robbing ourselves of the curious joy God intended families to be. Unreasonable expectations can get us in trouble. The son is expected to be like the dad or the daughter like the mother. But the truth is, people within the same family can be as different as night and day. We're all individually wrapped. You are not doomed to repeat the mistakes of your parents, and you are not a bad parent if your child loses his or her way. Life is bigger than that.

I think it might help us appreciate our own families if we learn from the attitude of our grateful strays. They know the value of a good family, flaws and all, as long as there is no abuse. We might get all caught up in how the house is never clean enough, but a person who has never had a cozy or friendly place to come home to won't even notice. They just soak up all the living that's been going on in your house. To them it's not messy—it's home sweet home.

If you are blessed to have a family, remember you really are *blessed*! More important, we all have a family in Christ. We're part of the family of God, and in his family there are no strays. Indeed, this family is eternal. We are privileged children of God, and with that privilege, we can invite others who are lost or lonely. If you need family around you today, rest assured there are people of God waiting with open arms to welcome you to a family celebration! —k.m.

May 30
Why the Caged Bird Sings

In the LORD I take refuge. How then can you say to me:
"Flee like a bird to your mountain."
—Psalm 11:1

One of my very first pets was a yellow canary named Chirpy. Her cage had to be cleaned and lined with newspaper every other day. Her food and water trays needed constant cleaning, too. She was a messy eater and threw seeds all over the floor that had to be swept daily.

She would sing and trill, high and low and back again with the most beautiful melodies I had ever heard. Every time her cage was freshly clean, and sometimes even during the process, she would serenade me. She had a song in her heart all the time.

I sometimes wondered if she observed the wild birds outside her window and wished she could join them. But she seemed to really love her cage. In fact, she didn't ever sing outside her cage.

The cage must have made her feel secure. She didn't have to worry about food or having to watch for predators while she slept. She trusted in her provider to give her what she needed. What to me seemed like confinement was a shield of protection for her. Instead of worrying, she sang all the time!

The world might look at living a holy life like a cage. Seeking to live within God's rules might seem restrictive or hard, when really it provides safety and true freedom. For example, the law of gravity isn't a punishment, it's just a boundary, a truth that when ignored lets us hit the ground hard. Love is the cage we live in when we are God's children. He protects us, provides for us, and cherishes our song. And we delight in his concern for us and dance in his law of love. Holiness is singing in the security of belonging to God.—d.o.

May 31
Fear Factor

For God did not give us a spirit of cowardice,
but rather a spirit of power and of love and of self-discipline.
—2 Timothy 1:7

We know instinctively that if we want to get a frightened animal to come to us, we must be loving and patient, not fearful. Trustworthy kindness helps dispel fear.

Fear is necessary the way pain is. It lets you know danger is present and triggers responses that can save your life. Respectful fear is necessary for our survival.

We are also wise to fear the Lord. This kind of fear means respect and trust. It means, "Listen to this person; he's got your best interest at heart." It is certainly wise to obey someone who knows better than you do. A sharp command has saved many a dog's life when they were in the way of an oncoming car or too close to a trailer behind a truck.

But sometimes we misunderstand the fear of the Lord. Most people who don't know God are either scared of him or have the wrong impression of him, and they need love and patience, not more fear. God doesn't want people to come to him in fright because they are afraid of what he will do to them if they don't. How could any loving parent want a child to feel that way? He is our loving Father, and he evokes our respect, not our terror. In fact, he even tells us that we can come before God's throne of grace with confidence (Hebrews 4:16).

God will still love us if we don't receive it, but we cannot gain the full benefit of the love if we are too timid to accept it. If you give your dog a treat and she drops it on the ground, the treat is still hers, but she never gets the benefit of it. That's how it is with God's love.

Terror-filled fear is not a factor with God's love. God's purpose isn't to rule over a whipped and trembling world, but rather to empower us with his love.—k.m.

June 1
Going Forward in Reverse

Humble yourselves therefore under the mighty hand of God,
so that he may exalt you in due time.
—1 Peter 5:6

Poshee was a pro, and since I had not ridden much, the barn teamed me up with him for a trail ride. He was patient and let me ride him like the amateur that I was—until we reached the back tip of the field that would take us back to the barn. Halfway across, Poshee stopped and would go no more.

My riding companion continued a few paces ahead before she realized I was no longer beside her. She called back to make sure I was okay.

"He won't go!" I yelled. I gently tugged on the reigns, tapped my heel against his side, made a clicking sound, and then told him straight out that I wanted him to take me back to the barn. Nothing.

By then, my friend had turned and come back, and she said, "He's a dressage horse," like I knew what that meant. "He reads very subtle moves. You must've told him to stop." She tried to explain the go com mand, and I tried to do it. Nothing. I tried again, and he moved . . . backward. He walked me backward a half-length of that field away from the barn!

"You've put him in reverse!" my friend said. Nervous that we were going to repeat the entire trail ride on rewind, I started squeezing and tapping until he finally stopped again at the edge of the woods. My friend came over, took the reins, and toted us in while I clutched Poshee's mane, humiliated that a horse was that much smarter than I am. It occurred to me later that I had learned a gentle lesson about what it means to "humble yourself under the mighty hand of God."

It is in the little things, like the subtle movements that Poshee obeyed, that we learn to obey. The Lord may lead us to do a menial job, or to watch TV less, or to apologize to someone with whom we are angry, and at first, we may think we are capable of so much more. But it is when we obey in the small commands that he can take us on to bigger things, entrust us with more. He "exalts us in due time" and when that time comes, we are tried and proven, ready for undivided service motivated by the heart of Jesus.—k.m.

The Homing Rooster

Like a hunted gazelle, like sheep without a shepherd,
they will all return to their own people, they will flee to their native land.
—Isaiah 13:14

We have a friend who has chickens. She's not a farmer, she's a realtor. Her family moved to the country, and she thought chickens would be a nice "green" addition to their country estate. But those chickens multiplied, free-range and joyous because no one in the house wanted to make the pets into Sunday dinner, so before long, cockle-doodle-doos were happening at all hours of the day.

Since no one would agree to thinning the flock with a trip to the skillet, they agreed that at least one of the roosters, a polite white leghorn that was constantly picked on, should be taken to roam freely in a field a few miles down the road.

About four days later, looking down the driveway, our friend saw that lone white rooster coming into sight. Here he waddled, the returning rooster who had found his way home. He crowed, and quite frankly, his successful journey—one that was fraught with cars and yelping dogs—was a feat worth crowing about.

We can find ourselves in strange lands, with strange people, feeling rather abandoned sometimes. Have you ever felt dropped off? In a bad economy with home foreclosures and job losses at an all-time high, we can all feel like a lonely rooster left to scratch out an existence in unsure circumstances. Give God your worry. In a time of fear and loss, just keep walking down God's driveway. God will take you in. Let go of what you think you *have* to have and look at the possibilities God may have for you once you return to him.—d.o.

Who Let YOU In?

"How is it that you, a Jew, ask a drink of me, a woman of Samaria?"
(Jews do not share things in common with Samaritans.)
—John 4:9

I've often wondered why people jump to conclusions about a person's character so quickly, when they are so often wrong. We have a catalogue of templates in our heads, and we force everything to fit into one of them, making sweeping assumptions about people in the process.

I have noticed that some of our animals share this flaw with the human race. After all, the bird kingdom gave us the phrase "pecking order." Life in the wild is often survival of the fittest, and the fittest flock together. Bring a new horse into the field, and he will be bullied by the other horses until he has earned their respect. Add a new cat to the group, and she will refuse to associate with the others. Add a new dog to the pack, and things can get tense at dinnertime. But both human and animal can rise above these actions.

Veronique is our collie, and she is a most gracious hostess who rises above the natural instinct to insist that everyone get along. She tries to make sure no animal is shunned for being different. If a new dog growls at her, she whimpers sweetly and tries to get it to play. If a cat bats a paw at her, she nudges it with her nose and soon the cat is cuddled up next to her. She loves every new animal that comes to our farm.

I have seen churches that love the same way, where there is no judgment or assumption about race or sexual orientation and no raised eyebrows at someone who is divorced or at a young mother who has no husband. All are simply loved and accepted. All are welcome.

If dogs and cats and horses can all get along in the same family, why can't the human race? We're all part of the same kingdom, and God can give us the wisdom to know when to approach others with open arms. Today we may just have the opportunity to offer grace and acceptance to someone we've never even said hello to before.—k.m.

June 4
All we Like Sheep

There are different kinds of gifts, but the same Spirit distributes them.
—1 Corinthians 12:4

Did you realize that there are two different types of sheepdogs? The first, the herding breeds, are extremely important because a scattered herd is a lost herd. The border collie is a breed especially adept at creating something called "bunching." They bark and nip at the sheep to keep them together in a bunch.

Outside danger from predators calls for a different kind of sheepdog. Where the herding shepherd is small and fast-moving, the pastoral shepherd is large and blends into the herd as one of them. Eight- to ten-week-old Great Pyrenees pups are left with the herd to become imprinted. Herders work around the outside, but the pastoral dog works from within. The sheep bunch around the livestock guardian dog, pulling in close, protected by this unusually fierce member of their group.

Though these dogs can fight to the death against wolves and other predators, they usually use their booming voices to deter predators from coming near. The livestock guardian dog has unusually thick fur around the neck, so vital arteries are not left vulnerable. They have been given a flock to care for, and God gave them the exact features and skills needed to complete their job.

In churches, we have need for both herders and guardians. One person cannot fill all the needs of the people-herd any more than one type of dog can handle all the needs of a herd of sheep. You might be a herder by nature, or a guardian. God calls us to our place according to the gifts, talents, and personality with which we've been equipped. Now, you also might very well be the sheep, and the sheep must look to God, the Good Shepherd, for leadership and protection, always listening for his voice. But all are vital in God's kingdom, and God mindfully gives each person abilities to fit into his masterpiece.—d.o.

June 5
Sheep on Every Corner

*Woe to the shepherds who destroy and
scatter the sheep of my pasture! says the LORD.*
—Jeremiah 23:1

I haven't seen a sheep up close since my last trip to a petting zoo with the kids, or seen a whole herd since my last train ride across the Irish countryside. Most of us live among sidewalks and highways, shopping malls and neighborhoods. Counting sheep is about stress relief, not the number in your flock.

I am one of God's sheep, and I am a shepherd, not just to people but to God's creation. Pet lovers are the literal shepherds of our day. Our herd is made of dogs, cats, hamsters, parakeets, ferrets, and goldfish.

God gives a tall order to shepherds. We are to take our jobs seriously because the sheep really do need us. We are the hands and feet of God to people and to animals. Neglect or abuse of people or animals in our charge angers God. I would be angry, too, if my precious and beautiful creatures were suffering at the cruel and selfish spirit of those who were supposed to be blessing them.

Christians, especially, have an opportunity to be good shepherds. The heart of our message is love. Our mission statement is connection and unity (Matthew 28:19-20). I can't imagine God is pleased when we spend more time arguing about Armageddon than caring for his creation. We cannot know when the end of time for earth will come, but *we can* do something about taking care of our sheep. The Bible places more emphasis on the here and now of compassion and care and encourages us to follow its example.—k.m.

Fishing on Sunday

Remember the Sabbath day by keeping it holy.
—Exodus 20:8

One beautiful Sunday afternoon, after attending church with my grandparents, I packed up my little fishing pole—short enough for my seven-year-old arms—and headed down to the river behind the parsonage where my grandparents lived. It was a perfect day to fish, not too hot, not too windy, and I had hours before we needed to be back at church for the evening service.

I was almost out the door when my grandpa, Pawpaw, asked me where I was going.

"Fishing, Pawpaw. You wanna go?"

"We don't fish on Sunday," he answered.

"Why?" My young brain couldn't make sense of that. I understood why we didn't drink. I knew that smoking could kill you. Spitting and chewing weren't ladylike, and I knew that "whistlin' girls and crowin' hens always come to no good end." But, why not fishing on Sundays?

"This is the Sabbath," my grandfather began. "It's important to have convictions you stick to in life because when you get out in the world, it's too easy to be swayed. This is the day we take time to remind ourselves of what our convictions are."

As an adult, I have the freedom to do what I want, when I want, where I want, and with whom I want. Nobody tells me to put down my fishing pole. I don't have anyone to say, "Get up and go to church" or "Keep the Sabbath holy." My heart is *my* business.

We need a day because that's our way to reinforce the walls that are compromised and challenged during a hard week. Fishing isn't bad, but my grandfather wanted me to be strong enough in my convictions that others would see that strength and know who I am. My heart may be my business now, but every once in a while, when I'm extra tired or have too much to do, and I'm tempted to sleep my way past the Sabbath, I hear Pawpaw's voice in my head. Fishing, it turns out, was just a metaphor.
—d.o.

June 7
God's Snaggletoothed Hills

In the beginning God created . . .
—Genesis 1:1 NIV

In Tennessee the mountain ranges are snaggletoothed with glitches of gray dust. A coal mining company there employs about a hundred workers because that's all the manpower it takes to decapitate a mountain and harvest the coal; the dynamite does the rest. The sad news is that it is unnecessary devastation. A way exists to get the coal without destroying the Appalachian range that is home to generations of families and wildlife. Those mountains, and the life that teems within them, cannot be replaced. Only God can make a mountain.

Someone in the chain of decisions that takes place on the way to the dynamite store must have something personal to gain by blowing up the mountain. What is the thought in the mind of the guy who sets the charge, do you think? Maybe he pictures his hungry children at home or his wife who cries because they have no money for bills. He's just doing what a man's got to do, right?

But God has a better way, a way to carry godly and loving principles into every situation. It is possible, in fact, imperative, that right choices be made for the good of all concerned.

Action that either creates with God or destroys God's handiwork begins in the heart of individuals. We can help today by praying for leaders to change the legislation that allows the demolition of creation and by conserving energy and using up less of our resources. God has provided all we need, and there is nothing godly about wasting his gifts; there is plenty of fuel and energy to be gleaned in ways more gentle to the environment. And, find other ways to help. You can make the decision to turn off lights when they're not being used. It's a small thing, but it's one way to be a good steward of God's perfect creation.—k.m.

June 8
On Wings of Buzzards

Cast but a glance at riches, and they are gone,
for they will surely sprout wings and fly off to the sky like an eagle.
—Proverbs 23:5

I was at a beautiful campground sanctuary on the side of a mountain when overhead soared a beautiful eagle . . . or at least that's what I first thought. Looking closer, I realized it was actually a buzzard floating on wind currents, gracefully and skillfully. It's amazing how similar a buzzard can look to an eagle when it flies overhead, casting its mighty shadow. One is symbolic of life, shelter, and protection, while the other signifies death and waste cleanup. Yet, from a distance, all I could see was a great bird.

Sometimes I'll notice people with better cars and finer homes, and I imagine how great my life would be if I were like them. From a distance, everyone else seems to have it all together. It's easy to judge another person's life as better than mine.

That same distant point of view, when narrowed, might show a mountain of debt, worry over problems we aren't privy to, and family struggles kept behind closed doors.

We are not our bank accounts, the house we own or the one we lose, or the car we drive. We are children of a loving God who wants us to focus on the here and now of relationship with him and those around us. Those other things—the money, the house, the car—will pass by as quickly as an eagle will, but God's blessings are not easily lost. So on days when God sends an eagle or on days when we need a buzzard to help clean up the mess, rejoice in the abundance of love God supplies to us no matter what.—d.o.

June 9
Consider the Lilies

O LORD, our Sovereign, how majestic is your name in all the earth!
—Psalm 8:9

Loving creation is not the same as worshiping it. We are to love it, though, and see the majesty of God through it. You can't get very far through the Psalms without having a good idea which ones must have been the favorites of Saint Francis, a saint who loved nature and gave us the great hymn "All Creatures of Our God and King." In Psalm 8, we are instructed to look at the heavens, the work of God's fingers, the moon and the stars that God established, and to be humbled by the magnificence of them, knowing that the same God made us.

There is no need to be afraid because the world is suddenly placing such emphasis on the color green. Frankly, we needed the reminder; but there is a big difference between worshiping the Creator and the worship of creation. It is right and holy to worship the Creator and love the creation.

It breaks my heart when churches downplay the importance of loving the earth and all that is within it, as God made it. Some even call it pagan. The word *pagan* does not belong in a grateful acknowledgment of God's handiwork in the adoration of God, who could breathe such beauty into being. The sky is not going to fall on your head if you cry over a breathtaking sunset, and tree hugs and butterfly kisses are not heretical.

In his classic novel *The Brothers Karamazov*, Fyodor Dostoevsky says it well:

> Love all God's creation, the whole and every grain of sand in it. Love every leaf, every ray of God's light. Love the animals, love the plants, love everything. If you love everything, you will perceive the divine mystery in things. Once you perceive it, you will begin to comprehend it better every day. And you will come at last to love the whole world with an all-embracing love.

Go outside this week and just soak in God's beauty as seen in what he's made. Allow yourself to feel the excitement and passion of the psalmist, and maybe you'll find yourself repeating his words.—k.m.

June 10
Stingrays for Dinner

For we are God's handiwork, created in Christ Jesus to do
good works, which God prepared in advance for us to do.
—Ephesians 2:10

In one of our many trips to the Gulf Coast for a family vacation, one of my favorite memories was "floundering" with my father one night. We mimicked the vacationers we'd seen the night before, with lights on our foreheads and long gigs to poke and capture the nocturnal fish that liked to camouflage themselves under the sand in shallow waters. We were more freshwater fishermen, so the entire experience was new to us.

I had two jobs. The first was to be on the lookout for the hard-to-see eyes of the flounder and alert daddy to where to stab the catch. And then I was to hold open the plastic trash bag so he could drop the caught fish in.

I saw eyes. Dad aimed precisely and lifted his catch over his head, smiling proudly.

"Open the bag, honey! I've got us a big one!" he shouted like a playful little boy.

I saw the whip-like motion of the singular tail just as I began to open the bag, and I screamed, wrenching the bag away. "Daddy, that's a stingray!"

"Are you sure this isn't a flounder? I mean we went where they were catching these things last night, right?" My father's voice seemed small and so disappointed.

"Daddy, I'm completely sure. Don't you know what a flounder looks like?"

"Nope. Only saw one once in my life . . . and it was fried." He looked at me with his boyish grin.

That was the end of our flounder-fishing experience: one stingray, one grand adventure, and a priceless night with my father I would never forget. As we walked home with a brand-new tall tale to share with the world, I realized that God had created that particular stingray for a single perfect memory between a father and daughter.

Today look for the perfect memory-makers God has placed in your path, precious gifts from a treasure chest of divine creations that require only your willing heart and watchful spirit.—d.o.

June 11
Love Is Bigger Than a Donkey's Ears

My brothers and sisters, do you with your acts of favoritism
really believe in our glorious Lord Jesus Christ?
—James 2:1

Prejudice is a poisonous gas that seeps into the cracks and crevices of humanity, dividing as it goes. The racial discrimination that continued through the 1960s and 1970s, and even today with some people, is a dark example. The way women were and are often still treated on jobs and in marriages is another. Social classes look down on those less financially blessed, and people are labeled by a jacket or hairstyle.

The night two new donkeys came to live with us, the horses and dogs were beside themselves. The dogs looked to us for cues as to whether to chase these strange creatures off or round them up. The horses sniffed and snorted as Tucker pranced around with his tail in the air as though to show off for them. All were aware that these were not creatures we had 'round here before.

All were cautious, except, of course, the collie Veronique, whose first impression is always a loving assumption, but none seemed to say, "Donkeys? There goes the neighborhood!" Within the first week, the Tennessee walking horses and the donkeys were lying together in the field. The dogs calmed down and stopped chasing them, and the newest members of our family began approaching us affectionately. Those two turned our farm into a petting zoo, and even now their loud braying stirs up a joyous commotion.

The celebration of our differences has brought so much life to our farm. Why can't the people kingdom be a little more like the animal kingdom? Big ears, little ears; black, white; male, female; rich, poor—all things come together in Christ. Our job is only to love and accept. God can handle the rest.—k.m.

Crying Over Spilled Milk

*Godly sorrow brings repentance that leads to salvation
and leaves no regret, but worldly sorrow brings death.*
—2 Corinthians 7:10

My little grandmother was barely five feet tall, her tiny hands worn with the work of many years on the farm. Teaching me to milk a cow required extreme patience on my grandmother's part because she had been doing it so long. To her, it was like teaching me how to breathe. Those hands, pink from overuse, would wrap around the teat of that milk cow, and instantly, warm milk would hit the side of the bucket with a well-aimed ping. She made it look so easy. Both she and the cow appeared relaxed, my grandmother working smoothly, and the cow placidly chewing her cud.

My grandmother taught me where to put the milking stool and how to hold my hands on the udder, warming them first by rubbing the belly of the cow. The most important part of milking is where the bucket is placed. Cows are particular, it turns out, about which side is used for milking and bucket placement. A full milking can be lost in one fell swoop of a swift hoof.

The cow turned back to look at the unskilled hands trying to urge milk from her pink freckled bag. It took me forever to get even a dribble, but finally, after great effort, the bucket was a quarter full. Feeling proud of myself, I stood to get my grandmother's attention, and I heard a metallic thud. I looked down, and all I saw was the precious white liquid seeping into the soft dirt floor of the barn. Some mistakes you don't get a chance to re-do. That milk was gone.

Days are like milk, once spilled, once spent, they cannot be replaced. The enemy loves to remind us of our past mistakes, using shame to keep us repeating them. In God's world, our mistakes are answered by his grace and compassion, and the milk can be "un-spilled." God's gift of do-overs is new every morning, found in your surrender and your willing heart.
—d.o.

June 13
The Dog Didn't Do It

Love . . . bears all things.
—1 Corinthians 13:4, 7

When families divide, everybody's heart is broken, even the pets'. Life changes. Marriage is never just about two people because it connects families, children, communities, and animals. When it ends, the destructive effects—the shattered hopes and dreams—are far-reaching. Divorce seems to say that all of Scripture's words about love's strength simply aren't true.

Some of us realize too late that there was hope for the marriage; but there is hope within the divorce, if both partners are willing. Forgiveness is a little easier when you don't live in the same house. Even if you don't end up back together, friendship and good memories can be restored through seeking to show God's kind of love. It will be difficult to find the motivation to love one another when it was animosity that created the difficult circumstances in the first place, but God can intervene in ways we didn't imagine possible.

If this is your circumstance, start by trying to care about the innocent ones who had nothing to do with your breakup, but whose lives will be changed because of it. Think about how it felt to be a child and adoring both of your parents. Think about your puppy's eyes and tail between her legs as she hides in a corner to escape the storm. If you can't love each other right now, love the kids and the dog enough to overcome your anger and hurt. Allow love for *them* to guide your conversations with your partner. Love will have the chance to grow, then, and the war will end, one unselfish act after another.

Love *does* always work and *does* always win. Try it. Your children, your friends, and your dog will thank you.—k.m.

June 14
When Is Too Many Too Many?

In everything I did, I showed you that by this kind of hard work we must help the weak.
—Acts 20:35

When TV began spotlighting the problem of animal hoarding, I remember getting a visit from a neighbor who accused me of hoarding. Animals have always helped me through the most painful experiences of my life, and in my darkest moments, I have sought comfort from God's creatures, and they have blessed me with loyalty and love. But the accusation said I was irresponsible, inconsiderate, and somehow less civilized than everyone else in the neighborhood, and I suddenly felt like everyone's eyes were on me.

Animal hoarding is often indicative of pain that has gone untreated. Mental illness, obsessive-compulsive behavior, and depression are linked to the over-collection of animals kept in unsanitary or unhealthy environments for either animals or humans, known as hoarding. Animals wrap around our souls, so we feel loved when we feel unlovable. They make us feel less alone, less ugly, less obese, less unwanted. For me, collecting animals was a response to a world where many people had hurt me.

After asking God to help, God supplied me with complete compassion. He taught me to let go and find compassion for others who suffer from this same affliction of the heart.

If someone you know is having trouble caring for themselves or the animals they love, reach out in love. Don't swoop in and remove their only source of peace, but ask God for new compassion, less judgment, and more understanding. Then ask others for help and resources to ease your friend to a healthier lifestyle.

When we fall into a trap, we must always remember that God has compassion for us in each of our different weaknesses. We all have them, and God just wants to free us from any bondage that keeps us from living joyful lives.—d.o.

Sackcloth and Grace

Better a patient person than a warrior, one with self-control than one who takes a city.
—Proverbs 16:32 NIV

L ife is burlap. Its threads are coarse and rough, scratchy to the skin, so thick you could make a stencil of the crisscross pattern, and so sturdy you can use it to hold a sack of potatoes. A cat can lie on a burlap sack like it's as luxurious as silk. We, on the other hand, are not so fond of the rough places. When we make our beds on sackcloth, we always wish for satin.

Peace comes when, like our pets, we accept our circumstances with patience, knowing that someone greater than us has our best interests at heart. I always marvel at the way our dogs display that most difficult fruit of the spirit: self-control. They'll sit by a grill, jowls dripping, lips quivering, licking their chops, whimpering under their breath . . . and wait. Their restraint requires an extraordinary amount of trust. They obey because our love and respect are more important to them than a steak. Barely, maybe, but that counts!

Why is self-control so much harder for people? We consistently fall prey to our bad habits and desires. We smell the steak cooking and *have* to have it. We are unwilling to suffer the discomfort of longing. Overeating, charge cards, unhealthy but exciting relationships, or worry habits can be our big, juicy, medium-well, irresistible steaks, and we just want to leap on to the grill and seize our prize.

The dogs who have been lovingly trained are the ones that resist the steak. Like them, we can overcome many of the problems that wreck our lives if we allow God to help us or, should I say, *train* us. His word tells us in 1 Peter 1 that the trying of our faith teaches us patience. As we learn, we grow in grace, in patience, and in self-control. When we seek his help, moment by moment, God will fill us with his qualities, so that we can respond like God, no matter the temptation.—k.m.

June 16
So Huge, So Fragile

He called out to them, "Friends, haven't you any fish?" "No," they answered.
—John 21:5

In the American Museum of Natural History in New York, you can walk underneath a replica of a giant blue whale, known as the largest mammal living on this planet, reaching a length of over one hundred feet. Yet, this uber-mammal of the sea is on the endangered list. They are disappearing from the earth. They once filled the oceans in the Antarctic, numbering over two hundred thousand. Now, because of years of overhunting by whalers, their numbers in the Pacific, Indian, and Atlantic oceans are hovering around five thousand.

They spend most of their time alone, sometimes pairing up with a mate, but even alone, their song communicates to whales across the ocean, allowing them to travel in a vast joined-yet-separate social community.

Now that hunting has been outlawed, the real danger for the great blue whale is the disruption of their communication system. Sonar from shipping vessels and ocean noise that is increasing with traffic on the seas interferes with the navigational abilities of the whale. When they can't communicate, they get off-course and end up trapped unintentionally in nets, on beaches, or just stranded in the wrong place at the wrong time. They need to be able to communicate to navigate. When communication is broken, even the biggest and strongest beings on earth become fragile and weak.

Communication with God keeps us on the right navigational current too. We are bombarded, much like the blue whale, with increasing noise around us. Our quiet conversations with God are disrupted by our busy schedules. Cell phones and wireless webs entangle our thoughts, and we can drown in the mire of clear, earthly communication while heavenly conversation remains a garbled message. If we are to survive, we have to find time to shut down and listen, uninterrupted, to the ancient voice that echoes deep within us, guiding us the way we need to go, calling us home.
—d.o.

June 17
"Bow Wow" Means "God Loves You"

Let your speech always be gracious, seasoned with salt,
so that you may know how you ought to answer everyone.
—Colossians 4:6

Christians say certain phrases a lot: "The Lord is our strength." "All things work together for our good." "I'll be praying for you." Those ideas often sound strange or even trite to someone who has not been on the "inside." When Christians say these phrases without really thinking about their meaning or their effect on someone else, Christianity can seem like a clique full of people who presume to hear from God Almighty and have all the answers to *your* life. It's enough to send any sane person running the opposite direction.

I'm one of the Christians who uses those phrases, but I don't throw the words around lightly. We need to realize that the concept of God being "the Lord," and the Lord being "our strength" is not something everyone will connect with. Depending on the situation, religious language can be about as useless as telling your poodle, "The Lord is your strength!" while a German shepherd is chasing him. Better to pick Fluffy up into your safe arms than to recite ancient poetry at a time like that. Yet, that's what we do to people in need sometimes. They can be hurting or lonely, and all they get from God's people is an arbitrary, "The Lord be with you," when they really need someone to listen and understand.

Our pets don't take our words seriously until they can firmly associate them with kind actions. The same principle works when we offer words of hope to someone who is hurting. When we walk the walk instead of just talking the talk, acting as Jesus would, loving as he would, then God's glory is displayed in our lives. People can see firsthand that God is real, God is love, and God cares about them. Only then will our words bring comfort, filled with the strong reality of God in our lives.—k.m.

June 18
Out of Control

Will the wild ox consent to serve you?
Will it stay by your manger at night?
—Job 39:9

Control is a funny thing. We all say we don't do it. We all say we hate it. Yet, when we feel we are losing it, we grip tighter and tighter at all costs. As sure as one can be about a wild mustang that has been rescued and tamed, there will come a moment when instinct will rule, and no matter what has been taught, the mustang cannot be controlled.

A horse trainer once told me that you can't ever control anybody, whether a dog, a horse, or a person. We all have brains and hearts and wills, and nothing's going to change that. Animals can be told or taught what you would *like* them to do, but the only way they'll do it is if they want to. When a horse goes from a running walk to a canter at your command, it is simply agreeing to your request.

When we walk around with expectations, we really are lugging a great big bank account of potential resentments. If I expect my horse to get on the trailer, and I've got a time deadline, I might get resentful when fear makes the horse balk for an extra hour before loading. Which of your expectations are consistently being unmet? Life is constantly reminding us that we are not in control.

Frustration over people, places, and things not hitting exact spots at exact times are the enemy's way of getting us to focus on needing control, instead of trusting God for the outcome. God wants us to focus on him because no matter what we see, God is always in control of what happens. Are you frustrated with a rebellious child or a distracted spouse? Ask God to change their hearts and watch over them in the process. Are you worried about a life change? Ask God for his peace and control in the situation. We can't force those around us to do as we desire, but we can give them up to the God who loves them more than anyone else could.—d.o.

June 19
Could I Have a Doggie Door in My Mansion, Please?

And the street of the city is pure gold.
—Revelation 21:21

What you believe about heaven and what you believe about your pets' afterlife can raise some fun new questions about our futures in Christ. Many people don't have any trouble imagining that our pets will be in the place of glory with us; others just sincerely hope that they will be there. Our pets don't have to say a sinner's prayer, go to an altar, apologize for getting the couch dirty or for tearing down another fence. Nonetheless, the picture the Bible paints of heaven and the new earth in cludes all kinds of images—streets of gold, glorious living in God's presence, and animals. Wonder if they'll like the mansions?

But, the Bible does not say our Father has many mansions. The verse so often quoted in John 14 says that our Father's *house* has many *rooms.* Perhaps some people will be disappointed. "What? No mansion built just for me?" Maybe *we* are the rooms. Or maybe you just get a room. I can't imagine it will matter to us then.

Regardless, I hope there will be grass for the rabbits, holy shavings and bedding for the guinea pigs, and vines for the monkeys. Scripture places the animals in heaven but offers no details about how that is supposed to work. An automatic pooper scooper moving along the streets of gold? And I often wonder if "streets of gold" is an analogy too. Perhaps every step we take in heaven will be pure. Gold always symbolizes cleansing and refining. To say we will walk on streets of gold must mean we will at last walk as Jesus walked—strong, beautiful, and perfect in God's eyes.

We are not given the answer as to what heaven is exactly like, only glimpses. I trust that it is bright, poetic, full of music and furry angels. I don't care whether there are literal streets of gold or literal mansions; I just want to see my literal loved ones—and my literal Savior.—k.m.

June 20
Faith by Fear

"How will this be," Mary asked the angel, "since I am a virgin?"
The angel answered, "The Holy Spirit will . . . overshadow you.
So the holy one to be born will be called the Son of God."
—Luke 1:34-35a

When the broodmares are in foal, they seem to know that life is growing within them. They change position, nuzzle their bellies, and nicker softly. Something in their eyes is more knowing and wise than before. As they swell and become robust, they sigh deeply getting enough breath for two.

I often wonder when Mary first felt the movement of the Savior of the world within her. Was it the moment she said yes, or was it like mortal pregnancies, where she wouldn't feel life move until somewhere in the third month? Did she seek counsel of the other women in her village? Did the synagogue ladies give her a baby shower, or did they whisper as she walked away about the young, unmarried girl with a baby on the way? Did she feel alone or did she feel more connected to God and creation than ever before?

When God asks us to do something, it is often filled with equal amounts of faith and fear. It's been said that we can't have both present at the same time, but I believe that faith can be present only *with* fear. In the face of our greatest fear and moving through it with God as our shield is when faith is born within us.

All mammalian creation is knit together by divine design in a female womb, and each birth is a symbol that God sees our fears and provides all we need to protect us even through the hardest journeys. The faith comes through that fear when we hold God's hand and say yes, just as Mary did—though we might be discouraged, threatened, and cast out of relationship with some. We answer knowing that the Most High's power will overshadow anything the world can do.—d.o.

June 21
Honey Jargon

Oh, how I love your law! It is my meditation all day long.
—Psalm 119:97

The Word of the Lord is not just words on a page translated hundreds of times throughout history. When the devil tempted Jesus to break his fast before God had given the okay, Christ responded that we don't live by bread alone but by every word that comes from God (Matthew 4:4). Jesus wants us to know that our souls are as important as our bellies for sustaining life, and that God's word is the only source of nourishment.

The psalmist writes about the word of the Lord, too, in the longest chapter in the Bible. In that passage, we learn that God's word is a lamp to our feet and a light to our path, so we get to experience how God's word is multifaceted and not just letters on papyrus. The poet in Psalm 119 writes that God's word is sweeter than honey. God's word is the substance of insight and understanding; it is comfort, full of promise, and packed with hope.

We've also seen how God uses his word creatively. God spoke, and all of life was born on the breath of the love behind his utterance. God spoke, and dragonflies and bobcats, black bears and goldfish existed. The same word of God that is honey to our souls is life to all creation. God's amazing word is worth thinking about all day long.—k.m.

June 22
Never Too Old for God

When Elizabeth heard Mary's greeting, the baby leaped in her womb,
and Elizabeth was filled with the Holy Spirit.
—Luke 1:41

When I was a little girl, my grandfather gave me a plaster cast of a black horse with four white stockings. I had asked for a horse at every birthday, every Christmas, and anytime I was given a chance to say what I dreamed of having one day. Grandpa told me to look at that horse every day and ask God for my dream. So, I would close my eyes to pray for a big black horse with four white stockings.

Years passed, and I still had never owned a horse. Then, when I was thirty-five, I went riding with a friend. When my mount appeared from around the corner of the barn, I gasped. She was a living, breathing exact replica of the black horse with white stockings I had prayed for as a child.

It turns out that she was just an old horse on the farm, and they were glad to let me buy her for almost nothing. This old Tennessee walker was a gentle, retired broodmare, too old for anything worthwhile, they told me. I felt a nudge from God that he had plans for that old black horse and me.

I named her Maria, and before long, I had groomed back the sheen of her beautiful, neglected coat. Getting her feet back in healthy shape took a bit longer, but she seemed to realize that I wanted to love and care for her. Then she began to love and care for me, helping me get back on my emotional feet.

When we pray, God hears us, even if years pass before we see him changing things. Be patient and wait for God's answer in his time. We are never too old for God to work in us, use us, or create a miracle through us, just as God created a miracle in Elizabeth's "too old" womb. We are forever valuable and worthwhile to our Father, so even if we feel like we're not enough—we're too young or too old or not talented—God can do incredible work through us, if we're willing to listen for his direction.
—d.o.

Finest Bread

"This is my body that is for you. Do this in remembrance of me."
—1 Corinthians 11:24

Nobody appreciates a great feast like an animal. Like horses to apples, dogs to pepperoni, or cats to tuna, we are encouraged to long after God. The human heart needs God not just to survive, but really to live, and fulfilled life is God's thing. He designed us to need life, to want it, to give it, to live or die by it, and there is plenty to go around—a veritable worldwide feast. So why are so many people and animals lonely and abandoned?

At the root of all sin is selfishness, and selfishness creates loneliness and heartache. In a world whose ruler is the enemy, we quickly change the focus from God's mission of full life to me, me, me. Nothing personal, right? But when we're downsized, having food on the table becomes pretty personal. Even so, we have to stop asking, "What's in it for me?" and begin asking, "What's in it for God's kingdom?" Otherwise, we'll be stuck in the cycle of worry, unable to grab on to the satisfying life God has offered through his Son's sacrifice on the cross.

Selfishness is not the only thing ruining God's fiesta. Laziness is at the root of much evil. The work of knowing yourself is hard. Learning to forgive others, getting over bad memories, and helping the helpless requires effort, extra planning, and lots of tears. Perhaps that's why God's Word says we must *labor* to enter into God's rest. Peace comes when the work is done, but the tender, loving care of the Holy Spirit helps us every step of the way, breathing his life into our actions.

A hymn, "Here I Am," or "I the Lord of Sea and Sky," says, "Finest bread I will provide, till their hearts be satisfied." Every time I sing that line, I remember Jesus. He is the Bread of Life. When we allow God into our hearts, we have accepted his invitation to God's fulfilling, satisfying feast.
—k.m.

June 24
The New Cat

With words of hatred they surround me; they attack me without cause.
—Psalm 109:3

Driving in late from out of town, we stopped to gas up the car. As the tank filled, an insistent meow caught our ears. An unusually beautiful, yet bedraggled cat ran up to us. She was definitely a stray, so we decided she at least needed a place to spend the night. When no one called to claim her, we gave her a permanent home.

The other cats never accepted her. She was the out-cat, the one that no one liked, and for no reason we could see. Have you ever walked into a new job and felt resentment rising against you for absolutely no reason? Ever been new at school? New in town? People react to perceived threats because of their own insecurities, but that knowledge doesn't really help if you are the attacked one. So, how do we combat illogical and cruel behavior? We love.

We follow Jesus' example and love people the best way we can based not on who they are, but whom God made them to be. Ask compassionate questions, smile, invite them for coffee, try anything to make a first step, a second, or a third. Jesus has given us so many examples of how to reach out, always with prayer as the foundation. We aren't solitary by nature, so mirroring bad behavior will never render a bad situation better.

"Kill 'em with kindness," a friend of mine used to say. "It may not make them friendlier, but the rest of the world will see you're trying." If we repay unkindness with the same kind of unkindness, we play right into the false testimony that the enemy goads us toward daily. When we take up Jesus' cross, responding to unjustified hatred as he did, the way is not easy. But he will be with you, giving you the same strength he used when everyone abandoned him to the cross. He rose from the dead to redeem the earth, and we are left his legacy, to reflect his glory.—d.o.

When God Gets Angry

If any of you put a stumbling block before one of these little ones who believe in
me, it would be better for you if a great millstone were fastened around your
neck and you were drowned in the depth of the sea. Woe to the world
because of stumbling blocks! Occasions for stumbling are bound to come,
but woe to the one by whom the stumbling block comes!
—Matthew 18:6-7

The words from Matthew's Gospel bring harsh words from the Lamb of God. Our Savior is compassionate and understanding, but intolerant of mistreatment or misguidance of others, especially those who are younger or under our responsibility. God accepts no excuses for the abuse or neglect of the innocent.

Often, God steps in where adults fail. He knows every whimper a dog cries as it searches for shelter and food on a stormy night and the terror of a cat that is vulnerable and lost. Imagine a horse that has given his very best effort to win blue ribbons for his master, but is then considered disposable, or the pony whose family wants to be rid of him once the kids are grown and sells him for slaughter. God is always on the side of the weak. He never forgets the tears of a little girl whose parent hit her, and he sees the anguish of a boy whose father told him he could do nothing right.

God does not throw his anger around like a super villain. He preserves his wrath for the true injustices. God's concern is always that love prevails, so that which goes against love is the only thing that provokes God's fierceness, and nothing goes against love quite like the abuse of the innocent.

We cannot erase the abuse, the hurtful words, or the neglect we've experienced, but God can heal in the most miraculous unassuming way—through the love of another who knows how you feel. In God's kingdom, we as his warriors against evil need to protect the weak while they heal. If we are patient, consistent, and present, these little ones will grow up and one day stand beside us in the good fight.—k.m.

June 26
Magpie Funeral

My lyre is tuned to mourning, and my pipe to the sound of wailing.
—Job 30:31

Marc Bekoff recounted in *The Emotional Lives of Animals* a scene about a group of magpies that had just lost a member of their flock. Their comrade had been hit by a car and left lying on the side of the road. Each bird took a turn prodding to see if their friend was, in fact, gone. Then, one by one, they flew off and returned, laying grass over their lost friend.

In a photograph that circled the globe, Hawkeye, the canine pet of fallen Navy Seal Petty Officer Jon T. Tumilson, broke hearts as he lay prostrate in front of his friend's casket for the entire service.

Scientists have said that animals don't have emotions, that they just react to stimuli, but even the science world is becoming more and more aware of occurrences that can only be explained by emotional phenomenon.

We live in a world that pushes us to move on, focus on the positive, and keep our emotions in check. When did it become so important to get on with living so quickly that we can't feel anymore? We're not allowed to feel our loss, our hurt, and our pain as deeply or as long as we need, trained to think that grief is for the weak or imbalanced.

God hears the pain of the universe and never pushes us to move quickly through it to convenience him. God didn't chastise Job for mourning his lost children or tell him to buck up. In fact, God was and is consistently compassionate, urging us to bring our hurting spirits to him. In the demonstrative feeling of our pain, in the rituals of funerals, and in seeking God for comfort and solidity, God validates our needs, helping us find the peaceful passage to the next emotion.—d.o.

June 27

I will both lie down and sleep in peace; for you alone, O LORD,
make me lie down in safety.
—Psalm 4:8

If you ever observe your pets all day, you'll notice a lifestyle that is balanced with rest and activity. Granted, they don't have bills to pay and are not responsible for gathering their own food and water, but they harmonize their activities. Our pets do not work themselves into a frenzy or sleep their lives away in a dark room. The cat sleeps, explores, sleeps, eats a little, sleeps, purrs, sleeps. Okay, so they sleep a lot, but their patterns have a rhythm and balance.

Ever feel like a slacker or been accused of getting old if you need a nap? Ever need to sleep in on a weekday when your job accommodates, only to wake feeling guilty? Ever need to go to bed early but choose not to after your friends tease you about missing the nighttime fun? Wouldn't it be nice to sleep when you need to? Jesus did. He went to sleep in the middle of a storm, and he upset everyone's apple cart by doing it.

The key to a restful soul is a restful mind, so allow yourself to rest when your mind and body need it. Ironically, allowing yourself the proper rest enables you to be more efficient and get more done. We also need to allow ourselves our differences without judgment. Some people need less sleep than others. Some need a gracious plenty, and others are sleep grazers.

So, let the sleeping dogs lie and take a catnap because the Lord gives his children rest.—k.m.

June 28
Listen to Me when I Cry to You!

Yet give attention to your servant's prayer and his plea for mercy, LORD my God.
Hear the cry and the prayer that your servant is praying in your presence this day.
—1 Kings 8:28

When our cat Tyrone was just a kitten, he used many methods to get my attention. He would begin by crying softly, then louder if he didn't get the response he wanted. If that didn't work, the cries would grow more and more insistent, and he'd throw in a loud purr. When I still didn't acknowledge him, he would look for a glass, perhaps a glass of water on the nightstand, and turn it over with his paw. That usually got my instant attention.

Scientists who have studied the communication and emotion of cats have concluded that cats learn how to manipulate their owners by mimicking the cries of a human infant. They add purring and anything else they can to elicit a response from their humans.

The psalmist David was insistent that God would hear his prayers. He took it all to God. He brought his praise, his joy, and his anguish, and waited for God to answer. David would increase his pleas until he was certain God had heard his prayer.

Our Maker seeks communication with us with even more determination. God whispers to us in the gentle breezes, or he shouts in the flames and in the dark, stormy clouds until we have heard his voice. God gave us the Scriptures because communication with our Maker is *relationship* with our Maker. We need harmonious unity in our prayer life, our daily life, our love life, our family life, and in every segment of our being, so we keep seeking until we find it. We must live insistently for God, as God goes to all lengths to insistently be near us.—d.o.

Bark Nicely

But now you must get rid of all such things—anger, wrath, malice,
slander, and abusive language from your mouth.
—Colossians 3:8

We have a friend whose dog can say, "I love you." She's been on television, in commercials, and circulated in video across the Internet. I think that if my dog was able to talk, "I love you" would be what I would want her to say. For a determined terrier to utter the syllables correctly takes great effort and lots of practice. An *I* or *Y* is a tricky business for the canine tongue.

Even so, I don't think I want my dog to be able to converse. Think about how often words get in the way of what we mean. Without a single word, my dog is one of the clearest communicators I know. With the wag of a tail or the move of an eyebrow, she can make me laugh or break my heart. I know if she's sad, happy, hungry, lonely, or concerned about someone. If I am sad, she will do silly things to cheer me up. She sits quietly with me on the porch when I write or play guitar. Words could ruin all that.

Words are a powerful gift and responsibility. We can use them as weapons—manipulating deals, arguing points, or cutting others down. Or we can soothe a hurting friend and inspire people to positive action.

We need to put the meaning back into our words, choose them carefully, and not waste so many. The Bible says our words should be "seasoned with salt," so that what we say is poignant and important, carrying authority to change people. Jesus promised the disciples the Holy Spirit would give them the words to say that would help deliver the good message of the gospel to people.

So start with something simple and pure to learn to speak words that are life-giving and healing. Our friend's dog has the right idea: let's tell God, others, and ourselves, "I love you."—k.m.

June 30
360 Degrees of Praise

Let all creation rejoice before the LORD, for he comes.
—Psalm 96:13

A photographer told me about an exercise he would do when inspiration eluded him. He would walk into the middle of a field, city sidewalk, or suburban park, lift the camera to eye level, and snap pictures in a complete circle around his location. Then he would circle again, taking the circle of pictures looking up, then again looking down. The camera would catch what he had begun taking for granted.

We live in time-lapse miracles every day, and we just plain miss them. But all of creation is alive and rejoicing in God every moment of every day.

To communicate on this visual level, find just a few moments to walk outdoors. Close your eyes, and let your body inventory every sound you hear. Hear each noise as praise to God. Now, open your eyes, and catalog every single person, object, animal you can see within your 360-degree circle of vision. Imagine each detail in a praise motion to God.

Breathe in the smell of creation. Take off your shoes and wiggle your toes in it. Ask God to reveal himself in the slices of creation within your sense's reach. Ask him to help you realize how full each second of life is on this glorious planet brought into being by God's hand. In the heart of a bustling city, baby birds are being fed by their mother as they dangle from the side of a blinking neon sign. In a country field, baby rabbits hop from a thicket to enjoy the sunshine.

Give yourself a fast from all things God did not create, just for a moment. Let the quiet become louder within your heart as *all* creation praises him.—d.o.

July 1
Low-Sodium, Please

For the Lord disciplines those whom he loves, and chastises every child whom he accepts.
—Hebrews 12:6

A slug was the creature that taught me compassion for all living things. Actually, it was my mom's experience with a slug. I came home from school one afternoon to find her sitting despondently on the couch. She said, "I did a terrible thing today." It had rained, and she had noticed a slug making its way across the sidewalk. She ran and got the saltshaker from the kitchen table, and shook the grainy poison from the heavens onto the helpless creature. Apparently, the slug's reaction was fascinating, but she soon realized that water would not wash the slug clean and end the slimy torture game. She was mortified. Thankfully, he died quickly.

My mom learned that to cause a living creature to suffer intentionally wounds your soul. Somehow, she had not thought slugs could suffer, but as she watched it die, she knew that those tiny antennae were attached to a harmless and living, albeit ugly, creature.

Perhaps Mom's regret was God's loving discipline, and he used the situation to teach both my mother and me an important lesson: respect what God created. And expect his discipline when you disobey! God allowed my mom to feel sadness for the slug because he loves her and wants to shape her into the woman he created her to be—a woman of compassion.

Now I try to think of slugs as homeless snails; it helps me to remember to respect the lives of even the ugliest creatures. I don't think I'll ever pour salt on a slug, and recalling my mom's expression when I came home that day, I don't think she could take another one suffering!—k.m.

July 2
Calling All Creatures!

He said to them, "Go into all the world and preach the gospel to all creation."
—Mark 16:15

She stood in Washington Square with a portable megaphone, handing out pamphlets that were immediately thrown to the ground and trampled by busy people with important things to do. "We must save our rain forests!" she shouted. People didn't even acknowledge her as she yelled facts that affected each and every one of them. Their apathy was infectious. They had heard it all before.

Opposite her in the square was an older gentleman, also with a megaphone and handwritten signs of Scripture passages like John 3:16 and Romans 3:23. People walked past him as well. They tossed down his salvation literature and walked over the texts.

I realized at that moment, as I took in the cacophony of megaphoned sounds, that I was in the midst of *callings*. And this pair, whether people listened or not, was successful in God's eyes. God's callings are not incumbent on the outcome. Our job is to take the message. God handles the rest.

Saying yes to God gives us the ability to face the rejection of the world and completes us in a way nothing else can. God knows the dots he's connecting. He knows that the one dog that gets adopted today might be the glue that holds a little boy's family together tomorrow. He knows that one person who understands the importance of saving the rain forest might actually help do it. And God knows the one person who needs to know Jesus' love might just realize it when he pulls a scrap of paper from the sole of his shoe.—d.o.

July 3

A Fish Story

For in him we live and move and have our being.
—Acts 17:28

Three young fish were swimming around one sunny day in the clear tropical waters. They swam from coral reef to sandy shallows, dancing and flipping and bumping the surface to touch the big light they could see above them. The water was so warm and exciting that a little fish could explore all day long to his heart's content.

As they played, a shadow approached from the murky deep. They were not afraid, only curious. Out of the dark mysterious beyond emerged a big fish, an older and wiser fish. He saw the three friends, and he moseyed over by where they were playing. Without stopping, he said, "Water's nice today, isn't it, boys?" and continued on his way.

The youngsters were puzzled. One turned to the others and said, "What's water?"

"I don't know," said another, and then to the other, "Do *you* know what water is?"

"Nope," replied the third gleefully, and the three little fish swam off into the big blue ocean in which they lived, and moved, and had their being.

A lot of people in this world have no idea that everything they've ever done, from breathing to winning a Nobel Prize, would not be possible without God. The story of these little fish reminds me not to judge others who don't know whose water they're swimming around in every day. All of humanity may think it's a human world and that it's making plans and doing its own deal, but we know whose world it really is. Our job as witnesses for God's kingdom is to point out how great the water is!
—k.m.

July 4
The National Turkey

Whoever walks in integrity walks securely,
but whoever takes crooked paths will be found out.
—Proverbs 10:9

Myth and history often go hand in hand, and from their union, a legend is born.

Have you heard the story of how Benjamin Franklin lobbied for the wild turkey to become the national bird of the new America? If so, what you've heard is probably not quite as history would tell it. Ben wrote a letter to his daughter and complained that the eagle was lazy and had no integrity or work ethic. In what sounds like Ben's notable sarcasm, he would have preferred the wild turkey. His letter says about the turkey, "He is besides, though a little vain and silly, a bird of courage, and would not hesitate to attack a grenadier of the British Guards who should presume to invade his farm yard with a red coat on."

The letter, when gossiped about, became, Benjamin Franklin would have the wild turkey as our national symbol, rather than the eagle.

The story reshaped and changed with retellings, just as stories from the Bible are often reformed through inaccurate perceptions and understanding. We listen to people give their versions of Scripture, laws, and stories, and often take their word for it. We share these incorrect versions with people, sometimes even snaring people spiritually, whether purposefully or accidentally, and the truth is lost.

Quite a few tales have become legend through the retelling of God's Word these days. Phrases are spouted out of context, and Bibles are used to bash particular groups. If we aren't careful, pretty soon the gossip will reduce Jesus to a chauvinist who didn't like working with women and preferred to throw fits in the temple and tell people to stop sinning rather than heal them.

On this day of commemorating American freedom, let us celebrate by letting God's Word speak for itself, and let the integrity of the text speak with God's voice to your heart. Use your freedom to discover the truth about the eagles and turkeys for yourself.—d.o.

July 5
The Importance of Spaying

Fools think their own way is right, but the wise listen to advice.
—Proverbs 12:15

My neighbor, Melinda, taught me how to train my dog. I was ten years old when I got her, a beautiful collie named Shane. It was the same year I was baptized at Pinecroft Baptist Church, for which I also have Melinda to thank. She invited me to church every week.

Melinda said, "You HAVE to teach Shane not to go in the road." She advised spanking her in order to teach her, but said NEVER use your hand. The idea was to discipline her lovingly, so Melinda rolled up a newspaper and said, "Always use this. Never hit her hard enough to hurt. It's the popping sound that will get her attention." It worked, and probably saved Shane's life. Ironically, though, Shane eventually died an untimely death because another bit of Melinda's advice was ignored.

Melinda told me the importance of spaying Shane, but my parents opted not to do it. So, to protect Shane, I kept her in the garage when she was in season. During those times, I got up before school and walked her with a leash, and after school I raced from the bus stop to walk her again and give her some sunshine.

I married young, and before I was twenty-one, my husband and I moved to New Orleans. Shane stayed at home, but her needs were soon lost in the shuffle of busy lives. One day, Dad called to tell me Shane had become pregnant, but because she was older, neither she nor the puppies survived.

My animals now benefit from the hard lessons for which Shane paid the greatest price. All of our pets are spayed and neutered, and it is my hope to always help people the way Melinda helped me—to teach them what I know about loving our pets.

If you have a good friend like Melinda in your life today, be sure to treasure that gift. Also, ask God to help you be that kind of good friend to the relationships God has given you. We need one another, and need to share "wise counsel" with each other.—k.m.

July 6
Praying for a Move!

Therefore I tell you, whatever you ask for in prayer,
believe that you have received it, and it will be yours.
—Mark 11:24

Colic is an awful problem for a horse. Everything from a change of feed to overeating or stress can bring on colic, and if not caught quickly, the results can be irreversible. When our horse Fancy developed colic we were devastated. We called everyone, friends and family, to help us walk her round the clock. The vet came immediately and then returned two days later and repeated the treatment. We pumped her full of shots and oil—anything that might help—and two days later, she still had no relief.

"If nothing happens tonight, we have to consider the . . . other option," the vet told us. We knew that meant euthanization.

That night, our little prayer group of twelve held hands and we prayed over people with cancer, those without jobs, and children who were sick. Then we prayed for our Fancy. We prayed specifically for her intestines and their healing in Jesus' name. We stood in agreement that God is a healer, and we asked for him to relieve all pressure and we asked God to help this sweet old horse to, well, have a bowel movement. There it is. We prayed for a great and righteous poop.

Believing in the prayers, we rushed down to the barn after prayer group, and, sure enough, God had answered our prayers. God is so compassionate, and so into the details that he was willing to answer our prayer for horse poop just like he is delighted to answer prayer about healing cancer. Even though the request felt a little silly, and less important than someone suffering from disease, God wanted us to believe that he would still respond.

As Fancy trotted out to the pasture, happy and whole, we gave thanks to our God, who never turns his back on our prayers, no matter how messy our needs are.—d.o.

July 7
The Bear in Your Backyard

For you have delivered my soul from death, and my feet from falling,
so that I may walk before God in the light of life.
—Psalm 56:13

My dad moved from North Carolina to Naples, Florida, where he bought a home in a new development surrounded by some wild landscape. Now, when I think of southern Florida, I think of alligators and pelicans, not black bears. But apparently, the black bear can take the tropical heat, because one visits my dad's backyard on a regular basis. And that bear knows it's his turf. Since people don't expect him to be anywhere near Naples, they don't lock things up tight. Trash cans full of table scraps invite the bear to feast, and he has decided to accept the invitation.

"Black bears" sneak up on our souls sometimes. We need to be aware of the potential dangers lurking in unexpected places, because the enemy loves to surprise us into sin. You think there are things you would *never* do; you don't even expect something to be an issue. And then, one tiny bit at a time, the action you declared you would never do becomes justified in your mind. Often, by the time you realize you have a problem, you're already nose to nose with the bear.

What do you do when a bear's in your backyard? First, acknowledge that the unexpected has happened. No matter how unbelievable the problem is, it's real, and now you have to deal with it. Dealing with mistakes always involves saying I'm sorry and then making a decision to change. Once it's appeared, getting rid of the bear may seem impossible, but we have to remember that God is walking with us through what we can't walk on our own. But we have to make the decision and trust him to help. The bear has to go. Don't feed it, or it will hang around and invite more bears to the picnic.—k.m.

July 8
Cute as a Box of Puppies!

For just as each of us has one body with many members,
and these members do not all have the same function, so in Christ we,
though many, form one body, and each member belongs to all the others.
—Romans 12:4-5

W ell that's just cuter than a box of puppies," a lady at our church used to exclaim when she found something particularly adorable. I love how a litter of puppies can all come from the same mom, but each is so unique. Even in a group of the same color pups, there will be definitive differences. Some will be fat, others aggressive, some sleepy, and some you just know will be a pack leader.

One night, my neighbor's hunting dog gave birth to a diverse litter. One of her little ones took to water immediately. One looked like the blue heeler down the road. Another was a fat black and red and white-spotted puppy that howled like a beagle. Every puppy was different and seemed to have been gifted with dissimilar abilities.

As they grew, their individual gifts all worked together to fill the needs on our neighbor's farm. The heeler rounded up the livestock, the beagle helped sniff out the rabbits, the Lab brought in the ducks during hunting season, and the big fluffy one kept predators away.

Even if you look at the people in your church or small group and think, *This will never work*, remember that God has placed us purposefully, with a job for each and every member of the body. When a room full of people from all walks of life can work together toward the same vision, maybe God sees a creation collection that makes *him* smile and exclaim, "Now, *that's* as cute as a box of puppies!"—d.o.

July 9
Quacks Like a Child of God

The LORD upholds the righteous.
—Psalm 37:17

Ducks float for several reasons. A gland that secretes oil keeps their feathers from absorbing water. Ducks also have a system of internal air sacs. When they want to dive for food, they have to squeeze the air out of the pockets in order *not* to float. Also, their bones are hollow. These traits are not unique to ducks, but ducks know how to make use of them.

We use the phrase "water off a duck's back" when we want our hearts to be impermeable against hurtful words, which are often disguised as "friendly words of advice," or they just come straight as jealousy or criticism. Sharp words may sound petty, but they can stop us in our web-footed tracks just when we were beginning to paddle in the right direction. When someone tells you that you can't do something you know God has called you to do, don't let their words wipe the oil from your feathers and force you to sink. Instead, with God's promises, let these words slide right off.

The Bible talks about the oil of gladness, the oil of anointing, and the oil of the Holy Spirit. All of these hold us above the water when we think we might drown. The joy of the Lord strengthens us because we can be free to be joyous and confident when we know that God makes everything right. The anointing of the Lord gives us the touch of God's presence and favor as we persevere in the face of hardship. The Holy Spirit guides us in wisdom, integrity, and truth to know how to respond in difficult situations.

Ever wonder why a duck on the water always looks so peaceful? He doesn't struggle to stay afloat; he is held up. And so are we. You can take God's anointed ones to the water of misfortune or disaster, but you can't make them sink!—k.m.

July 10
One Day at a Time

But you must return to your God; maintain love and justice,
and wait for your God always.
—Hosea 12:6

July is National Bison Month, the celebration of the American buffalo. When European explorers set foot on American soil, some thirty to two hundred million of these animals roamed freely. For thousands of years, the bison was hunted by Native Americans, who used every part of the animal. But as the century turned, wasteful killing for sport and hides by explorers, settlers, and commercial interests had decimated the herds of these magnificent beasts. By 1880, the breed was almost extinct, with only a thousand left by the beginning of the twenty-first century. Now, because of private farming and government protection, over four hundred thousand bison live, and the herds are growing.

These animals make their home in wide open spaces, and they have an interesting habit. They like to wallow. Wallowing creates either dust or waterholes, depending on the wetness of the ground, and as they move from one wallowing hole to another, they carry life-producing seeds with them. When the bison almost became extinct, many of the prairie grasses they had reseeded with their wallowing almost disappeared as well.

Some scientists believe the native bison was the first water purification system of our grassy plains through their creation of watering holes in the wallows within wetter areas. God gave this animal so many amazing jobs, and yet greedy thoughtless people almost put a stop to one of God's custodial plans.

Humanity has realized and begun to rectify our mistakes with the bison. As the rebuilding of a species begins, there is no quick fix. We have to wait for God to work through the hands of the environmentally called—and the bison themselves. Just as we often wait years for a prayer to be answered or a relationship mended, we need to be faithful in our efforts to care for God's handiwork. As humankind works to correct our mistakes, we must wait for God to replenish the splendor of his creation.
—d.o.

July 11
where's Jelly?

You search out my path and my lying down,
and are acquainted with all my ways.
—Psalm 139:3

Jelly is a Pomeranian with a tricolor bouffant, and the personality to match.

Jelly likes to play hide-and-seek. We're always amazed how long that typically yippy girl can be quiet when she sets her mind to it. One day, we were pet-sitting Jelly and Phoebe (her sister). We were in charge of watching her, and then making sure she was safely locked in her cage before we left. When it was time for us to go, we told Phoebe good-bye with hugs and kisses, and then looked for Jelly to put her in her safe place. But she was gone. We called. But we didn't even hear a yap from her. Our hearts raced as we imagined all kinds of terrible things that could have happened and the sadness of this sweet family if they lost their little princess.

At last, out came Jelly, walking calmly out of her hiding place. It was a calm surrender, like she had thought it through and accepted that we were there to take care of her and that she should let us do that.

We also have our secret places, the corners of our hearts where we think God cannot find us. He searches for us and seeks us so we will experience his waterfall of love. God pursues us not in order to be punitive, but in order to help us. Those habits and dark places only damage our souls and our relationships with God, others, and ourselves. Sometimes we even place our health or well-being in jeopardy by the secrets we carry. But God wants to make us whole.

The good news of the gospel is there is nowhere too far or too hidden for God to find us. As long as you hide, God will seek you, reminding you of his love, that he created you, and that your life has purpose in his kingdom.—k.m.

July 12
Show Up!

When a man makes a vow to the LORD or takes an oath to obligate himself by a pledge, he must not break his word but must do everything he said.
—Numbers 30:2

When we look at huge problems in our world, we can so easily feel overwhelmed, and when we try to contribute, we feel undervalued or unable to make a dent. When one hurdle is crossed, we want to pull back, pull out, and go on to something easier or go somewhere we can feel important and effective. It is so hard on us to feel ineffective. Have you ever noticed that when you decide to get involved in anything unselfish and giving, someone will always appear out of nowhere to say how pointless your efforts are in trying to effect a positive change?

There are many stories to the contrary of how one person took on the insurmountable and began a tidal wave of change. For example, at Awareness Day at our city's local animal control, volunteers helped clean up our dilapidated facility. Because one person spawned the idea, inspiring others to sign up and show up, petitions were signed, and companies matched funds bringing the attention of an entire community to the need for a new facility. Dogs, cats, puppies, and kittens found forever homes that day, and ground was broken on a new, more civilized building less than a year later. All this happened because one person helped others catch the vision and they brought friends!

We may not be able to influence a stampeding herd alone, but if God has put it on your heart to stand in front of the stampede, you better believe he is prepared to stand in front of you! Be the person who steps up to the plate and says, "Yes, God! I will!" Show up, and let God show off!
—d.o.

July 13
Roller Skating in a Buffalo Herd

Enter through the narrow gate; for the gate is wide and the road is
easy that leads to destruction, and there are many who take it.
—Matthew 7:13

If you spook one buffalo, the whole group will take off. Sheep, horses, deer are all easy to round up or run off because they go with the crowd. Just like these animals, we, unfortunately, tend to follow the herd even if it's going the wrong way.

People will commonly compromise their good standards for self-preservation, and those around them nod in approval and laud the courage it took to "do what you've got to do."

However, as God's children, we are called to make choices that please God first. You can often judge which decision is correct by whether it is loving or not, since we know that God's defining marker is love. I know a girl who worked for a corporation that sold insurance. Her superiors told her to charge some elderly people for things that could not possibly apply to them—hidden costs that would be perfectly legal on paper. She refused to comply and follow the herd in cheating innocent people of money they depended on, and she lost her job.

She says that God took care of her. Soon after she lost her job, she lost two hundred pounds of the weight she had put on because of the emotional stress of working there. God continued to help her to depend primarily on him, and not her paycheck.

God doesn't just warn us away from Easy Street and toward the brambly path; he helps us through the trials that come when we run the opposite way from the herd.—k.m.

July 14
Sweet Dreams

He said, "Listen to my words: When there is a prophet among you,
I, the LORD, reveal myself to them in visions, I speak to them in dreams."
—Numbers 12:6

God's Word is filled with dreams and visions, and using animals as symbols in those dreams has been a tried and true method of reaching humankind through all time. Whether it is a talking donkey that has visions or a man's dream of animals coming down from heaven in a sheet, God uses animals and dreams to help us understand his messages.

When God speaks this way, we experience the dream as if we were walking in God's very presence. And God doesn't waste words, so we should seek to understand what he says.

Do you feel that a dream is trying to tell you something? Have you had a recurring vision about a particular animal? Perhaps God is calling you to his Word to examine that animal as it has been used in the Scriptures. What are the personalities of the animals? Did they speak? Did they speak or emphasize a command that appears elsewhere in God's Word? Are there characteristics in these animals God is bringing to light that you need to pay attention to?

A snake might suggest God wants you to watch where you walk and with whom you keep company. A spider in your dreams might be God's urge to tap into your creativity, by bringing to your mind one of his most creative creatures. Whatever the dream, whatever the animal, if you feel in your heart that God is sending you a message, ask him to continue sending it until you fully understand. In the Spirit, we see much more clearly than in our human ability. So lean not on your own understanding; look to God and let him bless you with dreams that instruct, heal, and bless you.—d.o.

July 15
Don't Eat Yellow Grass

Beloved, I pray that all may go well with you and that you may
be in good health, just as it is well with your soul.
—3 John 1:2

Someone told me a long time ago not to worry if my dog or cat ate grass because it just meant they needed the nutrients that are in the grass to settle their stomachs or supplement what else they've eaten. Not all animals are so savvy about their health. My collie will eat some odd things that, thankfully, don't stay down, putting toxins in her or plugging up her system. One of the horses would eat himself into oblivion if we let him.

People don't always eat well, either. Marketing schemes and advertising use catch words like *light* and *healthy* to make us feel good about buying products. We have to be vigilant to take care of ourselves. We're worth it.

Taking care of our bodies is godly. It is right. It is a responsibility we all have. God created flesh and bones, and he called them "good." Who are we to judge as unimportant what God loves? Some people believe that when we die, we will be waiting for eternity as a disembodied soul, so they start to think that the physical body doesn't matter. But it does! That's why Jesus healed so many people. He could have just sent them on to heaven, but he valued their bodies, so he made many people whole physically.

God has given us ways to maintain good health. His intention is that we be whole. We are not split into body, soul, and mind in his eyes; we are one being, one person with a body, a soul, and a mind that each work best when they work together. So, show that you respect God's creation that is your body by maintaining good health.—k.m.

July 16
Storm and Snake Season

Who gives the ibis wisdom or gives the rooster understanding?
—Job 38:36

When I was in high school, my class read the story called *The Scarlet Ibis* by James Hurst. It was a story that inspired me to be a writer as it began with these words: "It was in the clove of seasons, summer was dead but autumn had not yet been born, that the ibis lit in the bleeding tree."

In reading God's Word for the writing of this book, the ibis again lit in the bleeding tree on the pages of Job.

Ibises have great variety; they are white, gray, bald, straw-necked, and scarlet birds that wade through water and live on crustaceans, frogs, and reptiles. Resilient in storms, they are the last to seek refuge in a hurricane and the first to fly after.

Legend places the bird as one of the first Noah let go after the Flood. The historian Josephus said Moses used ibises to fight serpents in Ethiopia. Pliny the Elder, a natural scientist, recorded stories of the Egyptians also using flocks of ibises to destroy snakes.

In the story by James Hurst, the scarlet bird had ended up off course in an escape from a bad storm and lost his way. The bird came to two brothers in the story as a symbol, showing them that wisdom, when ignored, leads to death.

Wisdom is not born within but gained without. Listen for God's urge to fly or his advice to stay home. Is God telling you that the storm is about to pass and you will be ready to fly soon? Or is God warning you that you are about to see some rising waters? God will guide us, but only when we ask, bringing all his wisdom to us when we do.—d.o.

July 17

A Mouthful of Learning

The wild animals will honor me, the jackals and the ostriches;
for I give water in the wilderness, rivers in the desert.
—Isaiah 43:20

Certain subcultures of America make it impossible to keep weapons out of your son's hands. You can lay down the law, set the rules, hold firm, and then you'll look out the window and see him with a BB gun aimed at a squirrel.

Hunting, they say, is sometimes necessary for the health of the animal community. But to kill any animal for selfish gain or pride cannot be right. "Sport hunting—the killing of wild animals as recreation—is fundamentally at odds with the values of a humane, just, and caring society," said one leader of the Humane Society.

The Humane Society of the United States campaigns against wildlife abuse. When people are in danger, or starving, circumstances will dictate the choices, but often more choices are present than we realize. Killing only for the sake of killing is always wrong. How can a head mounted on a wall honor God? No lives are saved when a deer's meat is rendered useless as food by buckshot. Motives matter.

The Native American Indians prayed over their kill, giving thanks for the provision, and they honored the life that was sacrificed. Because they so respected the life that had been given to feed their children, they made sure to use every part of the animal; nothing was wasted. In the same way, many Christians say a blessing before meals, and parents encourage their children to eat all the food on their plates, as they have been blessed with enough. When we give thanks to the one true God and use his provision well, we're reminding ourselves not to take for granted that sometimes life must be lost for another's life to be preserved.—k.m.

July 18
The Last Song

Do not pollute the land where you are. . . . Do not defile the land where you live and where I dwell, for I, the LORD, dwell among the Israelites.
—Numbers 35:33-34

God created everything. We know that. Rocks, rivers—really, every-thing organic is God's handiwork. Scientists have done some amaz-ing creating, too, but nothing like the wonders that naturally have been given.

On the other hand, the things we cannot create, we most definitely can destroy. Pouring toxic waste into rivers, blowing the tops off mountains, and bulldozing grasslands are just a few ways that humanity can maim what only God can create.

Despite the clear command and obvious expectation God has for Christians to use the earth wisely, protecting our environment has become a political issue. Tax dollars become more important than the cost to the environment and it's all right to remove the natural landscape, as long as people are employed to do it and we don't have to pay anything extra in our taxes for endangered animal safe havens. When money becomes the decision-maker, God's creation loses, and we have everything to do with what we see being destroyed by our decisions.

Maya Lin, an amazing designer and architect of great memorials around the world, including the Vietnam Veterans Memorial, created what she calls her last memorial. *What Is Missing?* is an ongoing display we hear in-stead of see. People, two at the most at a time, can enter a sound cone and listen to the sounds of creation that are leaving us. The haunting cry of the loon, the beautiful song of the humpback whale, even the chirp of the prairie chicken is dying, and we hear the distressed call. Some of the animals are already gone. The sound of the earth is changing, growing emptier.

God lives on the earth with us, and he filled it purposefully with the noise of diverse and lush life. Take an aural tour of our world today and imagine what will fill the void as more of creation ceases to be. What will replace the sound of a waterfall? What will replace the song of the loon, the wind in the prairie grass, or the echo from a mountaintop? What song will we hear when the earth is silent?—d.o.

July 19
Quantum Faith

He has described a circle on the face of the waters,
at the boundary between light and darkness.
—Job 26:10

The world is made of more than meets the eye. Jesus tried to make that obvious to people through stories and even direct speech, but they still didn't get it. When Einstein opened the portal to understanding some things, such as the nature of energy and mass and quantum physics, he may have been seeing with spirit eyes more than we realize, tapping in to information that only God could have revealed.

Animals make it easy to expect the unexpected, which is really all a miracle is—the unexpected. They break the rules of science and theology and give us plenty to ponder and learn. It's fun to imagine that the animals look at *us* with wonder, marveling at the way we complicate things with our categories and preset expectations, when God has given us a world full of visible and invisible mystery to search out.

If events or discoveries are properly presented to us today through media blitz and hyper-focus, we generally accept them as true, no matter how outlandish they seem. Technological advances alone are enough to make one's head spin. Though I think the organic discoveries are a little harder for us to accept these days, things like healing through natural means, walking on water, or the mending of a broken family. But, we need not exclude science when we give praise for the incredible world God has created. Science can lead the way with some real blessings for theologians to expound upon.

I love to tell people about God's astounding universe with reassurance that the God who creates spiral galaxies and constellations is the same God who gives us holiness and peace. Even though the two areas of study sound opposed to some people, the physical world we see is a picture of the supernatural world at every turn, so Christians don't need to be afraid of science, and scientists don't need to avoid listening to Christians.

Discovery is fun and reminds us of God's strength and majesty, whether we learn something new about his creation through a telescope or a prayer. God is our guide, our wisdom, and our vision, helping us to use what he's made to light our understanding. All we need to do is stick close to him, asking him to open our eyes to see what we couldn't see before.—k.m.

July 20
Saving a Wasp

As surely as I valued your life today,
so may the LORD value my life and deliver me from all trouble.
—1 Samuel 26:24

The horse's water trough is a dangerous place for the insect world. But for some reason, they tempt fate. One hot summer day, I saw a red wasp struggling to get out of the water that had become his death trap. I'm allergic to wasps, but watching him twitch and thrust, desperate to live, I couldn't help myself. I lifted the bug from the water with a stick, and he flew off, awkwardly, but very much alive.

The next day, in an adjoining stall, I was grabbing a pitchfork when out of nowhere came an angry red wasp that stung me three times! My first thought after getting the antihistamine was, *Fine thanks I get for saving you!*

How many times does God reach in to save us and we end up stinging him the next day by falling into the same predicament again? Have you ever been rescued from debt collectors by a helpful relative, only to pull out the old credit card when a sale was too good to resist? When we know that there are foods or substances that are unhealthy for our bodies, and we consume them anyway, we're acting as though we've forgotten that God has called our bodies "temples." God cures our cancer, and we continue to smoke.

So many times, we feel we have God's favor when we do things we shouldn't and we don't get caught or have to pay consequences. God knows our mistakes, even if we aren't forced to live in the mess we've made. Just as the wasp couldn't save himself from the water, we can't always manage to save ourselves from our messes, but God's grace—his unmerited favor—covers us even when we make the same mistakes.

We have so much to learn. God is working out his perfection in us, bringing us closer to him every day, as we strive not to land back in the water trough. But if we do, grace fishes us out, reminding us that God is always reaching for us, even when we don't reach back.—d.o.

July 21
Pearls and Peace

As you go, proclaim the good news, "The kingdom of heaven has come near."
—Matthew 10:7

I learned from my mother that virtually everything in life is an opportunity for a spiritual lesson or a helpful analogy, especially for understanding places or ideas we've never seen, like heaven. Life is one grand parable to her. Read Matthew, Mark, Luke, and John a few times, and you'll have the same impression of Jesus.

Jesus used parables to explain the kingdom of God, giving his listeners the opportunity to perceive what's between the words, the *real* story. But when he taught the religious people—and that's who probably needed to hear the parables most—they already believed they were heaven-bound. They just didn't seem to get the *point* of their own sainthood, which was to lead others, not condemn them.

Jesus spelled it out for them over and over again. The kingdom is like a tree where birds rest. It is like a pearl of great price. It is like a treasure you want so much you'll dig for it.

Jesus was talking about how to show love and joy here on earth. He was talking about compassion and understanding, right now, shelter for the homeless, and food for the hungry, whether they are human, dog, cat, or horse. That tree Jesus spoke of is a place to call home in God's kingdom, people you can count on and trust, and a place to be where you matter. We can do our part every day to help God bring that kingdom on earth by committing to compassion for others. Bring heaven near to someone who is hurting or stressed or even to someone who is okay, but whose life has lost its color. You are God's spokesperson to remind people that they *can* have one foot in heaven, living a vibrant life in God.—k.m.

July 22
Flutter by Me, Oh Gentle Savior!

*Sovereign LORD, you have begun to show to your servant your greatness
and your strong hand. For what god is there in heaven or on
earth who can do the deeds and mighty works you do?*
—Deuteronomy 3:24

Butterflies are God's colorful bursts of art that flutter in a frenzy. But every single motion of what seems like erratic flight is a practical design. From caterpillar to the waiting grace in a chrysalis to transformation loveliness, they follow an exact regimen created by God.

A butterfly has flight muscles, tuned to work best when around eighty-two degrees. Constant movement means increased temperatures, and all that flapping creates wind, which cools the muscles. So the butterfly finds a car hood or shoulder on which to bask until their muscles have cooled to eighty-two degrees again.

Butterflies are more colorful in warmth, and they can fly in the face of hungry birds without fear because the color toxins oozed from each wing tip alert predators that the insects are foul-tasting.

When temperatures drop in the evening, a butterfly's wings cannot move at all, and the toxin defense doesn't work, so God added illusion to the armor. The "eyes" on the wings of some butterflies scare away small rodents who might be searching for a nocturnal snack. These built-in designs protect the butterflies when they are totally defenseless.

We are protected by a design as intricate, as complicated, and as delicate as a butterfly's. God never leaves us defenseless. In times of vulnerability, he has equipped us with his strength, with family or friends, or with what we've learned from the hard times of our lives.

Are you feeling a bit defenseless today? Do you need time to bask and warm up in God's light? A walk in the sunlight, a few minutes on the warm sand, even a nap to replenish our overstretched minds can be therapeutic and give us the time to bask in the amazing things God has done for those he loves. What might seem to others like an impractical use of time might be part of God's plan to warm up your wings, so you can fly again.—d.o.

July 23
What Do You Think?

And we take every thought captive to obey Christ.
—2 Corinthians 10:5b

What you think about is important. You cannot always control your thoughts, but you don't have to let them control you. Martin Luther said it this way: "Your thoughts are like a flock of birds; you can't keep them from flying over, but you don't have to let them nest in your hair."

What do you do when the wrong thoughts invade your otherwise peaceful mind? Paul doesn't leave us hanging with questions, but says we should set our desires on things heavenly or good.

Now, some people have a real affinity for the darkness. It seems more interesting, like a grab bag of adventure. The mind set is that we should eat and drink (and be merry) for tomorrow we die. Shakespeare didn't say it. The Bible did. God knows how we think, even when we are being rascals (Isaiah 22:13; Ecclesiastes 8:15).

God's desire is that we be whole, living in happy, healthy peace. He is not seeing who he can catch thinking bad thoughts and doing bad things, but *is* seeking someone he can show compassion to. When we ask for his help, God will begin to infuse our thoughts with his light.

God will direct our desires toward what will make us whole, and we begin to want what he wants. He works on our selfish streak, and with every step of obedience we take, he heals our thoughts more and more until we truly do start seeing things the way God does. And then we can discover who we really are—who we were created to be! The first step is to ask, and keep asking, that God will help you focus on good things that lead to healing.—k.m.

July 24
Armor Up!

All the believers were together and had everything in common.
—Acts 2:44

In many cities throughout our country, we face seemingly insurmountable evils. Animal control facilities are underfunded, understaffed, and overpopulated. As a result, many become a sick and horrible final experience for animals. In rural counties, as the economy dwindles, animals are commonly overbred, malnourished, and neglected. Abandoned animals, starving animals, and cruelty cases just keep increasing in number. Even watching the late-night public service announcements breaks my heart as they show animals looking sadly out of nasty cages, begging for help. And all this is before we even mention starving children, poverty-stricken areas, and whole communities destroyed by extreme weather.

As compassionate people of God, we are called not only to share our problems and concerns among ourselves, but to reach into the heart of the world and be God's hands.

We sometimes forget the power of the fellowship of like spirits. God is constantly, gently urging our faithfulness, but his instructions have been misconstrued into faithfulness in church attendance or how many church events we can chair. The church is neither a building nor an attendance record. The church is the defender of creation, of what is right, and love. With God's blessings also comes responsibility. "Look out for number one," when transformed by God's grace, becomes "Look out for everyone." Connect—with other Christians. "Armor up" against the difficult causes you see in your universe by reconnecting with like minds, and the God who gives you his strength will accomplish great things. If God has called you to do something, he has probably called others to help you. Together, you create a positive army that can solve even the unsolvable problems in the world!—d.o.

July 25
Gray Stray Days

Jesus answered them, "This is the work of God,
that you believe in him whom he has sent."
—John 6:29

Sometimes when you rescue strays, you can just tell by their eyes and the way they cower that they have lost faith. They don't believe in people, nor do they trust any other animal.

Faith has a way of slipping away one day at a time as prayers seem to go unanswered, and life just gets harder. But God will give an animal discernment when the right person comes along that can help them. When life finally gets so bad that even pessimism seems positive, a sixth sense seems to kick in to let animals see through to the heart. After running from so many people, they suddenly know that you're the one who can help.

People have this gift too. It's the reason you *know* that a stray dog or cat is choosing you, or that you *have to* talk to a particular person. You can't really explain it. You're sent to help restore the faith of this animal, or you're the one who's despairing when you finally really see a friend who's stuck by you the whole time.

If you've ever had faith, you probably haven't lost it completely; it could just be very, very small. But the good news is that God never lets us go. Jesus said that faith as tiny as a mustard seed goes a long way in God's kingdom. So, with whatever you have, believe in God's promises, and he'll give you more faith. And if you've *never* had faith, God hasn't let you go, either; you just didn't notice he was there. Now that you see God, believe! Hold on to your faith, and on the days when it seems too hard, let God hold on to it for you.—k.m.

July 26
Trial by Fire

And Elisha prayed, "Open his eyes, LORD, so that he may see."
Then the LORD opened the servant's eyes, and he looked and saw
the hills full of horses and chariots of fire all around Elisha.
—2 Kings 6:17

We live in a world where crime and cruelty walk around like a hungry lion. I read a horrific story about a cat named Bernice that had been maliciously burned alive and left to die in the downtown area of a city.

Why does God allow this kind of suffering? Why does evil always seem to get the upper hand? We tend to only see the suffering, but we can't forget that God isn't in the suffering; he's in the restoration. God brings together his saints and uses them to do his work on earth. God doesn't *create* suffering, he *heals* it.

Bernice's story of healing began with one person who called for help, then volunteers, doctors, and rehabilitators who answered by working round the clock to save her life. She grew stronger, learned to walk again, and was poked and prodded, allowing treatment that was totally out of her comfort zone. Her story spread, and God turned the evil into an outpouring of love. Bernice has become a symbol that God does not abandon us. God sends angels. God heals bodies. And we can take heart that we will not be consumed by the fires of life.

Bernice looks to be well on the path to complete recovery with only scars to show that she has a survivor testimony to God's love. God did not wish for this animal to be tortured, so what evil meant for pain and suffering, God has turned into a wave of unforgettable goodness. If God hears the cry of one small cat, lying in a dark alley in a very large city, you can feel the power of knowing God most certainly hears you.—d.o.

July 27
Ink Blots on the Moon—what Do You See?

Praise him, sun and moon; praise him, all you shining stars!
—Psalm 148:3

The moon never sleeps. If one side of the world is awake and in motion, then the moon shines on the other side that slumbers. The giraffes in Africa see the same moon over their desert as the dolphins see shimmering down on their ocean. People and animals everywhere see the same moon, but not all see the moon the same. Some can make out a man on the moon, and others say it's a rabbit. Once you know both are there, you can see whichever you want because, when you get right down to it, it's all just craters anyway.

Faith is a way of seeing. Some see a benevolent God, others see a wrathful one. People can focus on avoiding hell, or getting into heaven. Some pay more attention to healing and gifts of the Spirit, while others go to every country of the world to teach and help the lost, the poor, and the hungry. Whether we are socially conscious, discipleship-conscious, or concerned about avoiding the world altogether to stay holy, we must know what the "craters"—reality, the nonnegotiables—are. No matter how you look at following God from your part of the world, some parts just *are*.

So, I see a rabbit on the moon, and you see a man, but we're all looking at the same craters. Our craters are these: we believe in one true and living God, who became a man through his son, Jesus, who forgives our sins. We believe in God's Holy Spirit, who teaches and guides us daily. We agree that followers of God need to band together for support, encouragement, and accountability. We believe in the resurrection of the body, and life everlasting is a promise we have to look forward to. We believe that God is love. He is just and fair. He cares about people and puppies and all of the earth, and through God we learn that same way of seeing and are called to that same care. Amen.—k.m.

July 28
Design 1, 2, 3

In spite of all this, they kept on sinning; in spite of his wonders, they did not believe.
—Psalm 78:32

Did you know that within the pattern found in the spiral of a seashell, in the cone formations of a pineapple, and in the cells that layer like bricks within our human body lies the same exact numerical pattern? In 1202, Leonardo of Pisa discovered a numerical sequencing formula that now bears his common name, Fibonacci. The mathematical formula dates back to the Orient in the year 200 BC, and it deals with the multiplicative formula of how in nature, things grow with the same numerical expansion.

The Fibonacci sequence occurs in trees as they branch, the circle of seeds within a sunflower, the birth pattern of rabbits, and so on. Scientists keep finding the formula in different segments of life. Architects have copied and used the formula in designing famous buildings, and school-age children have used the formula in math class.

Is the formula just a natural structure that developed through the years all by itself? Or is God leaving us some proverbial breadcrumbs to help us understand divine creation? Could it be a blueprint for sharing the gospel?

The natural pattern multiplies into infinity, strengthening as it multiplies. What if we could apply the Fibonacci sequence of nature to God's message of love? If we share with one person and they share with one, then each new person shares, and so on until God's truth circles the globe, love multiplies into infinity in a spiral so great that nothing can penetrate it. See how you can set this sequence in motion in your circle of life today.—d.o.

July 29
Abandonment Issues

For he has said, "I will never leave you or forsake you."
—Hebrews 13:5b

Whenever we come home from a trip, we can easily tell which of our animals have had hard times in their lives before us and which didn't. Veronique, the princess collie, greets us gently and goes back to whatever she was doing. She's glad we're home, but she knew we would be. She takes that for granted in the most wonderful way, as she should. Veronique's only had one home, never been lost, and never been abused or treated badly by anyone. She's been pampered.

Josie and Jesse, on the other hand, spent some time on the streets. They know the dangers out there, and they remember a hungry, hugless life. So, when we get home, they jump on the car before we can even get out of it.

God can heal those old memories and hurt places inside us. He does it with gentle kindness, just like we do with our dogs. We let them come inside to feel reassured, and we give them extra hugs and attention until they understand that we're home to stay. They trust a little more each time we go through the process, but if they always need the extra TLC, that's okay. Love isn't so hard to give. Josie and Jesse need all the pampering they can get to help them remember what it's like for them now in the *real* world, the world at home on our farm.

As much as we want Josie and Jesse to know that we're never going to leave them, think of how much more God wants all of his children to trust his faithfulness and feel at home in his presence. He wants us each to know that we are precious to him, the apple of his eye. As we learn, time and again, that God is always there for us, trust grows, and so does our love for him.—k.m.

July 30
The Happy Hugger

Do not be afraid; you will not be put to shame.
Do not fear disgrace; you will not be humiliated.
—Isaiah 54:4a

Our friend Adam, an adult living with Down's syndrome, has a dog, Janie, who's always beside herself when thunderstorms crash. The thunder frightens her to the extreme. Adam understands Janie's fear, and when she starts whimpering, he puts his arms around her and holds her close until she is calm and the storm has passed. He doesn't scold Janie for being afraid. He doesn't explain to her that she has a roof over her head, so there is nothing to be afraid of. He doesn't tease her for being silly, about how she feels safer with her head under the bed. He holds her and comforts her and understands her fear is real.

Children and animals do not *try* to be truthful, they just are. I'm hungry. I'm sleepy. This hurts. They don't ask for advice, reasons, or explanations for their needs. They just want comfort. Because they are children and animals, they probably are given comfort. This changes in adulthood, where pain, fear, and humiliation come with judgment, suggestions, and recommendations on how the problem can be overcome or managed, or how nothing is as bad as it seems.

We often miss what adults in need are actually asking of us when they are hurt or scared, trying to fix the problem rather than heal it. People, just like dogs that are scared of thunderstorms, need to be held and comforted until the storm passes. Comfort, rather than advice, can go a long way in helping someone you love through a hard time, and it never humiliates them or makes them feel ashamed of how they feel. We could learn so much from Adam in how to *comfort* during a problem, instead of trying to solve it, allowing God to heal simply through our hugs!—d.o.

July 31

Inviting God

Search me, O God, and know my heart; test me and know my thoughts.
See if there is any wicked way in me, and lead me in the way everlasting.
—Psalm 139:23-24

Do you ever wonder if our pets appreciate our stupid human tricks? We have some crazy ones at our house. We got the dogs to imitate people by teaching them to shake hands or speak, and now we sometimes imitate all of our animals by ascribing voices to them. We dub cartoon-like voices to match the personalities of the cats, dogs, and donkeys, and even a mouse that got into the house received his own soundtrack as he cleverly maneuvered around our set traps. But what do these creatures really think?

Have you ever wondered if God really knows every thought you think? Scripture does not portray God as a mind reader, but the psalmist suggests that we invite God into our whole being. I want to invite God to search my heart and my thoughts, where problems originally come from most of the time. But, I know that's asking for trouble. It means I'm probably going to have to face a thing or two about myself that makes me uncomfortable. I may even have to give up something I love. But if that loss means I come that much closer to who I was meant to be, then it's worth it.

God, in some sense, knows my thoughts when I read his Word. In Hebrews, we are told that God's Word is a discerner of our thoughts. Through his words, God can direct us to an answer or a comforting embrace, depending on what we need. When I read my Bible, I'm not just reading God's Word, it's reading me.

I don't think we're really so far off with the scripts we write for our animals, but I'm sure God is a lot more accurate than we are when he reveals our thoughts. God probably smiles at the whole lot of us. I'm sure he likes being invited to the party: to the things we say and share, and what we think.—k.m.

August 1
Bless the Beasts and the Children

As for me, I am establishing my covenant with you and your descendants
after you, and with every living creature that is with you, the birds,
the domestic animals, and every animal of the earth with you.
—Genesis 9:9-10

My three cats are my children," the teacher told her class when she made her preliminary introductions. She wanted them to know this fact about her. She related the story of what happened when her town was flooded by relentless rain, how she and her husband got the cats out of the house before any of their possessions when they realized all were in danger. Her love for her pets was the first impression she wanted to make on her new students.

People with children, even animal lovers with children, often misunderstand sentiments like hers, and are sadly judgmental sometimes. But God sends our pets to us just as surely as he directs any person to a particular person or place. God loves us enough to know each person's unique need. He understands *why* we feel the way we do. There are those who, for whatever reason, cannot have children, and a cat or a dog, a parrot or a horse, might be the only way to fulfill the part of their heart that longs to love with parental love.

Those who make their pets a high priority don't undervalue children. They have big hearts and tender souls and are able to love with a caretaking love that respects and cherishes all living things. In God's kingdom, we don't have to pick—kids or cats.

God never saw the need only to love one or the other. When Noah left the ark with all the animals of the world, God made a promise of protection and blessing over them as well as Noah's wife and sons.

When your pets are your children, God promises to watch over you and your family just like any family. You can trust in that promise today!
—k.m.

August 2
Someone Else's Cat

Are not two sparrows sold for a penny?
Yet not one of them will fall to the ground outside your Father's care.
—Matthew 10:29

For a decade, our friend Denise had a cat that wasn't hers. The little cat showed up in her kitchen windowsill one night, crying for attention. She let the cat in, gave it love, attention, and some food, and let her out. It wasn't her cat, after all.

During a bad divorce, this little cat showed up again, but even while my friend held the purring feline for comfort, it wasn't her cat. During a storm, the bedraggled kitty meowed loudly at the back door. During her lonely nights, it stayed and kept her company.

Denise provided for her vet care and feedings, and she always kept a litter box for her friend, but everything was just temporary because this really wasn't her cat. Years went by, and Miss Kitty became an integral part of her life. She was great company in between Denise's business trips. And every time the suitcase was opened to pack for a new trip, Miss Kitty would jump in, as if to say, "Purrr-lease, take me with you!" But Denise didn't because, of course, this wasn't her cat.

Miss Kitty weathered storms, a new happy marriage, and lots of life. Her small body showing all the signs of kitty-aging, Miss Kitty let her "temporarily permanent" mommy-person know it was time to cross the bridge. Together, Denise and her husband tearfully said good-bye as the vet humanely released the cat from her pain.

"How would you like me to take care of final arrangements for your cat?" the veterinarian asked.

Denise burst into tears as she said, "But, she isn't my cat."

A little urn of ashes now represents how God's provision comes to us. Denise felt totally alone, but God saw her tears and sent Miss Kitty. We are gifted with what and with whom we need, and it is totally up to us whether we accept.

Life in all forms on this earth is temporary. God loans us our children, gives us a life-mate for as long as we or they are given life. We have no guarantees of how long anyone's term on earth will be, but we are guaranteed that nothing we suffer is unseen. We are all someone else's too. We belong to God, and he cares for us so deeply that he watches over us every moment, mourning and celebrating with us.—d.o.

Promises, Promises

He is the source of your life in Christ Jesus, who became for us wisdom from God,
and righteousness and sanctification and redemption.
—1 Corinthians 1:30

God demanded faithfulness to his covenant law, which is and always shall be love. Jesus said *all* of God's commandments are summed up in one: love God with all your heart, and love your neighbor as yourself. That's how we say yes to God.

The children of Israel never could keep their commitment to God, so even with Israel's sweet deal, God had to keep his own end and the people's end of the bargain. Paul wrote to the Romans, "What if some were unfaithful? Will their faithlessness nullify the faithfulness of God? By no means!" (Romans 3:3-4a).

In order to have relationship with his people, God had to give them faithfulness. Throughout Israel's story, God forgave the people again and again, until at last he added a whole new dimension to that covenant man had failed to keep—he sent Jesus. Over and over we are told in both the Old and New Testaments that God himself will make us faithful. *God* will make us holy. *God* will make us blameless. God fulfilled his own covenant.

I watch our animals say yes to God every day. They rest. They wait expectantly to be loved. They surrender to the goodness shown them, and I always notice how surrender and gratitude go hand in hand. Perhaps I should start with their example, surrendering so that I can see all that God has done for me so that I can be filled with that same gratitude.
—k.m.

August 4
Mine, Mine, Mine, Mine, Mine, Mine!

Rather, be openhanded and freely lend them whatever they need.
—Deuteronomy 15:8

Selfishness is not just a human character flaw. Animals of all sorts will show signs of greed or aggression over food, and they'll fight over chew toys.

Rescued animals that have been starved or malnourished might be very selfish when it comes to food, even after years of wonderful care. But have you ever had a pampered pooch turn on you for taking your new shoe away from him? Dogs that have everything and dogs that have nothing are both capable of self-serving behavior.

Where one seems justifiably motivated by a traumatic past, the truth is, selfishness can show its ugly face anytime. It doesn't have to be motivated by anything! One horse in the herd will rush through its food, and then aggressively run all the other horses away from theirs as if to say, "It's *mine*! All mine!" A cat might be a bit more calculating, showing its unhappiness with having to share the house with a new kitty by marking territory or refusing to use a litter box.

When we see it in animals, it's easy to see how ugly a character flaw can look. But do we see it when it sneaks into the mirror and looks back at us? Watch a family dynamic change during distribution of property. When a neighbor asks to use your brand-new lawn mower, do you hand him the keys, or say you don't make it a policy to loan your things?

God tells us to share freely. When we bury our talents or stack up our stuff, holding them tight and refusing to share them, we're blatantly rejecting what God's told us to do. If we have been blessed, we are to share our blessings. Whether you have everything or nothing, God requires the same sacrifice from you. God asks for our whole heart, and in exchange, he gives all of his.—d.o.

August 5
The Power of Love

For just as by the one man's disobedience the many were made sinners
so by the one man's obedience the many will be made righteous.
—Romans 5:19

When one of your babies suffers, you suffer. You wish so much you could take away the discomfort or pain. Sometimes you wish you could take it on for them, and they don't always know what is best for them the way you do. The kitty cat, for example, thinks you're torturing him when you make him endure a car ride only to end up at the vet; and the dog simply cannot understand why she can't have pizza every night for dinner instead of the kibble you know is better for her.

God loves us so much that before he ever required "what is best for us," he took our sin upon himself. He is not asking us to do anything he has not already done. With the supernatural power of love he obliterated sin so that we could be free from it. Jesus walked in our shoes so that we could walk in his.

God never desires that we suffer, and he never causes it. He walks with us through the painful process we are called to of dying to self so that we can be made whole.

God intervenes to make us righteous when he is invited to do so. It's a true miracle when a soul turns round, from darkness to light. Transformation begins in your heart, changing your motivations, intentions, everything!

Being made righteous is being made over, but you can be sure Jesus has led the way with grace. You are going to be happy deep down inside with the outcome when you realize what a marvelous gift God made when he made you.—k.m.

August 6
Duck Soup

Then he is to release the live bird in the open fields outside the town.
In this way he will make atonement for the house, and it will be clean.
—Leviticus 14:53

One morning I awoke to the sound of quacking, *loud* quacking, and it was coming from our living room, which was odd because we didn't have a duck. Wiping sleep from my eyes, I went downstairs, and something blasted by me so fast it almost knocked me over. Turning, I saw the duck, black, white, and red, trapped in our living room.

"Hurry, there's a duck in the living room!" I yelled.

My dad was on the scene first, told me it was a Muscovy duck, and started doing the duck call. *Zoom!* There it went, right at my dad. Brooms came out, then a fishing dip net, but my mother put a stop to things when my dad lifted his pellet gun

"Not in the house, Charles!" she exclaimed.

My father captured the frustrated duck in the dip net and got him outside, where he flew off to the lake.

The duck had probably flown to the chimney and fallen down the fireplace. Lucky for him it was summer! A few days passed before the living room was steam cleaned and sanitized enough for us to feel comfortable again. A lot had to be done to fix and clean the mess that had been created.

Our messes are usually a bit harder to fix, and with hurt feelings, unmet expectations, and promises not kept, our houses just get dingier. But for all those messes, Jesus made atonement. On paper, we might look as chaotic as that duck in the living room, a victim of wrong place, wrong time. But God takes one look at all of life's messes, and with a word, he cleans them up.—d.o.

Just Desserts

But God proves his love for us in that while we still were sinners
Christ died for us.
—Romans 5:8

Have you ever in your life seen one of your animals misbehave and think it should die? Of course not! Maybe there are some bad dogs, but "deserve" is an awfully harsh word to toss around regarding a living being. The message of the Bible culminates in God's vision for a world that reflects his glory. Before we make rash judgments, we need to let God tell the whole story in his Word.

God wants us all to live. You can tell by the way the story ends. Jesus is raised to new life, and so are we! And what's truly incredible is that no matter if I'm the worst dog in the pack, Jesus still offers life to me.

God is never about death. At the cross, Jesus conquered death, and that's the whole point. No death, no tears, no sorrow. And that scenario plays out in our souls too, as we die to ourselves so that we can be raised to newness of life. Heartbreaks, bad habits, depression, and whatever destroys you . . . God wants the power those things have over you to die so that you won't.

Most people, I dare say, want to be good. Animals too. Most are smart enough not to want to bite the hand that feeds them, so if they ever do, there is probably a sad reason they are going against the better side of their nature. But God, who is only good, breathed his life into us, knit us together in the womb, so there must be an inherent desire for good in each of us, though we've twisted it with our selfish desires.

You, we, our pets, all of creation receives God's love, not by our own earning but because God says so. Without him, all we have is death—no purpose in life, no hope in death—but with God, we are given life and value, and we discover we are worth much to him.—k.m.

August 8
Dolphin Chats

*Call to me and I will answer you and tell you great
and unsearchable things you do not know.*
—Jeremiah 33:3

Dolphin swims are one of my favorite vacation activities, but a swimmer needs to know a lot before entering the water. It's not like movie dolphins that are trained and do exactly what you want. You have to know your limits as a human in the water with these animals. An eight-foot tube of solid muscle flying through the water is a force to be reckoned with! So to be safe, while in the water with any dolphins, you should wait for them to come to you. If you try to rush them in your excitement, you could pay for it with your life. Dolphins love to play, but they don't know their own strength against our human vulnerabilities.

Dolphins are said to respond to vibrations, so when I entered the water, I began to hum "Amazing Grace." The dolphins responded in a wonderful way, like they were drawn to me. I was amazed that they could feel me humming through the water, and I wondered if the vibrations made them want to find the source as much as I do when I hear the vibration of grace.

We *feel* grace in our souls. God's grace is palpable and real, and when we hear God's voice by faith, we are forever changed. We yearn to know that there is a place where we are loved and welcomed no matter what, where we don't have to be afraid, but can just be loved for who we are.

It extends to all. God will go to any lengths so that we may fully appreciate the grace he holds for all of us. It is God's greatest hope that we share his grace with everyone, even those who have wronged us.

This grace, with all its beauty and hope for people, is mysterious. We don't understand why God even bothers with us, but because of it, we can't help following grace's vibrations through life to him. His grace is so amazing that all creation will sing about it one day. In my circles, many dolphins already have.—d.o.

August 9
Until You Know . . .

*Now to God who is able to strengthen you according to my gospel
and the proclamation of Jesus Christ, according to the revelation of
the mystery that was kept secret for long ages but is now disclosed. . . .*
—Romans 16:25-26a

Albert Einstein wrote: "The most beautiful thing we can experience is the mysterious. It is the source of all true art and science. He to whom this emotion is a stranger, who can no longer pause to wonder and stand rapt in awe, is as good as dead; his eyes are closed. This insight into the mystery of life, coupled though it be with fear, has also given rise to religion."

Our animals have a way of ignoring the silly lines we draw between each other and around what we think God is. They don't need any rationalization for the life they live—a dolphin swims in the ocean because it is a dolphin; an eagle flies to the mountaintops because it is an eagle. Mysteriously simple.

For us, our conversation gets us into trouble. Our gift of language allows us not only to say what we don't mean, but to say the opposite of what we mean. "I hate you" can mean "I love you," and "Leave me alone" can mean "I'm desperate for love." Mysteriously complicated.

The mystery of God is revealed in Christ. His life, death, and resurrection have both cosmic and personal ramifications for us all and for all creation. Knowing that the mystery is revealed, and that the culmination of God's plan for all time is Jesus Christ, changes how you walk through this world. God has a higher purpose. A connectedness joins all events throughout history. Step outside your own front door and recognize with awe that the Lord, our God, is in the midst of us, not because of anything we do, but because God has decided that of all the places in the universe, he wants to live in our hearts. Mysteriously wonderful.—k.m.

August 10
Truth Serum

At the place where they stopped for the night one of them opened his
sack to get feed for his donkey, and he saw his silver in the mouth of his sack.
—Genesis 42:27

Helmut was the perfect inside dog belonging to a friend of mine. Helmut only had to go out three times a day. He didn't chew the furniture and came right home when he was called. You can imagine the surprise when a neighbor came knocking to accuse Helmut of killing his chickens.

"Helmut would never do that! He only goes out for a few minutes a day."

"Well, I *think* it was him, but you say he's been here?" the man took off his hat and rubbed his head.

Helmut rounded the side of the house, passing into my friend's line of vision, and did a quick 180, but not before my friend noticed white feathers hanging from the dog's beard. Guilt is an awful thing. We carry it around our necks as if we can make up for what we've done just by feeling bad. When guilt hangs on, it is like a millstone keeping us from communion with God.

Resentment is the millstone that people carry *because of* the guilty ones in our lives. It's so easy to be the right one when we've been wronged. And in the midst of feeling pretty superior, we commit sins just as grave.

The reading from Genesis comes in the middle of Joseph's story. He had good reason for resentment after his brothers sold him into slavery. Resentment could have been followed by revenge, but Joseph chose to wear *forgiveness* around his neck instead. When he saw his brothers, he had a feast prepared for them. He turned so they wouldn't see his tears. He had been hurt beyond measure, by family members no less, yet he answered that hurt with love.

God does not say forgive when our enemies *deserve* forgiveness. We are told to forgive because resentment destroys our peace. The chicken was not coming back, no matter how guilty Helmut felt. But forgiveness from the neighbor and walking Helmut on a leash from then on resolved everything. Take the first step toward forgiveness today and see how, though it may not bring your metaphoric chicken back, it gives the new ones a better place to come home to roost!—d.o.

August 11
Home Sweet—where Am I?

How lovely is your dwelling place, O LORD of hosts!
—Psalm 84:1

The male golden bowerbird is yellow with a pretty brownish Zorro mask around its face and olive brown along its wings. He is simply beautiful, and his female counterpart, though a bit less flamboyant, is equally gorgeous. Native to the Australian rain forest, there is talk that they may need to be relocated because of climate changes. We know that some will be lost in the move, if it happens.

For once, humans are not entirely to blame. Variations in climate are a natural rhythm of life. But, as usual, humans do play a part in the problem. Scientists, however, are working hard to make us also part of the solution. Managed relocation, also known as assisted colonization, of a species is a drastic move, and so debates are cropping up about if or when to move the bowerbirds.

Change is not easy on any species. We like our homes and the way we do things. While wildlife must adapt to the growth and change in the world (including humankind's effects), people must adapt to their own progress. Technological advances alone create new stresses, new disorders, and new problems to go along with the good. Sometimes relocation can be sound advice.

And change doesn't always have to be in where you live. Relocate your thoughts. Paul constantly encouraged us to keep our mind on good godly things. Panic over schedules can be quelled by taking time to calm your thoughts. Giving too much time to social networking or virtual life can be balanced by spending time reading God's Word. Relocate your emotions. When tough memories sneak in, Philippians says to lay aside what is behind and focus on the things of God. If we can train our thoughts, then we create a suitable dwelling place for God, who lives in us and through us.

Meanwhile, we need to pray for the animals being affected by climate change. Pray for the scientists, too, that the right decisions will be made, and that if the bowerbirds have to move, the shift will go smoothly so that they can thrive in a new, safer dwelling place.—k.m.

August 12
Unstoppable Faith

When Jesus saw their faith, he said, "Friend, your sins are forgiven."
—Luke 5:20

The humpback whale is one of the largest mammals on our planet, with the most beautiful song, shared during mating and calving season. Before 1967, no one had recognized the song of the whale, but that year, scientist Roger Payne and his colleagues heard it, and in 1970, they released an album called "Songs of the Humpback Whale." Payne was the first to believe that whales communicated across oceans. The work of this one man is one of the primary reasons the humpback whale is not extinct today. His "Sounds of the Humpback Whale" was later credited with pushing forward the legislation to ban commercial whaling, which was finally realized in 1986. He believed. He saw more than big animals swimming around in an ocean. For all their size, he saw that they were quite vulnerable to trash, noise, seafaring vessels, and of course, fishing harpoons.

Those early recordings are still the best known recordings we have to date, the deep-sea creature joining with others to sing as a chorus when a new whale calf is born. They literally rejoice in the sea.

Have you ever felt like you were trying to convince the world of something imperative, yet no one would listen? You might feel like the friends of the lame man Jesus spoke to in the Luke passage. The lame man was a hopeless case, incurable as far as the medicine of the day was concerned. But he and his friends looked for any opening in the crowd, pushing and straining to get to the house where Jesus was staying. And when they didn't find one, they didn't despair. Instead, they made a hole in the ceiling. Because of their faith, an incurable man was healed. Because of Roger Payne's faith, an entire species was saved. What will be said of your faith?
—d.o.

August 13
Radah

And one called to another and said:
"Holy, holy, holy is the LORD of hosts; the whole earth is full of his glory."
—Isaiah 6:3

Seraphim, angels of the highest order, filled the temple in this passage from Isaiah, and they called to one another shouting of God's holiness. In the scene the prophet describes, the praise seems to burst forth out of these angels, as if they just can't contain it. The seraphs see a vision of God beyond the walls of the temple in this case, but they see his fingerprints over the whole earth. In fulfilling their responsibilities, the angels are privileged to see how God is enacting a beautiful, perfect plan to redeem the world.

We are created in the image of the holy God, separated from the rest of creation. Not even the seraphim have the same honor. And that honor comes with responsibility. Our "dominion" over animals and over the earth comes, according to the priestly tradition of the Old Testament, from our royal status as heirs with Jesus.

The Hebrew word for dominion is *radah*, which describes the kind of authority rulers have. God expects us to be benevolent kings and priests, not harsh or neglectful ones. To rule well, God's way, is to love big. It means being there for the ones you're responsible for, and it means making sacrifices. When we act in love, we get to see a piece of that picture God is painting. We'll begin to understand some of the work he's doing, and recognize daily that we get to be a part of it!

When we don't lead with love, then animals are driven to extinction or pets are abused and abandoned, and people have not lived up to their godly image, instead using that privilege for evil.

To recognize God in his holiness, full of grace and truth, benevolence and kindness, majesty and power, is the first step to realizing who we are meant to be. Jesus didn't come to take away our humanness—he came to show us what it means. For that reason, we sing with the angels about the only true and holy God.—k.m.

"One" Plus One

God is not unjust; he will not forget your work and the love you
have shown him as you have helped his people and continue to help them.
—Hebrews 6:10

I remember being told by a friend, "I can't walk into a shelter because I would just want to take them all home."

So she did nothing.

"It's just so negative to think about, and no one can figure out how to solve it," said a man to the organization working hard to help victims of human trafficking.

So he did nothing.

God said to go into all the world, which means that we have a responsibility to do impossible things every day. In the face of the impossible, we serve a God who makes all things *possible!* When we make one step, God makes two, or ten, or a hundred to multiply his plan through us. Every great accomplishment for good began as an impossible task. One person, with God's help, can create a wave of change so positive and so powerful that evil quakes in the undercurrent.

"Take heart" appears five times in the New International Version of the Bible. "Take courage" appears four times. The repetition shows that we need encouragement, and we need to be reminded that our good works are pleasing to God. No good deed escapes the heart of Christ. He sees all of the efforts we make because he's making them right along with us!

The outcome of our work is not our goal. Our goal is Christ, and he will complete the good work begun in you until he returns. Humorist Erma Bombeck said, "When I stand before God at the end of my life, I would hope that I would not have a single bit of talent left and could say, 'I used everything you gave me.'" I want to be able to say that too. How about you?

So, take heart, take courage, and be of the knowledge that you are pleasing in God's sight in dreaming and *doing* the impossible every day!
—d.o.

August 15

Good-Natured God

For you, O Lord, are good and forgiving,
abounding in steadfast love to all who call on you.
—Psalm 86:5

Animals have natures. Six puppies from the same litter can have six different personalities and a wide variety of propensities. Anyone with pets or who is around domestic animals for a while can see the unique qualities of each one. Some horses are hot-headed and some even-tempered. Some cats hold grudges and some are cuddle muffins.

People are the same way, each person with attributes that define their character, what you can expect from them in a given circumstance. A man might be dependable, someone you can count on to keep his word, while another might be predictably lazy or a con artist. We come to expect certain behaviors or responses of people and animals by what we know their nature to be.

A person or animal's nature can be specific to the individual, or it can be used in the broader sense. For example, it is the nature of dogs to tease cats, and the nature of cats to purr when they feel safe and comfortable.

God has a nature, but in God's case, we can assume it in the broad sense and in the specific one, because there is only one God. We can't say, "All gods make stars," or, "All gods are trinitarian," because there is only one God. Yet, our awesome God is a being, has a metaphysical existence, and so displays attributes of a personality, things that characterize him. God has told us who he is through his servants, who wrote down what he told them: revealing himself through Scripture. We can also see God's personality through his agenda, which is always to love, restore, heal, and deliver. And *that* is because God's very nature is love—specifically, broadly, whatever way you look at it. He cannot go against it. Love is who God is, what God does, how God plans, and why we exist.—k.m.

August 16
Winning the Chase

The ox knows its master, the donkey its owner's manger,
but Israel does not know, my people do not understand.
—Isaiah 1:3

Have you ever tried to catch an animal that does not want to be caught? We have a pony that thinks the chase is the most thrilling thing in the world. Now, add to that pony two little donkeys who run in tandem in the opposite direction from where we want them to go. The dogs think this is all a big game, so it's like a visual version of "There Was an Old Lady Who Swallowed a Fly." We chase the pony, the pony chases the donkeys, the dogs chase the pony and the donkeys, and I'm sure the cats join in because we all look like we are having the best time!

They might be remembering a time we chased them down for worm medicine or shots or for a bath that they didn't like so much. For some reason, they remember just enough to keep them running away from those who care for them and keep them safe.

Just like ancient Israel, we run from our safe place. Our loving God would never do anything to harm, yet we sometimes run from what is good for us. We have guaranteed grace that will always take us in, but guilt raises its ugly head and we run.

What we don't usually realize is that we run *in* the hand of our Father. We are his. Even if we make our bed in hell, God is with us still. There is no place so far or so fast we can go to escape his love. That's the given. That's the nonnegotiable. Your heart may be hurting and that pain keeps you running scared, afraid to trust in anything. You might be carrying shame for some destructive behavior in your past. But no matter what you've done, at the end of the chase, when you say, "God, come get me," God will finally have the chance to say, "I never left."—d.o.

August 17
Don't Lick at Me That Way!

God said, "See, I have given you every plant yielding seed that is upon the face
of all the earth, and every tree with seed in its fruit; you shall have them for food.
And to every beast of the earth, and to every bird of the air, and to everything that
creeps on the earth, everything that has the breath of life,
I have given every green plant for food." And it was so.
—Genesis 1:29-30

In this first of two creation accounts in the beginning of Genesis, God gives people and animals plants for food. He mentions nothing about them eating meat. Much later, in Genesis 9:1-3, God gives humankind permission to eat meat, and apparently he granted the same carnivorous right to lions and tigers and bears. I often wonder if it was God's original perfect plan for living creatures not to eat each other. It wasn't until Noah and his family got off of the ark that God authorized cookouts.

The economy would crash if everyone went back to the Genesis 1 model for food. Entire industries would die if we all quit eating cows and chickens, and BBQ festivals wouldn't be nearly as much fun. But there is a humane way to kill for food.

On another level, we might take the Genesis verse as a reminder to eat more vegetables, fruits, and nuts. When you put in the effort to eat healthy, you're taking care of God's temple, your body! Both our bodies and the food God has given to nourish them are blessings we should not take for granted.

So, educate yourself in both subjects: animal farming and healthy living, giving glory to God as you use what God gave you well. Oh, and one other thing—veggies grill up just fine!—k.m.

I'll Give You Six More Chances

Then the LORD said to Moses, "Go to Pharaoh and say to him, 'This is what the LORD, the God of the Hebrews, says: "Let my people go, so that they may worship me." If you refuse to let them go and continue to hold them back, the hand of the LORD will bring a terrible plague on your livestock in the field— on your horses, donkeys and camels and on your cattle, sheep and goats.'"
—Exodus 9:1-3

The Old Testament talks of God's chastening if people didn't obey. The punishment fell on people and their animals too! I wonder what an Egyptian's poor ox thought, working hard in the hot sun when all of a sudden he was covered with painful boils. Why did animals have to be punished right along with the obstinate people?

Humans always demand proof, at least when it comes to God. The Egyptians wouldn't listen, and the animals were their food. When the Egyptians got hungry, it was a tangible feeling. Did God want to make the Egyptians suffer for the sake of suffering? No, God just wanted them to let God's people leave the country. It was that simple. No plagues had to happen in the making of this movie!

Are we holding on to something out of pride that is detrimental to ourselves *or* to the creatures around us? We insist on holding on to harmful thoughts and actions, not even realizing they are holding on to us. You see, God loved the Egyptians too. But if you have two dogs you love, and the more powerful one tears into the weaker one, would you want to see the larger dog suffer to get his attention so that he lives peaceably with the other? God wants all his people to love each other, live in peace, and be in a love relationship with the Almighty. When we see all of God's chastening through the lens of love, we are less likely to fight for control or rebel for the sake of rebelling. In God's world, his bottom line is always love and within that love we are all free. If that weren't so, God wouldn't go to such great lengths to prove it.—d.o.

August 19

Abad

The LORD God took the man and put him in the garden of Eden to till it and keep it.
—Genesis 2:15

The Bible is a book of many books, so it gives a balanced perspective. That perspective makes the Bible rich, allowing us to see a more complete picture. We get to watch the way the heart of God's Word shines through, and the way God is consistently relentless with love.

Since the Bible was compiled over quite a span of time, it is full of genres and cultural differences. Also, we should realize that God's Word was originally told through oral tradition. The way the Bible came together, what it is, and why it is vital to our Christian faith is a long story worth a lifetime of exploration.

The original texts of the Bible, none of which exist anymore, were basically two languages, Hebrew in the Old Testament, and Greek in the New. Understanding the cultural nuances behind the languages helps us gain insight into the exact meaning the ancient author wished to convey, which brings us to one of the words in the Genesis passage. *Abad* means "cultivate." The Lord used it with Adam and Eve in the second creation story. Here, *abad* is used in an agricultural context, not in relation to the animals. It's a different twist on man's role in the whole story. In Genesis 1, the writer uses the Hebrew word *radah*, which has to do with ruling in kindness. So, *radah* is a word of dominance, but *abad* is a word of dependence. Adam and Eve were to till the land, working it so that they would have food to eat.

In understanding the dependence of *abad* we gain deeper understanding into the service of *radah*. How can we live in a way to observe both commands? Consider how you can, in your family or at work today, depend on others and on creation while you live as God's heir.—k.m.

August 20
Danger Ahead!

But those who ignored the word of the LORD left their slaves and livestock in the field.
—Exodus 9:21

When we see those we love doing something that will harm them, we warn them. When our sweet doggie wants to chase cars or won't stay in the fence, we have to train him. Sometimes that means a leash, and sometimes that means discipline of a tougher sort, but we don't ever want to inflict harm in that process. Pain is not the point.

When the point of discipline is love, warnings are an extension of that love. Warnings that come from love are not meant to control, enslave, or harm; in fact, they mean precisely the opposite.

God's Word is filled with warnings. He warns us not to cheat in marriages, not to steal, and not to eat or drink to excess. He warned people not to look back, not to go to certain places, and what would happen if they refused to go to certain other places. With all those warnings, and he gave many more than I listed, we can easily think that God is just spewing out rules to follow *or else.*

But purposeless dominance isn't God's goal, either. We have to remember that God lives in infinity. If God needs to show humanity a drastic illustration to prove an infinite point of love, then he might just do that.

Actually, God has done that. Noah and the flood and Jonah and the whale are stories of God's doing extreme things to prove that he loves all humankind but that relationships can't be fixed when sin is still an issue. When we disobey God's laws, we hurt God's heart. When God sees us coveting another person's spouse, he sees families that he formed, knit together himself, get broken. God sees how sin breaks our bodies when food, alcohol, or drugs control us.

God warned us so that we could live a full, complete life in relationship with him, but God's love is not reserved just for here on this planet. His love is forever. When we close our mouths before snapping at a family member or stop ourselves from eating that second piece of pie, let's focus on God's point in telling us to discipline ourselves: saving and loving us for eternity.—d.o.

August 21
Is This Seat Taken?

So then, a sabbath rest still remains for the people of God;
for those who enter God's rest also cease from their labors as God did from his.
—Hebrews 4:9-10

Josie thinks she is a lap dog, even though she's big enough to jump up and put her paws on my shoulders. The funny thing is, she can actually crawl up into your lap before you even know she's done it. And she can pretty much make herself fit there too! If we are on the porch swing, she eases her way onto it. If I am sitting in a rocker, she slips up, one paw at a time, with the most subtle of movements. If we are by the bonfire, she wiggles her way to full snuggle position and looks up at you like she doesn't know how she got there. She loves her farm, her family, and her life so much. She's the happiest dog in the whole United States of America because she is loved and wanted, and she *knows* it.

I think God would be very pleased if his children knew just how much he loves them and were willing to relax in his presence and soak him up. Obedience would be not a question or a challenge, but a response. Less time would be wasted deciphering religious angst and misconceptions, and more time would be spent sharing the love that would overflow from within us.

Knowing we are loved is a foundational stone for the Christian life, and faith without this knowledge creates a harsh, condemning religion. God wants us to be like Josie and crawl up in his lap just because we like him so much and love the life he gives. That's what the Sabbath rest is about. It is holy confidence. It is obedience and faithfulness springing forth naturally out of a heart that is home in God's presence.—k.m.

August 22
Goody Two-Shoes

And do not forget to do good and to share with others,
for with such sacrifices God is pleased.
—Hebrews 13:16

Have you ever been called a do-gooder? Have you ever been told that you are working too hard or doing too much that you're not being paid for? The life of a Christian is hard to reduce to logic, business-is-business mentalities, or accepted time management principles. Saying no to a hurting heart becomes impossible when we have the heart of Christ.

When we see an abandoned animal, and we're late to work because we helped capture and get it to safety, the business world might tsk-tsk as if we have lost our minds. Business and logic are no longer the primary filters for someone who has asked to follow Christ. Our common sense is now love-based. What would love do in this situation?

We can't charge extra to boost the company's profits any more. We can't deduct pay from a mother who had an emergency with her child. When our heart changes for Christ, everything, even down to the proverbial bottom line, changes. "It is no longer me, but Christ who lives in me" isn't just a statement we read. We *are* the statement.

What God sees is the time you spent time with an elderly neighbor, a homeless woman, or an abandoned animal. What God sees is every time you feed or clothe his sheep or share kindness in this world.

You might or might not get the rewards of success according to the world's standards, but God's reward is eternal, pure, and perfect, and it is waiting for all his servants during and at the end of a full life.

If you are facing criticism, unkindness, and humiliation for the good things you're doing, remember that walking in Christ's shoes on this earth is never easy. But if God is pleased, then all *is* well.—d.o.

The Hound of Heaven

Let us therefore approach the throne of grace with boldness,
so that we may receive mercy and find grace to help in time of need.
—Hebrews 4:16

Once you know Jesus, have had a revelation of who he is, and have committed your life to him, you can walk in that knowledge and grace. We don't have to rehash, rethink, and re-struggle. To keep going back into darkness and starting over is like asking to be reintroduced to the same friend again, someone who knows you well. God always knows where we are.

One of my favorite movies of all time is *Lassie Come Home*, which is about a collie that through a series of circumstances gets lost far away from home and the child she adores. She survives many dangers and meets interesting people along the way, some bad and some good, as she travels an extraordinary distance. At last, because her heart longs for home, she finally finds her way back. The reunion is the happiest moment you'll ever see, for both child and dog. That's how it feels to find your way back to God and the confidence he gives us, but unlike Lassie, we don't always realize how much we were longing to be home with him. God knows, though—all along our darkened way, he knows, and he won't give up on us.

A poem, written in 1893, by Francis Thompson depicts the way God pursues those who run from him with his divine grace. The poem is called "The Hound of Heaven":

I fled Him, down the nights and down the days;
I fled Him down the arches of the years;
I fled Him, down the labyrinthine ways
Of my own mind; and in the midst of tears
I hid from Him, and under running laughter.

I love that we can never be too messed up for God. Whether I've been the worst sinner or failed in my efforts to be squeaky clean, God always wants me back, and God wants you back too. God invites us to come near to him without fear because he's waiting to shower us with grace. Falling away doesn't happen overnight, but coming home can, because our loving Father is always waiting with open arms.—k.m.

August 24
Never Alone, Good Servant

For the LORD your God is a merciful God; he will not abandon or destroy you or forget the covenant with your ancestors, which he confirmed to them by oath.
—Deuteronomy 4:31

In the country, animal control is often handled one of two ways: a bullet or dumping. Both are cruel, uncivilized ways to deal with the overpopulation of animals, and I somehow doubt these practices are what God had in mind when he made the covenant with Noah and the rest of creation.

You have probably noticed companion animals along roadsides or left at rest stops, tail down and waiting for an owner who will never return. Mistakenly, some people think that leaving an animal to fend for itself is somehow more humane than euthanasia.

Animal cruelty laws are defeated in government every day in favor of a better bottom line. Somehow if animal care threatens to take from someone's pocket, even if it's just pennies, cruelty is condoned by lawmakers.

So how do we serve God in a world that reduces everything to money? We can begin by looking for a method of treating animals humanely that actually saves money in the long run. Using your voice to contact representatives and political figures in the local, state, and even federal government in regard to animal issues that weigh on your heart is the first step.

The perfect second step is to raise money and awareness for spaying and neutering because the process saves everyone money by increasing the health of animals and controlling overpopulation. Research ways to handle animal problems in your area and consider beginning a rescue shelter of your own. Ask for better laws. Ask for better treatment. Speak to anyone who will listen and share even with those who don't want to hear.

In this world, human and furry beings alike are abandoned and mistreated every day. You may be hearing the call to action. God may be urging you to become a warrior against the injustice you see, to battle with him to protect the covenant we've made together. And God will never abandon you in a fight he has called you to; God will be fighting right alongside you!—d.o.

August 25
Give Me Back My Gills

When I was a child, I spoke like a child, I thought like a child, I reasoned like a child;
when I became an adult, I put an end to childish ways.
—1 Corinthians 13:11

Some of the world's largest salamanders are the eastern tiger salamanders. They are amphibians who spend their childhood in the water and their adulthood on the land. However, for several decades some of these salamanders have lived in a water reservoir on a decommissioned, contaminated army base. These salamanders needed to adapt to man-made environmental issues that made it safer to stay in the water, so they grew legs, and then decided to keep their gills and the tail fins and stay in the water indefinitely. They didn't exactly "grow up."

It is not entirely unreasonable not to want to grow up. Remember *Peter Pan*? Many mourn the loss of the magical time in our lives called childhood, but some people weren't blessed with anything so magical. Sometimes, life is hard right from the start. You would think we would be eager to release our childhood if it was bad, but, like the salamander, we instead often hang on to it all the more. We are determined to relive it, hoping for a different outcome.

God doesn't want us to be chained to a difficult childhood, creating for ourselves a cycle of trying to un-break something. God can *transform* the hurt that is so deep inside us and set us free. The Almighty's grace will help us through the process, so we can live our lives fully, not enslaved to images, words, attitudes, or self-imposed reenactments of the past.

People who have had damaged childhoods often possess an unusual resilience, a unique ability to adapt to diverse landscapes, like the amphibians. It just goes to show that God can take what was meant for evil and turn it into good.

Cry your tears and ask God to help you grow. You don't have to be a slave to who you've been before or how people treated you. God can help you to put an end to your past and look toward the future with hope.
—k.m.

August 26
Dog Catcher

Before very long, a wind of hurricane force,
called the Northeaster, swept down from the island.
—Acts 27:14

Animals are incredible indicators that something big is about to happen. Before a hurricane or a major storm, marine life will swim out to sea to avoid the waves that can throw them to land. Birds will fly inland seeking shelter. The barometric pressure will have even our indoor pets acting out of the ordinary.

But, unfortunately, people don't have the same warning system that animals have, and storms end up leaving stories in their aftermath. One story on the Louisiana coast began when a young woman felt so burdened to help with storm cleanup that she just loaded up her car and drove to the coast to distribute water and to clean debris.

On her first day, she noticed a dog barking behind a chain-link fence. She didn't pay much attention because dogs bark behind fences all the time. The next day, he was still there, barking. She took a closer look, but that was it. But when she saw him again on the third day, she stopped. Turns out, his owner had lost his life in the storm, and the dog had no one.

The young woman brought water and food, and after a few days, the dog came to her and allowed her to apply medicine. She brought the dog home, opening her home to the refugee.

God calls us to see what and who blends in to the background, especially when so many are hurting—the dogs behind fences, the faces in crowds, the broken hearts hiding behind a confident smile. We cannot remain comfortable bystanders in a hurting world; we must watch for the winds that sweep into people's lives, so we can be the first to offer God's love to them.—d.o.

August 27
Name Tags

The name of the LORD is a strong tower; the righteous run into it and are safe.
—Proverbs 18:10

I've always thought it ironic that the name of the Lord is so emphasized in the Old Testament as a name to run to, when the children of Israel trembled at the idea of even spelling it out, much less uttering it. They spelled Yahweh Y-H-W-H in order not to profane that sacred name. The use of God's name is reserved for precious moments; it's not a word to be thrown around lightly.

A name is a personal connection. We feel special when our names are known. It's interesting how much our pets' names matter to them. Since we're the ones who name them, we see in them the characteristics of their names or namesakes—TV characters, playful funny names, or names that we find special and beautiful. They always make us smile when we call our pets to us. I marvel at the way older rescues, whose names we don't know, will take on a new name and embrace it as though we some-how guessed the name they always had.

While a dwarf hamster will be perfectly suited by the name "Fluffball," God's name represents too much to be encapsulated in one great big profound proper noun. Those who were faithful to Y-H-W-H called him *Adonai*. He was also called *Elohim*, which means "Strong One." They also called him *El Shaddai*, which means "God Almighty," *El Elyon*, "The Most High God," and *El Olam*, "The Everlasting God."

God wants us to know his name—his names. He gave us Jesus, who is the Door, the Healer, Wonderful Counselor, Prince of Peace, the Bread of Life, Son of God, Emmanuel, Savior. The passage in Acts 4:12 says, "There is salvation in no one else, for there is no other name under heaven given among mortals by which we must be saved."

To speak the name of God is an act of worship, a way of acknowledging who he is all the time. No matter whether you need the Strong One or the Wonderful Counselor, God is there to sweep you up, strengthen you, and shower you with his love.—k.m.

Now You See Me, Now You Don't

*Therefore you do not lack any spiritual gift as you
eagerly wait for our Lord Jesus Christ to be revealed.*
—1 Corinthians 1:7

Have you ever looked closely at a plant, only to realize what you're actually seeing is a well-disguised insect? Have you watched lizards change color or a rabbit blend into a woodland briar bush? Animals have to depend on the gifts that are given by God to help them be overlooked by predators.

Some animals smell horrible, and others have hurtful spiny needles, stinging tentacles, or an awful taste to keep the danger away. God knows the world in which each creature must survive, so he equips all animals with the tools they need. God has even designed protective partnerships like that of the stinging sea anemone and the clown fish that hides within its arms.

We, too, are equipped. Our greatest foe is the evil that attacks our soul, often spreading its poison to our bodies. Disguised in popular attire, evil will try to sneak into our most vulnerable places. But God has equipped us with spiritual gifts like discernment so that we can see evil for what it is. God equips us with wisdom, warns us with his Holy Spirit whispers, and lovingly pulls the teeth of the lion seeking to devour us.

Take stock of all the abilities that God has given you. Are you a gifted teacher, preacher, or doctor? Have you been told you are a wonderful listener or writer or that you're gifted in the arts? Sometimes we just need a refresher course in what we have been given so that we can remember how blessed and protected we really are.—d.o.

August 29
white Stones and ID Tags

To everyone who conquers . . . I will give a white stone, and on the white stone
is written a new name that no one knows except the one who receives it.
—Revelation 2:17

Understanding the importance of God's name helps me understand the importance of my own. It's not just a name; it symbolizes me, the life I've had, the things I've done, the character I display. When parents name a new baby, many look up the meaning and hope to include some attributes that will inspire their child to be a good person. When we name our pets, we try to characterize them, too, sometimes choosing a name that describes their physicality, and sometimes giving a name that fits their personality.

When I was a child, I couldn't understand why it was supposed to be good news that God was going to give me a new name. I liked my name. As time marched on, though, I understood a little better. My mistakes and memories began to define me in my own mind, and I began to wish that I could leave behind at least the negative events that my name represented.

God writes a new name for his conquering children. Jesus said that he has conquered the world, but with holiness and love, not with violence or wrath. In Romans, Paul says, too, that *we* are more than conquerors through Jesus. I can easily imagine that the stone in Revelation is Jesus. Receive Jesus—the one who conquers—and then we can conquer by faith in him. And the name on the stone connects us with God, like the identification tags we put on our pets' collars. We carry around the Rock of our faith—Jesus—so that we can overcome any struggles that come our way.—k.m.

August 30
Sit, Stay, Roll Over!

So then, the word of the LORD to them will become: Do this, do that, a rule for this,
a rule for that; a little here, a little there—so that as they go they will fall backward.
—Isaiah 28:13

Have you ever thought about what we expect of our pets when we train them? We count on them not only to learn the rules, tricks, or behaviors we don't want them to repeat, we make them learn the commands in *our* language. I often wonder what our dogs and cats think when we use baby talk and jump up and down when they tinkle in the right spot, or when we turn quickly to harsh words when they don't. We seem to have certain requirements for our pets to remain in our good graces, yet they have very few for us to remain in theirs.

Human beings tend to feel more comfortable with boxes, because boundaries make us feel secure. We write rules to live by, love by, drive by, and succeed by. We sometimes even try to reduce God's holy Word into a set of rules. We require of ourselves that to be a good Christian, you have to do x, y, and z. When we fail to be perfect, we end up throwing everything out the window. People judge themselves harshly and they never go to church again. Words like *hypocrite* are thrown about as if God has created a black list and we've ended up on it.

God does have a rule, and it's anything but damnation. God's *only* rule is love—that's the only box he created. The enemy can even hide behind a church system, waiting to throw the book at some of God's children in hopes of discouraging them enough to separate them from the fold. In these times especially, we need to reach out to each other the same way God reaches to us—with grace, patience, and love. God doesn't make us jump through one single hoop for it, either. And we should make sure that our church's welcome mat doesn't have a hoop to jump through.
—d.o.

Exploring Bears

Therefore they will be like the morning mist, like the early dew that disappears,
like chaff swirling from the threshing floor, like smoke escaping through a window.
—Hosea 13:3

On August 31, 1803, at eleven o'clock in the morning, Lewis and Clark set sail to explore the Louisiana Purchase territory. In journals of their findings, Lewis described his first experience with a grizzly bear as "a most tremendous looking animal, and extremely hard to kill." During the expedition, the party killed at least forty-three of the species, but at the time there were some fifty thousand bears estimated to be from the Plains to the Pacific Ocean, so they had little impact on the population. With a shrinking habitat in America today, however, those numbers have dipped to around one thousand. In the United States, they are listed as threatened under the U.S. Endangered Species Act.

Conservationists have suggested reintroduction programs, but their ideas have not been accepted. Meanwhile, numbers continue to dwindle as native grizzly grounds are overtaken by population sprawl. The biggest threat to the bears, as well as for most endangered animals, is from human contact. The illegal poaching and accidental killing by hunters of black bears and the ridding of nuisance bears are all contributing to the grizzlies' demise.

It is so easy to become oblivious to animals that we've grown accustomed to. Grizzlies are in movies and cartoons, and they're mascots for ball teams. An animal that popular can't ever disappear, can it?

The things we count on we often take for granted; they're easy to miss. We forget to tell someone we love them, when, in a moment, something that is a part of the fabric of our everyday existence can just cease to be.

Become a watcher. Have a gratitude checklist. Be vocal about protecting what's important. Let us be thankful for the grizzly bear that we want to be here for generations to come.—d.o.

September 1
Faith-Building Snake

But when he noticed the strong wind, he became frightened, and beginning to sink, he cried out, "Lord, save me!" Jesus immediately reached out his hand and caught him, saying to him, "You of little faith, why did you doubt?"
—Matthew 14:30-31

Snakes get such a bum rap. We have given them bad PR of biblical proportions. Paintings portray the fall of man precipitated with the deadly hiss of temptation by a snake. As close as we can get to the original translation of the biblical Hebrew word we now call "snake" is *serpent*, which may not be a snake at all. The story says that God would no longer allow the serpent to have legs, but snakes do not seem particularly unhappy with their pad-less existence. The lack of extremities comes with certain advantages.

We are afraid of snakes at our house, not for any inherent evil or symbolism, but for the places they can go and the speed and agility with which they can get there. If you don't know which are poisonous, best to leave them alone, so we try to do just that. But one day, a snake found us. It was the day we learned how to walk on water.

My son, my best friend (whom my son calls "Aunt Peanut"), and I had gone down to the river where there was a shallow crossing to the other bank. Copperheads live in our area, but we figured we would be safe in the river. So, with my six-year-old son between us, we held hands and started across. Suddenly, skimming across the water in elegant, swift *s*-patterns was a copperhead.

I yelled, "Snake!" and when "Aunt Peanut" spied it, she swooped my son up under one arm, and me under the other, like a couple of footballs, and ran across that water back to our shore.

Snakes remind me that I don't have to misjudge any of God's creatures, but that I also don't need to go swimming with all of them! I am grateful that our snake encounter that day taught me that we can walk, or run, on water. Sometimes it just takes a little faith and motivation to do the seemingly impossible. With God, ALL things are possible!—k.m.

September 2
God's Voice

Among my people are the wicked who lie in wait like men who
snare birds and like those who set traps to catch people.
—Jeremiah 5:26

An ongoing fight rages between trappers and the anti-fur people. Both sides say, "Animals are here for us," but to one side, that means *we can do anything we want,* and to the other perspective it means *we must protect them at all costs.* But when God made us custodians of creation, did he ever applaud destroying it at will?

Animals can be sacrificed for food in a clean and humane way. Trapping, in particular, is neither clean nor humane and has never been seen by Scripture as a positive custodial service to God's creatures. Why? Because cruelty has never been a holy concept.

When traps are left in the wild, caught animals are terrified and in pain, and they must wait, sometimes days, until the trapper comes to strangle or crush them to death. According to the sellers, any other kind of "coat-damaging kill" would be unsuitable for the industry.

But, the trap doesn't know the difference between the targeted animals and any other creature. So, a cat or dog can end up among the surprisingly large number of family pets who unfortunately wander into the jaws of steel. Endangered animals, as well as children and hikers, are harmed by hidden traps every year, too. All are explained away as "accidents."

God's Word likens a trapper waiting to snare the unsuspecting to the wicked secretly trying to entrap God's children. Life in any form is precious, so dishonest tricks to cheat, kill, and destroy are evil. *Disposable* is never a word God associates with any of his beautiful inimitable creation.

When we perpetuate industries or hobbies that use cruelty as accepted practice, we are guilty of the problem and its far-reaching impact on humanity. The voice of the unwavering Christian must stand strong against evil in all forms and to fight to keep God's world alive.—d.o.

September 3
What Angel Fish and Beavers Have in Common

So they are no longer two, but one flesh.
Therefore what God has joined together, let no one separate.
—Matthew 19:6

Animal lovers notice the similarities between animals and humans, but we also know we have much to learn from our differences, differences in which the animals tend to fare better on the integrity meter than we do. Animals, domestic or wild, can make no excuses—a nice quality that comes with not being able to talk or build rockets. They simply are what God made them to be.

And he planned for many animals to mate for life. Though not the majority in the animal kingdom, those that do exemplify faithfulness, fidelity, and companionship at its finest. Do you suppose God cares when animals are kind and loyal? Perhaps many are called to live this way, but few are chosen.

The few "chosen ones" in the animal world that mate for life include gibbon apes, gray wolves, swans, French angel fish, and albatross. Rodents are known for their promiscuity, but the prairie vole goes against the grain and forms monogamous pairs, even sharing duties in the upbringing of the babies. Bald eagles mate for life, making them atypical in the country they represent, where the divorce rate exceeds the happily-ever-after rate. Black vultures prove that there's someone for everybody, as even they, with their stunning bad looks, find mates who stay by them. They form loving lifelong bonds, and if anyone tries to interfere, the mate will fight to defend her matrimonial status. Turtledoves are known for their sweet, lifelong romance. Beavers, geese, and seahorses all mate for life.

Marriage is a mate-for-life thing. More than just a legal commitment, it is a vow before God, sealed by his blessing. Keep God in the center of your heart and allow him to guide your thoughts. If both partners live directed toward God, then marriage is an equation for love and happiness.
—k.m.

251

September 4
Dr. Schweitzer

Be sure you know the condition of your flocks, give careful attention to your herds.
—Proverbs 27:23

Hear our humble prayer, O God, for our friends the animals,
especially for animals who are suffering;
for animals that are overworked, underfed and cruelly treated;
for all wistful creatures in captivity that beat their wings against bars;
for any that are hunted or lost or deserted or frightened or hungry;
for all that must be put to death.
We entreat for them all Thy mercy and pity,
and for those who deal with them we ask a heart of compassion
and gentle hands and kindly words.
Make us, ourselves, to be true friends to animals,
and so to share the blessings of the merciful.
—attributed to Albert Schweitzer

A man can do only what he can do. But if he does that each day, he can sleep at night and do it again the next day," said Dr. Albert Schweitzer, whose commitment moved him to oversee the building of a hospital in Gabon, west central Africa, treating all living beings with respect, even those that caused problems. To him, even mosquitoes and snakes were not to be killed, but simply allowed to live and move on.

We often feel our chance to right wrongs is hopeless in the face of the sheer magnitude of need. There will always be another mouth to feed and another loss to burden those that choose to see. This simple prayer shows how Dr. Schweitzer took all of his one-man weakness and combined it with his all-powerful God to do what he could. He prayed and his daily life exemplified the commitment of his prayer.

He passed away September 4, 1965, and was buried on the banks of the river at Gabon, but his memory lives on in his hospital there. Because of his dedication to caring for those God placed in his care, many now share his passion. May we all live to inspire others by living out our prayers.—d.o.

You Don't Say!

Even fools who keep silent are considered wise;
when they close their lips, they are deemed intelligent.
—Proverbs 17:28

The old adage goes, "It's better to be silent and thought a fool than to open your mouth and remove all doubt." This phrase rings true whenever someone calls a particular smooth, gray-black dog a "hairless Chihuahua." No hairless Chihuahuas exist except for the poor souls with a skin condition. What they mean to call it, but probably can't, is a toy *Xoloitzcuintli*, so named after two Aztec gods. It's pronounced "show-low-eat-squeent-lee," and can be called Xolo for short. It is a separate breed, and according to the Xolo rescue site and the American Kennel Club, it was probably the first domesticated animal in the Americas.

Xolos are not the only dogs that are mistakenly called Chihuahuas. Another is the Chinese Crested. These dogs are believed to have evolved from African hairless dogs, but they sailed with Chinese mariners long ago. So, you see, you can't always judge a dog by its fur—or lack of fur.

The same goes for people. You can't judge a mother by the number of children she didn't give birth to (or did), or a man by the wife he doesn't have. A woman's worth is not in her husband, and a man's worth is not in his sons. Some people are specially called to be available to orphans and be friends to those who would otherwise have no one; and some people need to have some time to themselves, perhaps watching TV with the cat. Cats are brilliant conversationalists, you know.

When you see someone and begin to make a judgment call about who they are, remember first that, according to the Bible, Jesus didn't get married or have children. And several times he left his followers for a while to be alone and recharge. Instead of making an assumption about the people you're looking at, why not ask them about their story? Ask God to use you in their life or to use them in yours.—k.m.

September 6
Deer Ones

The Sovereign LORD is my strength; he makes my feet like the feet of a deer,
he enables me to tread on the heights.
—Habakkuk 3:19

One morning, as I walked out on the front porch, I saw a mother deer in the middle of the driveway. She turned to look at me, but she didn't run. When I looked to see why, I saw underneath her two spotted fawns, suckling with all their might. The three were very close to where I stood, so I took advantage of the morning light and this beautiful scene to watch them. Twins are not a rare occurrence in white-tailed deer, but these were the first I had ever seen.

A truck came down the driveway to deliver hay to our neighbor, but the mother deer didn't move. She was doing her job. The rest of the world was just going to have to wait. The truck driver and I watched, and when the last sip was taken, the threesome walked off into the high thicket.

With life, it seems that someone is always waiting for us. The most important things in life get put off because someone waiting might be inconvenienced, so we move along. How many important things have we put off for the convenience of others? How many precious moments have been missed because we simply couldn't make the time? How often have we met everyone else's time constraints so they could enjoy their family time, while we miss ours?

Let us take a note from the page of the mama deer. Put the necessary stuff on the wait list, and the important stuff, like a talk with your daughter, on the front burner. When someone is pressuring you to do something different with your time, think of that mama deer who calmly looked at the truck driver and me and finished what she was made to do.—d.o.

September 7
Leopard Spots and Works of Art

And let the peace of Christ rule in your hearts, to which indeed
you were called in the one body. And be thankful.
—Colossians 3:15

Some people are so bent on making everything perfect, they would change the spots on a leopard or the stripes on a tiger if they could and call it an improvement. A special knack for details can turn into a careful, tension-filled heart and frustrated relationships, as a controlling spirit becomes critical of others. But we must look through the Jesus filter first. He is perfect, but his holiness is loving and kind, not critical and rude.

Animals can't talk back, so they often receive the brunt of controlling spirits. Biting, kicking, clawing, and pecking are sometimes a reasonable response to an unreasonable command. God doesn't want us to break the spirits of our animals any more that he wants our spirits broken; instead, he wants us to surrender and accept his peace so that we can pass it on. Surrender in God's kingdom is not a broken spirit—it is a willing heart.

Control shows up in other ways too. Sometimes our creative spirit is broken when we become so critical of ourselves that we can't bear to finish that song or that book. We'll never go near that easel again because we think we can't produce anything that will be good enough. We find a million excuses, all while telling the world about all the things we could do or are going to do. It's really fear stopping us.

Maybe the reason the Bible talks so much about surrender and suffering with Christ, giving and servanthood, dying to live, and God's Sovereignty is to remind us that we are not in control, no matter how hard we try to be.

No doubt God knows every spot on every leopard, and is pleased with his handiwork. He did not, after all, finish creating and then on the sixth day say, "That's pretty good, but I can do better." God gave everything he made a thumbs up, and that includes you!—k.m.

A New Earth

The first living creature was like a lion, the second was like an ox,
the third had a face like a man, the fourth was like a flying eagle.
—Revelation 4:7

Have you stopped to listen to God's poetry? God's theater happens all around us, and it's free all the time. Watch an ant colony. It's alive with drama that we often miss. Sit on the front porch and take in a thunderstorm. Watch the beauty of lightning as it crashes across the sky. Feed the ducks at the city park. God is always beckoning us to partake of life.

In Revelation, the chapters read like a theatrical play of how God is constantly delivering a downtrodden Israel, raising them to him in a beautiful shining moment. That same beautiful, inspiring scene of all life coming together before God applies to all of us.

When so many are busy trying to sell books and movie tickets based on the fear the end times bring, the Alpha and Omega is trying to get us to understand that he is always breaking his children out of bondage, desiring to give us all hope, not fear. The story of Revelation is symbolically told and retold to reveal to us one thing: from day one into infinity, God is sovereign over all the earth! God is the Creator and the Savior.

When we finally really see God's glory, we will join the heavenly throng in praise, and alongside us will be the humpback whale, the lady from the third pew on the right, and your childhood dog, Spot. Think about what it will look like when *every* knee will bow, and every creature sings. What will heaven look and sound like when the only utterance of all creation is praise, love, and joy?—d.o.

September 9
Warfare of Dependence

Finally, be strong in the Lord and in the strength of his power.
—Ephesians 6:10

People fight spiritual battles. People and animals suffer at the hands of humans who lose those battles and fall under selfish influence. According to Scripture, our battles are not all of our own making. There are enemies warring against our souls, rulers and authorities, and cosmic powers of this present darkness, wrote Paul, spiritual forces of evil in the heavenly places. An evil force is loose in the world for now who would love to destroy as much of our happiness as possible before God puts a final end to it.

Spiritual battles can look like depression, an addiction, rage, or a thousand other responses that humans fall prey to. Ephesians says that God has provided us with armor so we can fight these battles. Our shield is faith, which pleases God.

We wrap truth around us, which we can find in Christ, and we exemplify it in honesty, integrity, and living out the principles Jesus teaches.

Righteousness guards the heart, and so it is our breastplate. Righteousness simply means "rightly related to God," lined up with God's purposes, connected to the chief.

Paul tells us in Romans that God gives us his righteousness, since we can't fix our relationship with God.

Next, we have the helmet of salvation, which is God's grace, and the sword of the Spirit, which is God's Word.

Finally, we are strengthened by prayer, fellowship, and the gospel of peace.

We are encouraged to stay alert and to wear all of this armor of God all the time. Have you ever noticed that all of our weapons are really about total dependence upon God? He fights our battles for us.

It is important that we pray and do the things God has told us to do. He has reasons for the way he guides, and we may not understand for a while, but we can trust that his ways are right and good, and for good reason. God is a life-giving, life-protecting force, and if we allow him to, he'll fight with us through every attack the enemy ever sends our way, strengthening us so that we can stand.—k.m.

September 10
Cat's in the Cradle

When I felt secure, I said, "I will never be shaken."
—Psalm 30:6

Do not ever take your cat for a ride without a cat crate. That sweet purring mass can turn into a laceration machine the second the ignition is turned. I learned this the hard way with a cat that, I thought, was as tame as a cat could be.

His name was Mongo, short for Mongolian Spare Rib. He was born to a cat under my back deck one winter, but the poor thing's mother didn't want to feed him. In fact, she kept removing him from the litter and hiding him. The only thing that kept him alive was a will to survive.

I would hear him crying loudly from some hidden place and have to go find him. This happened so often, I finally just kept him near me and fed him with a bottle until he was weaned.

When he was two years old, I thought it would be just fine to take him to the veterinarian down the street. He was so tame that I didn't think I needed his crate. He began to howl as I pulled from the driveway, cried the whole trip, and then when I walked through the door of the doctor's office, Mongo leapt from my arms like he was on fire.

Through the parking lot he ran, past a motel, under a chain-link fence, across a large drainage ditch, and toward the interstate, all with me breathlessly following. I finally caught him and got him back to the vet's office, both of us covered in whatever was in that ditch. The assistants handed me a box of baby wipes and tried not to laugh. I've never since driven any cat anywhere, unless in the safety of a crate.

When we feel insecure, we do some pretty stupid things too. We run from love like it is fire, not understanding that God has a secure place in his holy love that nothing can ever shake.—d.o.

God Bless the Horses

I have suffered the loss of all things . . . that I may gain Christ.
—Philippians 3:8

There are days that make history, days when events occur that change life as we know it. Jesus came to bring peace on earth. It is difficult to have goodwill for all men when *all men* includes those whose idea of a god requires the destruction of innocent people. Yet, even the most hate-filled radical is breathing God's air. That alone is something of grace.

A historic landmark lives in the United States now. It's nothing as sweet as Kitty Hawk or as beautiful as the purple mountain's majesty. It is known as Ground Zero, which is memorialized in New York at the place where the buildings of the World Trade Center fell. In honor of those who died, we need to remember and share the tears of the families for whom it will always have happened just yesterday.

It is not just people who remember. The New York Police horses have seen it all. They keep the memories with us and have done their part to help protect us. There is something organic and reassuring about those beautiful creatures clip-clopping on the city streets in uniform. The horses serve in a way that cannot be replaced or replicated with technology or industry, with heart and spirits that want to bless humanity with their God-given power and strength.

When the tears are cried, we move on in hope. Together, we share a vision.—k.m.

September 12
Unshakable Ashes

Tremble before him, all the earth! The world is firmly established; it cannot be moved.
—1 Chronicles 16:30

Okefenokee means "shaking earth" in a Native American language, and it is the name of a soft bog that trembles when walked upon.

Okefenokee Swamp is home to alligators, reptiles of all kinds, swamp birds, fish, turtles, bobcats, and the Florida black bear, and it has one of the largest collections of cypress trees in the world. The 680-square-mile area of water that feeds into the Suwannee River comprises this Georgia-Florida landmark. But this delicate ecosystem has had many challenges.

In the late 1800s, the Suwannee Canal was dug across the diameter in a failed attempt to drain the swamp. The land was later sold to a private family who extensively harvested and sold the beautiful cypress trees. The land was logged for pine and live oak by other companies, and the natural beauty was taken out on trucks and trains, piece by piece.

The now protected Okefenokee Wildlife Refuge experienced a lightning strike in 2007 that began a slow-burning continuous wildfire that blazed from May until July, consuming some six hundred thousand acres with smoke that could be seen not only in Georgia, but as far away as Orlando, Florida.

But what God creates, he protects. What could have spelled destruction, just spelled change.

In the aftermath of fires that burned away thickets and brush, now there stands an open area where sandhill cranes move through waters actually sweetened by the fallen ash, inviting more wildlife growth. New growth flourishes, and life changes, but most importantly, it goes on.

We can be encouraged that even when all seems lost in an ecosystem, God's grace is still evident. The Almighty is constantly proving that he can resurrect.

From the ashes we rise, with the help of a replenishing Creator.—d.o.

September 13
Feminist Chickens

Be subject to one another out of reverence for Christ.
—Ephesians 5:21

What God intended for human couples is clear in Ephesians. Marriage is about being servants to one another, respecting one another. God's Word levels the ground between male and female, just as it does between rich and poor, between nationalities, and between expressions of faith in God. Galatians 3:28 says, "There is no longer Jew or Greek, there is no longer slave or free, there is no longer male and female; for all of you are one in Christ Jesus."

Submission. That word does not have the best connotations these days, and it has been grossly misused in some religious circles. "Submit!" many churches tell wives, who are promptly shown Ephesians chapter five and dared to cross those lines. Sadly, the verse that asks wives to submit is taken out of context, isolated from the rest of the story.

On the farm, the most shining example I've seen of a submissive wife is among the chickens. They admire the rooster and trust him to take care of them. They allow him to eat the first and best of the food, but they also allow him to go outside the henhouse when they hear a commotion to see what that noise was.

One day, we checked in on the chickens after hearing a commotion in their vicinity, and there, tucked under the rooster's strong wings, were the two little brown hens. Those chickens knew that their rooster had their safety at heart. They knew they were safe. As for the rooster, he would give his life for them, and nearly has on several occasions.

We can't get around the patriarchal nature of the Bible—after all, the book is stories that are grounded in a particular culture. But rather than accenting the maleness of the Bible, we should note the *balance* God's love brings.—k.m.

September 14
Saint Francis's Vision

After this, the word of the LORD came to Abram in a vision:
"Do not be afraid, Abram. I am your shield, your very great reward."
—Genesis 15:1

The patron saint of animals is Saint Francis of Assisi, who gave up a life of wealth to serve God. Legend says he preached to the birds and prayed with a ferocious wolf who lay at his feet and never killed again. Many Blessing of the Animals Services use the following Prayer of Saint Francis:

> Lord, make me an instrument of your peace.
> Where there is hatred, let me sow love.
> Where there is injury, pardon.
> Where there is doubt, faith.
> Where there is despair, hope.
> Where there is darkness, light.
> Where there is sadness, joy.
> O Divine Master,
> grant that I may not so much seek to be consoled, as to console;
> to be understood, as to understand;
> to be loved, as to love.
> For it is in giving that we receive.
> It is in pardoning that we are pardoned,
> and it is in dying that we are born to Eternal Life.

This week in 1224, Francis saw a vision of an angel on a cross, who gave him the five wounds of Christ in a phenomenon called the stigmata, according to witness Brother Leo, who recorded this first occurrence of the stigmata. Saint Francis was treated for the next two years for the wounds and a chronic eye ailment, and passed away on October 3, 1226, after dictating his testimony during his last days and singing the words of Psalm 141. Legend has it that just before he died, Saint Francis thanked his donkey for being such a good and faithful servant, and the donkey cried.

We can ask God for a vision for our life as we seek a deeper walk with him. Read about how filled with passion and love for God Saint Francis was. His dedication was answered—God showed him the special job he had prepared just for Saint Francis. Carefully listen to people and animals that come into your life. Give often, forgive much, and love always, and God will show you, too, the vision he has to fulfill your life.—d.o.

Poetic Rain

And the shower of rain, his heavy shower of rain, serves as a sign on
everyone's hand, so that all whom he has made may know it.
Then the animals go into their lairs and remain in their dens.
—Job 37:6-8

Each day has its own rhythm, its own character, its own purpose. Some days are sunny and bright with moods to match, while others are too sunny, so hot that the whole world seems angry. Some days your dreams follow you around as though two worlds, visible and invisible, had collided in the night, and somehow, life seems surreal and impressionistic. I like those days the best, especially if it rains and especially if the dreams were good.

Life is poetic on those days, where in the abstract mist, my soul settles down to listen. After a rain, when the trees are dripping a syncopated song, the birds are quiet and settled, but present, and all of our animals sleep, the world feels calm, as though heaven had sent a theatrical memo to say, "Settle down and be replenished." As a child, I loved the storms that came at the end of summer. Those storms set the tone for the transition from play back to work, a little ominous and foreboding, yet exciting and unpredictable.

As an adult, taking time to sit and wait on God is not so simple as rocking with the rhythm of the rain. Too often, the show must go on. Work schedules and the business at hand are set in stone, regardless of God's daily vibe. Rain is not so lovely when it is complicating rush hours and dirtying floors from muddy tracks. Complaints abound, as though sunny days are all we ever want.

Thank goodness, God doesn't conform to the convenient stride of our template for productivity. Our Father knows what's best for us, even when we don't. The verse before the one above in Job says, "God thunders wondrously with his voice; he does great things that we cannot comprehend" (37:5). Sometimes the greatest things, and the hardest to really understand, are the simplest—like rain.—k.m.

September 16
My Sister's Lizards

A lizard can be caught with the hand, yet it is found in kings' palaces.
—Proverbs 30:28

O f all the pets my sister has had, her geckos were the oddest choice to me. On a day outing with her niece and nephew, they begged her, as children will do, for two leopard geckos from the pet store. Their mother would never let them have a dog or cat, but they figured a gecko would be fine. So, breaking the rule about checking with their mom, they dove headlong into the purchase of two geckos, heat lamps, hot rocks, terrarium, and mealworms. Shortly after the new pets' arrival at the house, my sister got a call to quickly come and remove the lizards.

So, my dear sister became the proud mama of two spotted, fat-tailed lizards. Interestingly enough, she became fonder of these little reptiles than she ever imagined. She would watch them, coax them out to enjoy a mealworm right from the tips of her fingers, and even ended up in the after-hours emergency vet clinic on several occasions for their sakes.

These creatures became symbolic for my sister. Every time she had to undergo a major change in her life, the lizards shed their skins. Now, the lizard is known for feeling vibrations, even subtle ones, and they have extremely acute hearing. In some Native American cultures, the gecko is the king of perception. As we send out emotional currents, this tiny animal is capable of perceiving on a level of which we as human beings fall short. Perhaps God provided this animal symbolic of change, perception, and intuition for just the time when she needed it.

Think of how many times God illustrated his meaning through animals in the Bible. When we cannot hear God's voice, he will speak in the language we can hear. Animals, stars, people, or even clouds can be God's messengers on this earth—we just need to be subtly perceptive of God's voice today.—d.o.

Stinky Dogs and Muddy Paws

Be perfect, therefore, as your heavenly Father is perfect.
—Matthew 5:48

When it rains, I sit on the front porch and write or play guitar. The dogs love it, running through the downpour to me, and reeking of wet-dog smell. I wouldn't dream of making them move just because I am overwhelmed with the aroma of wet farm fur. They don't know they're smelly, of course, so they expect the same hugs and affection. I've learned to wear clothing that goes nicely with muddy paws on rainy days. Even my car is marked by muddy cat paws that don't seem to wash off anymore. The car is their castle, the top of the world, and they seem so content there that I decided the car could just match my muddy-paws clothes.

Life gets dirty sometimes. Not unholy, not impure—just dirty. God's perfection is not cold, stainless steel; it washes into our messy world with grace. God lets us dance in the rain with delight. We can be drenched with the tears we cry, the art we make, the lessons we learn, and sometimes even our mistakes. Holiness isn't just about being clean. It's about wholeness, and God wants to touch our lives with healing, understanding, and guidance.

Sometimes we get the idea that holiness, as in squeaky-cleanness, is more important than love, but true holiness cannot exist without love. Love comes first. It's the first thing God told Israel in what is known as the *Shema*, the prayer repeated daily—love the Lord, and love others.

God says if we walk before him, we will be blameless, muddy paws and all. Blamelessness is a consequence of standing on holy ground, not a consequence of right action. The right action is born out of the holiness, as a loving response to a Loving Father. God's rules exist to protect love. People are like stinky, wet dogs sometimes. We need help sorting through all our messiness and being godly and clean, so God bathes us in his righteousness. All we have to do is get in the tub!—k.m.

September 18
Refrigerator Art

With my great power and outstretched arm I made the earth and its people and the animals that are on it, and I give it to anyone I please.
—Jeremiah 27:5

What's on your refrigerator? Do pictures of friends and loved ones grin at you? How about a picture of your pet? Maybe you've posted a child's drawing that makes you smile, or a favorite Bible verse to keep you inspired. Our creative expression on the refrigerator is a precious collection of life.

God displays his handiwork on this planet like a great big giant fridge, and every creature that walks this planet is a panel of that fridge. Have you ever been walking along the trail and caught a deer grazing quietly, close enough to touch? Did you stop to reflect? As I've cleaned the kitchen and looked out the window over the sink, I have been amazed at a mockingbird stealing a piece of dog kibble from the bowl and swiftly flying away to feed her young. While you were stuck in traffic, did you see and admire the sunflower that grew from a crack in the highway pavement? Stop to be amazed.

Displays of God's creativity will be all around you today. You might be the only person to see it, the only one able to capture the moment with your eyes, your ears, and your taste buds, and the moment may be subtle and easy to miss if you aren't careful. The enemy is full of distractions, so we miss the split-second glimpse of the grandeur of God. But if we consider that these glimpses of God exist to be special secret messages just for us, we can walk through each day hopeful, hungry, and yearning for more glimpses. At the end of today, think about what refrigerator art from God you collected today. Then, go look in the mirror and see what his favorite creative project is.—d.o.

September 19
Hummingbirds in the Rain

A cheerful heart is a good medicine.
—Proverbs 17:22a

Now and then, I wake up with a head full of memories and a heart full of sadness. Maybe it is a dream that brings it on, or maybe it's just time to embrace the gift of tears again.

Dreams and memories can seem very real, and even if an event is long past, the memory can affect us today. Our dogs have chased many a squir rel while never leaving the couch they're napping on. Jessie is the most avid dreamer. She'll dream bark and swing her paws as though she's running after something.

One day I woke up to a melancholy day. Nothing had changed from the night before, and nothing was bad. I wasn't depressed or broken, just sad. The rain brought me comfort. I imagined God knew I needed to cry, so he cried for me. The world was quiet on that day, so I had the chance to slide into the rocker on the porch, writing and praying.

Just above the rocker hangs a hummingbird feeder. The little birds are fairly regular with their meal times, and usually one or two will visit later in the day, but on this day, one after another came to feed for several hours. The rain was pouring, and they came all the more, while the blue jays and cardinals stayed in their hiding places. On my sad day, hummingbirds, which represent joy to many people, all came around. I couldn't help smiling, and the strange, happy-sad afternoon passed gently by as my soul found comfort in the beauty of God's tiny-winged creatures.

A wise person once told me that the only way past pain is through it. There are times when sorrows come like a deluge, and you think you'll hurt forever, but you won't. Don't be afraid to open up your heart to God today and let him know what's going on inside you.

Feelings are there for a reason. They're part of our humanness, inescapable. They make us real. Don't be afraid to open up your heart to God today and let him know what's going on inside you.—k.m.

Shining the Spotlight on the "Well, Duhs"

Teach me to do your will, for you are my God; may your good Spirit lead me on level ground.
—Psalm 143:10

Riding horses in natural outdoor environments like trails, in the woods, or across fields brings lots of opportunity to learn. When horseback riding, you're not supposed to run a horse at a gallop across a grassy pasture because a hidden hole could cause your horse to stumble. Also, riders are always to look ahead for low lying branches and snakes.

Riding is a good analogy for life because we live in a natural world. We go uphill, downhill, curve abruptly, and amble across gentle rolling slopes as we go through each day. We can prepare as best as we know how and follow all the rules of living a good holy life, and still out of nowhere comes a variable that we couldn't have foreseen.

On one particular ride, I crested a mountain that overlooked one of the most awesome valleys of beauty I had ever seen. My old mare, Maria, and I stopped and marveled. Everyone else seemed too hurried to stop and appreciate the vista.

Then, we began our trip down the mountain. It was steep, with slippery spots and rocky, treacherous hazards. I gave her the go-ahead, and we took the mountain slowly, one step at a time. Instead of heading straight down, we zigzagged a serpentine pattern that took us much longer than everyone else on the ride. We gently moved safely across all of the dangerous places until we made it all the way down to the level trail at the bottom of the mountain. We were the last ones down the hill, but we had the most interesting journey.

God may lead you in a path that departs from others, that goes slower than everyone else, or even charts a new way of getting to the goal, but if God leads you, the path will be sure. If you're willing to go where he suggests, God will bless you with times like our moment of rest overlooking that valley. The rest stop might be right before a long, twisting road, but God will strengthen you throughout the journey, giving you much joy to discover as you trust him to take you all the way.—d.o.

Can I Pay You in Catnip?

Owe no one anything, except to love one another;
for the one who loves another has fulfilled the law.
—Romans 13:8

If animals had to deal with money, I wonder if they'd do a better job of it than people. Judging by the way they treat one another over food, I would say not. Life would be simpler without it, but money equals food and shelter for us and our pets, so we can't escape it, or all the issues that go with it.

Each animal we take into our family is a lifelong responsibility. They need shots, food, shelter, and medical care. They also need time and attention. We have quite a few animals, and once a year we have the mobile vet come and give everybody a checkup. We stock up for the yearly maintenance, and when the vet doesn't have something, we run over and get it from the co-op.

One year, the animal account was empty, and so were all the others, for that matter. We'd made a commitment to all of these animals, and circumstances beyond our control made it seem impossible to take good care of them. Then, right on time, a miracle happened. An old friend appeared out of the blue, wanting to donate to a cause—and it was on her heart that our animals should be that cause! We received her large check in the mail, and it was almost to the penny of what we needed for our annual "Pet Health Fair."

There have been other times when, instead of the miracle of a windfall, God has given us the wisdom to know how to be frugal and work within a budget with both dollars and portions. We've all made sacrifices along the way, but that's what having a family is all about! The true miracle is the gift of love that sustains us through it all.—k.m.

September 22
Rainbow Bright!

Every living thing on the face of the earth was wiped out; people and animals and the creatures that move along the ground and the birds were wiped from the earth. Only Noah was left, and those with him in the ark.
—Genesis 7:23

People will say that incidents like the great Flood were a time when God rebooted the world, like one, colossal do-over. We can ask ourselves why God destroyed all the animals that walked on land, but not the fishes of the deep. But ultimately, lives were gained because God gave humankind a second chance.

We are at the end of God's rainbow, a living example of the faithful love of our Father. God made a covenant, a promise of the strongest measure, with humans, and with the animals too.

The rainbow shined across a brilliant sky and returns to remind us of the covenant God made that he will never again destroy the world by flood. It must be hard for God to watch things on his precious earth get so turned around, so sick, so judgmental, so painful, and so evil, when it was meant to be a perfect representation of his creativity. But by flashing a rainbow across the sky, God reminds himself of his promise to redeem creation.

God's covenant was with all living things, and now we, as believers, must carry it out by showing compassion and kindness and evoking healing in the world we've been left in charge of. "Be fruitful and increase in number," or "multiply" in the King James Version, is also about multiplying the goodness, the love, and the promise of God in all creation. God's colorful reminder is our reminder that we hold the future of the world within us, those who were given a second chance, and that future is the perfection of all God created in love.—d.o.

September 23
webisode

All things came into being through him, and without him not one thing came into being.
—John 1:3

We don't typically feel sorry for moths. They eat our sweaters. One day, however, I heard a story that made me smile about a moth rescue.

A friend stepped onto her front porch one day to find a moth caught in a spider's web. The spider was nowhere to be found, but the moth, knowing it would not be in this world much longer, struggled and squirmed, only getting itself more trapped with every move.

My friend felt compassion for the poor insect, but wondered if she should tamper with nature. "Spiders have to eat too," she thought. She called her husband out to see, and his heart broke too.

"What will it matter if this one moth lives?" she said, but quickly answered her own question: "It will matter to this one moth!"

So, they followed their hearts. The husband gently created a small opening in the web while she gently shook the moth loose without touching it, which would have created a whole new tragedy for this newly significant creature. The moth finally flew out, and quickly, they said, as though it knew it had been saved and wanted to grasp its second chance at life.

It may not be our place to tamper with nature, but perhaps such little acts of mercy don't upset the ecological apple cart too much. My friend's story is an innocent testimony of someone who is paying attention to creation, counting all of life as significant. I think she viewed that one insect's life as God would have, because every bit of life matters. And just maybe we've all felt a little like that moth sometimes, stuck in a bad place, needing help. But God is always there, ready and willing to untangle the web.
—k.m.

September 24
Woolly to Wonderful

The house he builds is like a moth's cocoon, like a hut made by a watchman.
—Job 27:18

The woolly worm report happens this time of year in some parts of the country where superstition is part of the weather forecast. I had never heard of a woolly worm when I first saw the Woolly Worm Lady giving her annual prediction of when winter would arrive based on a funny black-and-rust caterpillar. She knew an awful lot about these worms, having devoted a great deal of life to their study.

In Banner Elk, North Carolina, a Woolly Worm Festival takes place in the fall of the year with music, food, and a great appreciation for the larvae of the tiger moth, which has been 80 to 85 percent correct in winter weather prediction for the past twenty-some years. According to that town, more rust or brown color on the back of a worm is said to mean a fairer winter, while black means batten down the hatches!

God has created this species with unbelievable survival systems. These worms require the cold temperatures to complete the cycle to brilliantly colored moth. They contain a cellular antifreeze that they shoot through the cells just prior to wintering, protecting the interior material up to ninety degrees below. The rest of the animal will freeze, but the vital parts are maintained. In the spring, the pupa gives way to a beautiful Isabella tiger moth.

In observing this funny woolly worm, I've finally understood God's lesson: to reach our most beautiful potential, sometimes we must soldier through hard, cold winter seasons. We must depend on the talents God has given us and our families to survive predators and find the best shelter. If you are entering a tough winter emotionally, physically, or spiritually, stay in the shelter of God's wings and know that you have been given the mechanisms to persevere by God himself. And if you count on him, then the world will be blessed by the new "you" that emerges next season.
—d.o.

September 25
The Tortoise and the Gray Hair

With long life I will satisfy them, and show them my salvation.
—Psalm 91:16

Noah's grandfather, Methuselah, lived 969 years. Theories abound as to why people don't live as long now. But these days, many species do live longer than we do, such as turtles.

Turtles come in all sizes, from barely the size of a quarter up to the size of a Volkswagen bug, but the remarkable thing about them is their potential life span. One giant turtle in captivity lived until he was 170. Others have been supposed to be 200 years old. Two centuries. That's only thirty-five years younger than America! A turtle living today could have moseyed through Abe Lincoln's yard or munched on George Washington's garden.

Not everyone would be satisfied with long life, or count it a blessing. I can't imagine life would be very livable without faith that God is providing it, and that he will be with you every wonderful and difficult second to the very end.

With the way Christians talk about wanting to go to heaven, I'm not sure even they always think long life is a good thing. The knee pops, the back creaks, and the saints feel like traveling home.

I'd like to live 200 years, but to be realistic, I'll be content with 100. By then, I'll be wrinkled. I'll have enough good God-stories to write a book, and I'll be eccentric and cute, like my two great-grandmothers who lived to be 100. Old age is a gift that God wants us to enjoy. Gray hair, the Bible says, is an honor. It represents wisdom that comes from many years of seeing God's loving, saving work in our lives and in the world. There is no doubt in my mind that my two grandmother-matriarchs lived long because they loved living.

I wonder if that's how it is with those turtles—they do what God created them to do, they are fulfilled in completing their purpose, and they see God's hand all around them. They must love living.—k.m.

September 26
Unequally Yoked

Do not plow with an ox and a donkey yoked together.
—Deuteronomy 22:10

On an impulse, I fell in love with a horse in a field, and I scribbled a note and left it on the door of the nearest house: If this is your dappled gray draft horse, I'd like to buy him.

I left, thinking no one would call. However, the owner called before I even arrived home. The owner said not only was he willing to sell him, but he would let him go cheap—and deliver him. I should have gotten a clue right then.

Andy was delivered to the barn where I boarded my horses. No stall was big enough for the mammoth animal, so they put him in a part of the barn reserved for heavy equipment. The behemoth tore down fencing, took a bite out of a friend's shoulder, and ate four times the food of the other horses. Not long after Andy arrived, I got a note from the owner of the boarding barn: Find that big horse a new home!

Andy went on loan first to a jouster, but that only lasted until Andy was first faced with a jousting rod coming directly toward him and did a quick one-eighty, and that was the end of that. Then, he went on loan to the Mennonites for the plowing season. They tried him, and in two weeks, I got another call. Andy was much bigger than the other horses, so when they plowed with him, he took off with the team and dragged them to the end of the field. He was having a blast, but he was wearing out all the other horses. They were unequally yoked.

When we end up on a team that's unequally matched, we are also unequally yoked. We think it will work out fine, and the field might end up getting plowed, but everyone will be exhausted and discouraged afterward. We can trust the teams that are put together by God, and we should always ask him before we force a relationship into being. He knows each of us best, so he'll definitely know our perfect match!—d.o.

How to Run to God

Devote yourselves to prayer, keeping alert in it with thanksgiving.
—Colossians 4:2

E. M. Bounds was trained as an attorney, but never pursued a legal career. Instead, he became a Methodist minister. Ordained in 1859, he is best known for his books about prayer. He served as a chaplain in the Confederate Army during the Civil War, and was even captured by the Union Army once. Prayer was so vital to his life that, after his release, he started weekly prayer sessions where he had been held—in Franklin, Tennessee. In one of his sermons, Bounds said, "Prayer projects faith on God, and God on the world. Only God can move mountains, but faith and prayer move God."

Bounds relates a story told to him by a friend. The friend was out walking one morning when he heard hounds in pursuit of something. He looked out over the open field before him and saw a young fawn darting across. He could see that the poor thing was terrified and quickly running out of strength. It reached the rails of the enclosure, leaped over, and crouched within ten feet of the friend. Within a moment, two of the hounds appeared out of the woods, and when the fawn saw them, it ran straight to him. So, he lifted it close to his chest, swung around, and fought off the dogs. The fawn knew it was weak and the man was strong, and so in its desperation, it trusted the man. "So is it," says Bounds, "when human helplessness appeals to Almighty God."

Our weaknesses show up in so many ways, and so many hounds are chasing us all the time. When we are in trouble, prayer is the way we can run to the Father's arms. Bounds said, "When faith ceases to pray, it ceases to live." Prayer is not a rule, not a prerequisite or a ticket to heaven, but it's what you do when you want to talk to someone you love. And God always has open arms, just waiting for us to let him save us from the dogs.
—k.m.

September 28

Sight-Seeing

How great are his signs, how mighty his wonders! His kingdom is an eternal kingdom;
his dominion endures from generation to generation.
—Daniel 4:3

I've been confused reading about animals in the Bible and trying to visualize those animals thriving in the areas we know of today as the Middle East. In the time of the ancient writings, those areas contained rich, green flora and flowing water. Lions and ostriches roamed in Judea, and donkeys brayed in the wild. Now, you can see only deserts, tiny streams, and small dirty rivers, and many of the species that we read about have become extinct. When so much time has passed, we may find it hard to make the Bible come alive to us. Sometimes, the stories seem unimaginable to our modern eyes.

Have you ever returned to the place of your youth and found it almost unrecognizable? Areas, people, the economy, and industries do change; that is one of the only certainties we can count on in this world.

When our minds can no longer imagine how things were before and how they are to be now, God must paint the picture. That picture encompasses eternity, which is forever in *both* directions. Heaven is not a "destination" in the future. Christ came to show us that eternal life includes what you are living here on earth. We are not sent here to use up everything and leave. God's authority over and plan for everything extended from forever in the past, through the bubble of time we live in, and forever into eternity.

When we live as if our lives on earth are heaven, too, then we are participants in the divine plan. Extinction, destruction, and pollution were not supposed to be elements of life here; abundance, fullness, and joyfulness *are*! So, take note of all that God has done, is doing, and will do, and enjoy heaven today right where you are!—d.o.

September 29

The Gift of Tears

A voice is heard in Ramah, lamentation and bitter weeping.
Rachel is weeping for her children; she refuses to be comforted for her children,
because they are no more.
—Jeremiah 31:15

They think Claudio was born with a heart defect, and he died in his mother's arms, suddenly and unexpectedly. Claudio was only a three-month-old baby gorilla, and his mother, Gana, loved him more than anything in the whole world. She could not accept that he was gone, so she kept stroking him and trying to revive him as onlookers wept. The zookeepers couldn't get the lost child away from her for several days. She had to hope, deny, mourn, and hurt, crying gorilla tears and feeling the pain in her broken heart.

God gave us tears for times just like this one. Tears are powerful. Sometimes they are cleansing, and sometimes they somehow express what we cannot say in words. We need our tears. They can be joy or the drops of wisdom. When a mother, a father, a grandparent, or a guardian loses a child, those tears will flow for a lifetime, not with inconsolable despair, but with longing and remembrance.

Some children feel lost to us because they lose their way in life. In the tears we cry for them, we have hope. By bringing our children before God in tears, we stand in the spiritual gap for them and fight the battle with them from our knees, because no matter what it may look like, they don't have to be lost forever.

God knows that a mother does not weep for herself when her child is lost. God will grow a garden of grace in the broken places, and every time she cries again, it will be watered with love. I pray that God plants grace in all of your hurt places, so you can see the beauty he'll grow in you.
—k.m.

September 30
Weep, Willow, Weep

The birds of the sky nest by the waters; they sing among the branches.
—Psalm 104:12

When I was a child, and the wind caught the willow trees just right, their tears would wash my face. My dad would always ask, "Did you feel that? The weeping willow was crying."

God uses the willow for many purposes, and he even sent a parable to the people about a willow to give them hope and instruction.

A lover of water that grows some ten feet a year, the willow is a haven for all sorts of animal life. It's a food or shelter source for animals like crows, wild turkeys, deer, nuthatches, tufted titmice, white-footed mice, red foxes, opossums, and rabbits, among many others. A beaver can chew through the trunk of a five-inch-thick tree in three minutes!

In flood-prone areas, planted willows can drink up so much excess that they can rescue areas for use. Some species of willow are used as medicines to cure fevers and headache. The branches are used in furniture, crafts, building, and more. How amazing is God that he can create such versatile and helpful things for all of us? God is concerned with every large and small detail in our lives, in the lives of animals, and in the provision and protection of all creation.

Have you embraced the thought that the same life force that blooms in a willow tree, in the beaver that chews its branches, and in us is all the same? He uses each segment of his creation for many purposes. We can be compassion to a friend, support to a child, instruction to a student, or boldness to someone who's stubborn! Let God direct the ways you treat people. Be like his willow tree and be of many uses to him today.—d.o.

October 1
The Woman Who Didn't Like Cats

*Blessed be the God and Father of our Lord Jesus Christ, the Father
of mercies and the God of all consolation, who consoles us in all our affliction,
so that we may be able to console those who are in any affliction with
the consolation with which we ourselves are consoled by God.*
—2 Corinthians 1:3-4

I know a woman who didn't like cats. She named no reason—that was just how she felt about it. This woman loved God, and because she walked close to him, he taught her and gently led her, just as she begged him to do every day. Though she couldn't see all the places in her heart where God wanted to make love grow, he knew just what she needed and when.

She needed a cat. Or two.

So the Lord sent Francis, an orange stray that showed up and chose her to be his person. She didn't think he was cute or pretty, but he was "incessant with his attention and love focused solely on me." So, she did a good thing by petting him and letting him stay. He followed her around everywhere, he never caught a mouse, and he had fleas, but he loved only her. Soon, she called him a member of the family, not out of obligation, but out of love.

Francis grew happily old and passed away. Then one day, the woman opened the front door to find a calico kitten on her doorstep. It wouldn't leave. She and her husband took her in and named her Mocha Bella. Once again, the lady found herself irresistibly drawn to a cuddly, whiskered angel.

Here's the miracle of it all: Francis and Mocha each came to her after a miscarriage. She and her husband wanted children so badly, and her heart was twice broken. She says, "Somehow, these kitties knew I was the one that their love was meant for." She knows that God saw her pain and sent his love and reassurance in a tangible, personal way through Francis and Mocha. I wonder how she will use her story to pass on that reassurance to others.—k.m.

October 2

Talk to the Animals

But ask the animals, and they will teach you, or the birds in the sky, and they will tell you.
—Job 12:7

God has given all of us instinct, intellect, and imagination. Animals from the lowest to the highest order can give us a to-do list to protect ourselves and preserve our home. So, how do we listen to the animals and learn from them?

If you would like to apply God's will to your life in nature, begin by planting trees. Trees clean the air and provide shelter and food for animals and people.

Create a wild bird sanctuary, which is an inexpensive way to help nature and bring inspiration to your days. Keep a journal of the birds and animals that visit your sanctuary and spend time making note of those blessings each day.

Picking up litter is a very simple act that can teach children at a very young age the value of the beauty in God's world. So, take the kids out to clean up a park and share with them the exciting bugs or plants they find while looking for litter.

Also, we don't always realize that buying animals from a pet store can possibly aid puppy mill operations. An exotic animal in a store could have been poached from the wild. Avoid products made from wild animals or those that use animal testing to protect our planet's creatures. Check labels; ask questions.

And most importantly, use your pen. Writing letters, blogs, and supporting organizations through social networks and donations can help increase awareness of the many roles available to help love God's beautiful world. A letter or phone call to government officials can mean the difference between the passing or failure of a bill or ordinance that protects the environment and us.

God loves when we listen and take his desires to heart. When we listen to the earth, the animals, and our own bodies, we listen to God. With every human being who chooses to open his or her ears and then put the right foot forward, our earth is saved, one step at a time.—d.o.

October 3
The Cocoon Intercom

This is my commandment, that you love one another as I have loved you.
—John 15:12

Imagine little voices echoing from the formative halls of two cocoons as one caterpillar calls to another: "You shouldn't be just lying around like that! You're supposed to be flying!" The other one might reply, "Point a leg at me, and fifteen are pointing right back at you!"

Many Christians have learned how to withhold hurtful judgment. They have spent enough time in the cocoon of transformation to know how hard it is to face ugly things about themselves, own up to faults, and go through heart-wrenching trials; and through it all, they've developed enough wisdom and strength to flex those wings and get out into the open sky. So they can extend the grace they've received, instead of harsh judgment. Religion, for them, is not a military institution; rather, it is an art form, an expression of faith. And study for them is not a template by which to make qualifying declarations about the fate of every soul. The study is their faith in search of understanding.

In *When the Heart Waits*, Sue Monk Kidd compares the metamorphosis of the butterfly with the transformation of the soul. We must collaborate with grace, she says. Grace is still a gift, so our striving doesn't produce grace. What we have to do is wait, which creates an arena in which grace can take place. It takes time to make a butterfly.

And we must be patient with other butterflies-in-the-making too! Perfection takes time, but God's got all the time in eternity. He is the one who transforms us; his love makes us mature and able to choose love over quick judgments. As we work with the Lord to bring about his best in our lives, we are able to see him doing the same for others. Don't worry, the day will come at last when he gives us our wings.—k.m.

October 4
One God, One Creator

And when you look up to the sky and see the sun, the moon and the stars—all
the heavenly array—do not be enticed into bowing down to them and worshiping
things the Lord your God has apportioned to all the nations under heaven.
—Deuteronomy 4:19

We live in a world of big commerce, big business, and big money—
the kingdoms that modern life has put high on the list. Creation
care, loving animals, protecting the environment, and speaking up against
the destruction of silent, dying species are enemies to those who think
money first. Big companies who may be thwarted by small forces of heart-
first thinkers will cast doubt by calling the earth protectors everything
from tree huggers to pagans.

The enemy has sneaky ways of entering government buildings and corporate offices and making God's Word seem stupid and ridiculous. God
is very clear throughout his Word that human beings are to take care of
everything he has given us on this planet.

How unfortunate that we live in a world where Christians who agree
to that covenant to protect creation have been portrayed as creation worshipers rather than creation caregivers. In the words of Dawn Coppock,
a Christian environmental activist in Tennessee, "calling creation care ac-
tivists creation worshipers is like calling pro-life believers fetus worshipers."

Be wary of all imposters who try to pull you off the narrow road. Do
not let the enemy (using commerce and destructive lies) deny the importance of God's call to protect creation. Spend time in God's Word and he
will illuminate his will for you. And above all, love only one God—the
one who created all those things we agreed to protect. Love him with all
your soul, all your heart, and all your mind. Acknowledge God as the
source of your ability, and he will direct your path.—d.o.

I Want to Be Where You Are

You show me the path of life. In your presence there is fullness of joy;
in your right hand are pleasures forevermore.
—Psalm 16:11

When you really love someone, you want to be with them. You can't help it. Their being, their vibe, their spirit, and your history with them draw you. The way they love you delights your heart and leaves you wanting more.

Of all our animals, certain ones just can't get enough of us. One of the donkeys will follow us anywhere, and the pony and his big brother, Tucker, will playfully sneak up and steal your hat right off your head or your work glove out of your back pocket. Veronique, Jessie, and Josie would go with us anywhere, stay with us all the time, and do anything to get to where we are. All of these actions are natural, God-given responses to love.

I want to *be* where God is, in a state of constant communion, in a state of being loved just for who I am. I want to be wanted. And I am, and so are you. It doesn't take a committee of theologians, philosophers, and scientists to tell me this part. My heart knows that God adores being with me.

Christians talk about the presence of the Lord. We ask him to be with us, even though we know he always is. We agree with the psalmist that we find the fullness of joy when we're with God, but we are blessed to be in his presence right here, on our earth, in this body.

For King David, the Lord's presence was only in the inner court of the temple. That's where they kept him. God, as it turned out, could not be kept. According to Jesus, he now remains with us everywhere, all the time. He's with you at the grocery store, the vet, the park, your workplace. . . . He wants to be where you are, so that you can *be* where he is.
—k.m.

Hay, Hay Everywhere, but Nary a Stalk to Eat

Though the fig tree does not bud and there are no grapes on the vines, though the olive crop fails and the fields produce no food, though there are no sheep in the pen and no cattle in the stalls, yet I will rejoice in the LORD, I will be joyful in God my Savior.
—Habakkuk 3:17-18

The drought in Texas drove people thousands of miles away to get hay for horses and cattle. Countless trailers with Texas license plates were loaded on Tennessee highways to move the food south. In the desperate times when some see opportunity to charge more and reap the benefit, others take a different stand.

Disaster brings out the worst in some people, yes, but it also brings out the very best in others. As each flood, hurricane, or tornado occurs, God is in the wake with love, helping hands, and food delivered by the truckload.

Have you ever noticed that the first on the scene of most disasters are groups of God's people? Church workers, volunteers, builders, water bearers, healers, and huggers are available to do whatever needs doing. Some are professionals, but most are just good people who gather in a church parking lot and get in a van loaded down with supplies.

When someone asks, "How could God let this happen?" a reasonable response could be, "He did not *do* this. But it happened, and now God is calling his people to shine."

When shortages arise, God supplies, and he usually does it with the hands of his people. So when the world ridicules organized religion, let the criticism roll off your back, and put on your work gloves.—d.o.

October 7

Noses

And through us spreads in every place the fragrance that comes from knowing him. For we are the aroma of Christ to God among those who are being saved and among those who are perishing; to the one a fragrance from death to death, to the other a fragrance from life to life.
—2 Corinthians 2:14b-16a

All dogs are descendants of the gray wolf, yet the domestic dog may be the most diverse species of all. If I didn't know better, I would never guess that the Great Dane and the toy poodle are related.

For example, consider the noses of dogs. My collie has a nose she could blow to Wisconsin, but my grand-dogs have petite Pomeranian noses. Pugs have nose inversions, while schnauzers have bearded schnozes.

But noses are not really about aesthetics; they're about smelling things. Some species know the power of smell for survival. No, that wasn't a black cat with a white stripe under the bush, it was a skunk!

People probably take the sense of smell somewhat for granted until something pungent wafts in the air, but we rely on it, too, for knowing when the food is good or when the house is on fire.

God likes things that smell good. Our definition of "good" and God's can be quite different, but Paul explains that those who love God emanate a sweet fragrance, a holy fragrance. Our prayers smell good: "Let my prayer be counted as incense before you," wrote the psalmist in Psalm 141:2.

The most poignant biblical nose analogy is the passage above from Corinthians. We are God's fragrance to the world. We smell like God from hanging out with him. And some people think we reek of God, while others think we're the best thing they've ever smelled. I guess we not only need eyes to see what the Lord reveals—we also need noses to smell.
—k.m.

October 8
Do It, Jesus!

He performs wonders that cannot be fathomed, miracles that cannot be counted.
—Job 5:9

A woman let her small dog out to take his morning break. When she heard insistent barking, she saw a grizzly with her dog hanging from his mouth like a salmon. Without a second thought, she ran out and punched the bear in the nose, and he promptly dropped the dog in her arms and ran off the other direction.

The dog had some minor bites, but was otherwise healthy. When asked about her actions, the young lady responded that she didn't think about her actions, she just acted to save her dog. We all are capable of doing seemingly stupid things in the name of love. At the source of every unbelievable rescue and every amazing miracle, God is our shield. We are always empowered by God to do the impossible, even when we don't realize it. I may not feel worthy of God working his incredible power through me, but God didn't put "worthiness" in the job description. God asks for one thing to be his miracle worker: a willing heart. That's all God needs.

When the day seems bleak and a problem seems hopeless, you get to put on the God cape. Cling to the promise that you can do all things through Christ who strengthens you, and you will be covered in a power so strong that all the forces of hell will shake in their boots.

Sometimes God sends a miracle, but it's not the one we wanted. People don't always live, and problems don't always disappear. Miracles happening all the time are defined by God and granted through God's big-picture lens. One day, we will see all of our miracle prayers in completion. Until then . . . keep asking, look for the miracles that you didn't have to ask for, and don't forget to wear the cape.—d.o.

October 9
Uniqueness of Christianity

Jesus said to him, "I am the way, and the truth, and the life.
No one comes to the Father except through me."
—John 14:6

Some say there are many paths to God, which sounds reasonable these days with society's emphasis on tolerance; however, it doesn't stand to reason with the words of John 14. Jesus said he is *the* Way, *the* Truth, and *the* Life. He is the *only* way to get to God. Try to explain that to your average, politically correct person, and you're likely to be labeled a fanatic. You're not, of course. Jesus said it, not you.

We must realize that Jesus did not say being a Christian is the way to God; he said that *he* is the way to God. Remember that Jesus was a devout Jew. He knew the Torah by heart and could teach it with authority by the time he was twelve (Luke 2:39-46). So, as Jesus' followers, we are Judeo-Christian, a combination of our forerunners, the Jews, and those who answered God's call across the rest of the world.

We live in a global world that wishes that whatever good things it does will make it worthy of happiness and life. But definite distinctions exist on its religious landscape, not allowing the wide road to salvation. Three religions claim Abraham as a forefather—Christianity, Judaism, and Islam—but they don't get along very well. It's like someone took all the animals of the Outback and all the animals of the Smoky Mountains, and threw them together in the same forest. And now kangaroos are hopping around with the black bears.

It is important to be aware, but not necessary to worry over such things. As long as we don't fall into the trap of thinking that other ways exist to fix the relationship with God, then we can trust that God knows what he's doing. True Christianity is unique because of Jesus and his love; God has it all under control, so we don't need to condemn those who think otherwise. Our job is to keep shining his light, and to love as he loves. God will bring them around in God's time to see the joy of the truth.
—k.m.

You Are My Favorite . . . And So Are You!

Keep me as the apple of your eye; hide me in the shadow of your wings.
—Psalm 17:8

I pick favorites. I can't help it! After hundreds of rescues, certain animals took bigger pieces of my heart. Finding Daisy the Dalmatian on the road and nursing her to health after she was hit by a vehicle ended up being a gift for me. She was sent to remind me that even when we've been left for dead by the world on a road out in the middle of nowhere, God sees us, hears us, and will help us.

All those animals that forgive our every mistake and still look up at us in adoration even when we feel like a screw-up are God's reminder of his love. God knows that we don't always hear him when he tells us that we are forgiven and loved. When we won't receive his love, he might send a dog that licks us right in the face, so we can't help feeling loved.

As I look back, most of my favorites came along at the worst times of my life. When I was in an abusive relationship, God sent an abused dog that showed me how love could heal. When I lost my job, God sent me a miracle in my cat living through what should have been a fatal accident. God showed me that he could provide even in an impossible situation. When I felt fat and ugly, God sent me a golden retriever that looked at me as if I personally hung the moon. Yes, I have picked favorites but mostly when they picked me first.

God sent each and every one of them because he knew exactly what voice would reach me. He never gave up, because I'm his favorite. And what's incredible is that he gives the same, individual attention to every single person. So I'm his favorite, and so are you!—d.o.

That Which You Take, Takes You

No one can serve two masters; for a slave will either hate the one and love the other,
or be devoted to the one and despise the other.
—Matthew 6:24

A cat decides to check out the world from a bird's-eye view and climbs from branch to branch one careful, curious step at a time. At last she perches, feeling smug because those sparrows have nothing on her. Then she looks down. What was she thinking? Thus begins the classic scene where the firefighter comes, climbs the ladder, and rescues the terrified feline, who fights him every step of the way.

A dog decides that pick-up trucks are more fun than Frisbees and decides to catch one. Hopefully, he won't, because his bravado could get him killed. He'll get dangerously close, though, biting at the wheels. Is he brave or stupid?

They act just like us sometimes, chasing after things with great passion that will only do harm. We start out feeling in control of the situation, but we're usually only looking at the immediate picture and not scrolling to the end. With great determination, we pursue a substance, an ideal weight, a relationship, a career, or whatever, only to realize too late that what we were controlling now controls us.

Ask God what he thinks. When our desires line up with his, things go much better. Life is designed to run best when run God's way, and he has plans—plans to bless and to fulfill his purposes on earth and in your life. Anything short of doing things his way is less than the best.

We can live in radical dependence upon him. He wants to guide us in all things.

That which you take, takes you, so take and be taken by God.—k.m.

October 12

The Spittin' Llama and the Randy Emu

If only they were wise and would understand this and discern what their end will be!
—Deuteronomy 32:29

Llamas have always fascinated me. I have wanted one as long as I could remember. Then I went to visit my friend Dave, who lived next door to a llama farm. Just knowing the experience would be wonderful, I slipped through the fence and went to meet Mr. Llama. He came right over to me, and seconds into my fantasy moment, he globbed a big stinky spit-lugey on me. It was awful, and then he began to paw and put his head down, and I heard a voice yell, "Run! He's comin' after you! That's the mean one!"

I ran for my life, as this evil creature chased me kicking, snorting and rearing with his front feet circling toward my head. I have never cleared a fence like that before. After I cleaned off the slimy llama spit, I was not happy!

On a similar scale, a friend had to get rid of his beloved emu, because he didn't realize he wasn't allowed to keep a full-grown emu in his backyard in the city limits.

As the shelter attendant led me back to meet the emu at the animal control facility, I was warned to be careful. I didn't know what to be careful of. Then out of the blue, the bird went nuts. Before I knew what was happening, some big arms pulled me from the cage.

"He must've really liked you!" the attendant said. "He needs to be neutered. He gets really amorous."

I am so grateful for all the times God showed me wisdom (and provided arms to pull me out before a dangerous encounter) before I made the mistake. Happily, I am llama-less and very happily emu-less, and my wisdom is growing leaps and bounds as I listen more to God than the impulse thoughts that fly by. Today, give God all your requests and ask him to give you the wisdom to make the right choices.—d.o.

October 13
Cleanliness Is Next to Impossible

Wash me thoroughly from my iniquity, and cleanse me from my sin.
—Psalm 51:2

I had big plans for Veronique. She was only three months old when I got her, so from the start, I determined to develop clean habits with her. I was sure she would love it too. We'd be like those people you see on TV, where dog and owner are inseparable, and just like their dogs, her long collie coat would be silky and shiny all the time, never a mat or tangle in sight. She wouldn't have fleas or ticks, and I would be able to take her anywhere, because she would smell freshly bathed all the time. I assumed she would greatly appreciate this lifestyle, because she was from royal show-dog blood. Grooming was in her genes.

As it turned out, flaky dry skin from baths made her miserable for days on end. I tried doggy shampoo for sensitive skin, but to no avail. No problem, I thought, she'll just be an inside dog, then how dirty can she get? But she pined for the outdoors. She whined; she ached for the green grass under her paws, the sunshine, and the freedom from the leash. So, I let her play outside for short periods of time. She decided at that point that "bath" meant "go roll in something nasty," which she always did. I finally gave up on the frequent bath plan, and you've never seen a happier dog.

Sometimes you just have to let a dog be who she is. I kept demanding that Veronique live up to my standards of cleanliness, when it wasn't her appearance that mattered. She is a happy, obedient dog, and does everything I ask her. She's got a clean heart, that's for sure.

Instead of scrubbing our skin raw, trying to make ourselves look clean to the world by never showing who we are, pretending that our lives are perfect, we need to reorient ourselves to God's definition of cleanliness. He's not fooled by our clean coats, but he'll take what's truly dirty in us and make it right. And the best part is that when *God* makes us clean, we discover exactly who he intended us to be.—k.m.

October 14
Missing a Loyalty Chip?

Your guards are like locusts, your officials like swarms of locusts that settle in the walls on a cold day—but when the sun appears they fly away, and no one knows where.
—Nahum 3:17

Have you ever been betrayed by someone you thought loved you? I have always felt that God sent animals to humans to show us how to *do* loyalty properly. We could all take notes on animal life and realize an ancient way to live correctly by others.

For instance, while half of the marriages between people end in divorce, species of geese, swans, falcons, wood hens, loons, and even buzzards mostly mate for life. In fact, 90 percent of all birds are monogamous for life.

But how do we handle the pain of infidelity with our mate? How do we forgive and forget the trespasses of a friend who proved not to be a true friend?

When we walk into a relationship of any kind with another person, we have to ask God for the same wisdom and discernment he gives us in all other areas of our lives. We tend to find it harder to listen to the wise counsel he sends to help us make the right choices in partnerships. We enter the situation with our physical longing, we go against what we know to be right, or we ignore the signs that God sends to help us avoid making painful mistakes.

Then, when arguments break out or silence reigns in our houses, God still eagerly waits for us to turn to him and let him help. And God can do the impossible! But sometimes only half the pair is willing. When we end up with a broken heart, God is always there to comfort us and pick up the pieces. He never leaves, no matter how many times we ignore him when we should ask for direction. And he never lies in wait to say "I told you so."

If someone has been unfaithful to you, ask God to help you find forgiveness and to set up barriers against resentment. Ask God to help you move on in love, in grace, and in hope. Until that day, take a walk with your furry best friend and remember as you look at that darling animal that it is just a picture of the faithfulness and love God has toward you!
—d.o.

October 15
Race You to the Top

And not only that, but we also boast in our sufferings, knowing that suffering produces endurance, and endurance produces character, and character produces hope.
—Romans 5:3-4

High Point, North Carolina, is a twenty-minute drive from where we lived in Greensboro, but since it was another town, it somehow seemed longer to me. One day, I decided I would bike to High Point. A friend agreed to go with me, though he thought it was a silly idea, and a waste of a good lazy afternoon. I think he was worried I would take off by myself, which I would have.

We kept a good pace, finding adventure in every mile. Just as I came to the "Welcome to High Point" sign, I learned why it was named *High* Point. I was facing the steepest hill I'd ever seen. I took a deep breath and started pedaling. Just as I was about to hop off the bike and push, my friend yelled something from below. Before I could turn to yell, "What?" I knew the answer. Two snarling German shepherds were bounding toward me at full speed.

Thank God for adrenaline, because I suddenly had the strength to fly. I looked straight ahead and pedaled up the rest of the hill as though it were a flat racetrack. I could feel their breath on my heels, but I didn't take time to look. Somewhere before the peak, the barking had stopped without my noticing, and I continued pedaling to the top. When I got there, I looked back. They were sauntering back down the hill with nice-dog greetings for my friend. He was laughing hysterically.

I was proud of myself for making it up that hill at record speed. I was exhilarated and terrified by those dogs that day, but thanks to those shepherds, I have taken much longer rides up much higher hills. They gave me the opportunity to realize I could do something I didn't know I was capable of before.

I've learned that this applies to more than physical stamina. There is a spiritual principle at play. When you feel like you're losing the race against anger, shame, or whatever the trial may be, it can be character building. I didn't feel prepared for the sprint up that hill before I left that day, and I had already pedaled for several miles, but God encouraged endurance in me to get through and then grew that endurance to serve me well on other trips. God will do the same for you.—k.m.

October 16
Sing in the Sunshine

Six days you shall labor, but on the seventh day you shall rest; even during the plowing season and harvest you must rest.
—Exodus 34:21

Our plucky pony, Geronimo, loves the sun. He doesn't miss a second of good sun to wallow in the soft dirt pillows he's fluffed to perfection in front of the barn. If even a ray of sun shines through, you can be assured that he will be in it, rolling around until it warms every part of him, then napping to appreciate it completely.

Horses are not often comfortable with a display of complete, unprotected abandon. They don't usually lie down in the presence of "two-leggeds," because they don't feel secure. However, on one crisp autumn day, Geronimo was splayed in front of the barn, back on the ground, legs relaxed in the air, sun on his belly as he snoozed. He wasn't just sleeping in the sun, he was soaking in it!

Are you overwhelmed by stress, fear, or schedules? We can have our worry chips on overload very easily, and that's exactly the vulnerable place the enemy wants us to be! Fever pitch is not a feeling that God has *installed* in us. Even in our busiest, most trying times, God tells us to rest, trust, and even enjoy. Even during one of the busiest times of the year for his people—plowing season—God told them to stop working and rest. God wants us to trust his word and allow him to bless us with rest, joy, and sunshine.

I don't always understand the economy of time that allows me to take five minutes or a half hour to sit in the sun or take a walk or a nap, and my busy work becomes more productive. I may not understand it, but I won't forget it!

Today, look for the unexpected sunshine, the unscheduled naps, and the unwinding walks that can be helpful rest stops enriching your day and foiling the enemy's ploy to keep you too stressed to be happy.—d.o.

October 17

Eeyore

Why are you cast down, O my soul, and why are you disquieted within me?
Hope in God; for I shall again praise him, my help and my God.
—Psalm 43:5

Remember Eeyore? He was always sad. His friends in the Hundred Acre Wood wanted so much to cheer him up, but in some sense, Eeyore was happy with his sadness, not in a miserable sort of way, but in a life is happy-sad sort of way.

We may fantasize about a life with no sorrow, but sadness is just part of the deal. When life hurts, we are healed through our tears when we grieve. Sometimes we can help others grieve too. That's what compassion is. Its literal meaning is "to suffer with."

In the Hebrew culture, groups of women are assigned to the task of crying. They take the sorrow of the broken in the culture, and they weep openly, wailing their prayers. Jeremiah calls that the work of tears. It's like grief intercession. These women cry for everyone; they cry for those who can't. We can realize from this that tears are a necessary balance to joy.

We can't ignore pain forever. If you don't cry when it's time to cry, your soul will be sickened by grief. God gave us tears for a reason. Though the physical tears may be uniquely human, some say that chimpanzees, elephants, dogs, and bears cry too. Animal lovers know that all animals grieve in their own way when something goes wrong. I remember an episode of *Winnie the Pooh* in which all the friends tried to cheer up Eeyore. The animals ended up making a day go very poorly for Eeyore as they tried to force him to be something he's not—cheery. At last, they gave up and said, "We were just trying to make you smile!"

Eeyore responded, "I *am* smiling!" They finally learned to accept their friend and his gift of sadness. In a way, he was quite brave, brave enough to face the tears. Sometimes, bad circumstances aren't the end of the world, they just mean that it's time to cry again, and then wait for the joy that comes in the morning.—k.m.

October 18
Save Some for Everyone Else

When you reap the harvest of your land, do not reap to the very edges of
your field or gather the gleanings of your harvest.
—Leviticus 19:9

Our friend's dog believes that all the toys in the house are hers. She collects them, keeps all of them beside her food bowl, and watches them, as if they'll disappear if she's not careful.

Abundance is a blessing we are given by God, not created by us. God is forever asking us not to hold on to life with clenched fists. The ancient Hebrews lived by a concept of generosity, taught not to harvest the edges of the fields to supply those who had nothing. Sharing brought more abundance. As care was taken to help others, there was enough for everyone. Leaving the edges of fields not harvested to bless others wasn't just a nice practice; it was a law.

In modern-day farming, not cultivating to the edge of the field is called a buffer strip. The buffer allows natural plants to grow and keep farming runoff from entering waterways, which causes sediment pollution and kills wildlife. The barrier of natural plants makes a habitat for wild creatures, such as pheasants, doves, and prairie chickens. It's a habitat where they can grow, multiply, have safety, and find nourishment.

Grabbing all our possessions, clenching tightly, not sharing with others, taking what someone else has, or thinking that our actions only affect us are examples of a selfishness that opposes God's commands. You have the opportunity to be a living connection between all things and their Creator. As you go through your day, think of yourself as a conductor of abundance, and God as the single-source provider. If you are open to sharing what has been given, God will open the floodgates for more to flow through you. In God's plan, there is always enough for everyone.—d.o.

October 19
Well-Worn Path

Trust in the LORD with all your heart, and do not rely on your own insight.
In all your ways acknowledge him, and he will make straight your paths.
—Proverbs 3:5-6

We have a big, wide yard, and still the dogs and cats have worn a path from the back door of the house to the front porch. The path is narrow and goes along right beside the bushes, as though carefully planned. It amazes me how those padded paws can wear away every stitch of grass. From big dog Jack to tiny cat Paddy, they all follow that path. They will round the corner in single file if they have to, just to stay on the path.

We are encouraged in Scripture to follow a well-worn path. The path was forged when Abraham believed God, and over time, the grass was pushed back, and the earth beneath became more and more apparent. Moses carved it out a little more, with commandments given by God that were all about loving God and others. After years, God's people finally discovered that the path led to Jesus. And, as it turns out, its source is Jesus, *and* it will lead to him as we keep carving it out.

Step by step, Jesus leads us in righteousness and truth. He set the example while he walked on earth, and he helps us, correcting our course when we lean off the path. We would be wise to do as animals do, who just seek a path to follow, even if distractions and seemingly more exciting options are available. Every human follows some path, but only one has the footsteps of our Creator. You either follow God or follow the darkness. Which path are you following?—k.m.

October 20
Honor Creation

As long as the earth endures, seedtime and harvest, cold and heat,
summer and winter, day and night will never cease.
—Genesis 8:22

Billboards in major cities across the country announced with certainty and doom the time and day the earth was ending. Many people were convinced and believed the story. They lived life as if they knew the end was certain, only to find that they had carried gloom on their shoulders for nothing.

God doesn't ask us to waste our lives figuring out when the world will end—in fact, he specifically tells us *not* to do that! He's told us, instead, to see the beauty of creation, including ourselves, and literally dance in the joy that bursts forth! God is pleased with the incredible world he created, and he wants us to share in his pleasure.

But when we think of creation as finite, we can easily treat this period of eternity as disposable. In God, there is always tomorrow. Tomorrow may be with him in heaven or tomorrow may be here on earth. The gifts we find on the planet—beautiful sunsets, intricate canyons, waterfalls, great apes, chipmunks, whales, and red-spotted frogs are gifts not only to us, but to all those who come after. God wants us to enjoy all he has created, not selfishly using up creation so that our children will never experience it.

How can we preserve the beautiful sites we take pleasure in today, so that our great-grandchildren can see the same beautiful site? How can we increase our vision to a tomorrow a thousand years from now, realizing that, until the earth ends, it is still here and needs to be preserved?

Today, look for a sparrow. Watch how they enjoy the life they have been given. Fallen twigs make a home, puddles make a bath, and a dropped ice cream cone is dinner. They just live here and now in the world that God provides. When people speak of doom, end times, and fear, you can respond with a sparrow's hope for today!—d.o.

October 21
Contemplative Kitty

He who did not withhold his own Son, but gave him up for all of us,
will he not with him also give us everything else?
—Romans 8:32

A cat who lived in the fourteenth century was called to the ministry of mousing. All we know about this cat is that it belonged to Julian of Norwich.

Julian was an anchoress, which means she lived in contemplative solitude inside an "anchorhold," a special room built alongside a wall of Norwich Cathedral, with a small window into the sanctuary so that she could hear church services. She became an anchoress through a solemn and dramatic rite of enclosure performed by a bishop. The door to her room was ceremoniously bolted from the outside, and the anchoress was declared "dead to the world"—in it, but not of it.

She had a second window where people could come and seek wisdom or prayer. She wrote about what God revealed to her, and what she probably shared with those who came to her, in a Christian classic called *Revelations of Divine Love*—the first book ever written in English by a woman. In her book, she said, "All shall be well, and all shall be well, and all manner of things shall be well." Hers was a message of hope, and confidence in the God "who loves and delights in us." Though she lived in a way that sounds unappealing to most today, she experienced God's never-ending love.

Julian had a third window accessed by a servant who brought her food. She was allowed a cat to keep the mice away, but she and the cat became best friends. We can tell because it is pictured with her in most portraits of her. One can only imagine that the kitty cuddled up with her through the long nights and lonely times, purring and reminding her that the God she served had given her a better gift than she could have ever dreamed.

—k.m.

October 22

Fall Pastures Are Not Green

Be patient, then, brothers and sisters, until the Lord's coming.
See how the farmer waits for the land to yield its valuable crop,
patiently waiting for the autumn and spring rains.
—James 5:7

Pasture grasses are not planted in the spring or summer. Experienced farmers and gardeners plant as the leaves begin to fall and the green is disappearing into the cold grip of winter. Putting fragile seeds into the ground as everything is beginning to die seems out of order. But God has a plan in all that seems to confound the wise.

God asks us to be diligent in planning ahead. If we want the horses to eat in the summer, we must make the plan months in advance. Seeds sown today will need to weather a few storms, feel the freeze of death, and rise to new life in the spring, just like God's analogy, and Jesus' example, of dying to self to be resurrected.

Good, deep roots and hardy plants such as the pasture grasses and the bulbs of the crocuses, tulips, and daffodils need the cold months of reflection to rise and blossom in the warmth of the sun. And think of how beautiful the result is after their quiet months.

We sometimes feel forced into waiting. Our patience is challenged, and we scream, "Why, Lord? Why have you forgotten me?" But God did not forget you. He is planting you deeply in rich soil that will yield stronger fruit, filled with the joy of life.

If the grass doesn't get planted now, the entire grass-eating menagerie won't have green grass in the spring. Without the wintering of our souls, we never release the full blossom when the sun shines. And if you don't reflect during that dark season, others will miss the blessing God has planned through you. So expect the deep and hidden things God wants to plant within you, and prepare for it with eagerness so that your harvest will be bountiful.—d.o.

October 23
Wesley's Compassion for Animals, Part 1

*The creation itself will be set free from its bondage to
decay and will obtain the freedom of the glory of the children of God.*
—Romans 8:21

John Wesley was the founder of Methodism, and from his ministry, quite a garden of faith grew. The Church of the Nazarene, the Wesleyan Church, and others all have roots that tie back to this humble man, who would likely be mortified to have his name up in theological lights. Nonetheless, the whole-hearted legacy he left is a treasure. Love of God, love of people, and love of creation were his only agenda.

In a sermon called "The General Deliverance," Wesley expounds spiritual, biblical insight about the relationship between God, people, and animals. He begins with the passage in Romans 8:19-22 which says the creation itself is waiting for God's people to be revealed because it knows that all of the death and destruction it experiences will disappear too. The passage is clear, says the preacher, that God cares for all of his creation.

In the beginning, God didn't just say that man was good; he placed animals in the garden, as well. Wesley sees in the story of Eden a portrait of animals choosing to live in the goodness that God had proclaimed. Wesley says no one can deny that animals are guided by their understanding. They can certainly love us, and what love is there apart from God?

Appreciate all of creation today, and in so doing, you're acting on creation's behalf; and when you look around at all the beauty, remember, you shine with God's glory too! It is as we embrace the reality of our identity that we bless creation back, maybe even more than it blesses us. Search God's Word and ask him to show you how you fit into his plan to redeem creation.—k.m.

Wesley's Compassion for Animals, Part 2

They will not hurt or destroy on all my holy mountain; for the earth will be
full of the knowledge of the LORD as the waters cover the sea.
—Isaiah 11:9

In his sermon about loving the animals and creation, John Wesley made reference to a book called *The Wisdom of Solomon*, where it says that God did not make death and has no pleasure in the death of anything living. Rings true, doesn't it? God is about life, not death, and so in God's economy, death only leads to more life.

The Bible teaches of a death necessary for life, like a seed in the ground that dies before it grows, or the leaves that die so the tree can live. Likewise, we must die to selfishness and sin. Paul said the price of sin is death, meaning death of the soul, death of goodness in one's life and purview, death of joy and peace, and even untimely death of the body. Wesley suggests that just as people are created for life, not death, so are animals.

Wesley suggests in his sermon "The General Deliverance" that God created people to be the "great channel of communication" between God and animals, so in essence, when the Fall occurred, humans dragged the animals right along with them. The animals were robbed of a blessing when humankind chose sin and death.

Wesley did not follow the mainstream Christian tradition of his day. His theology affirmed animals as worthy of the Creator's love and redemption. That may sound outrageous to some even today, but if you search your heart, I know you'll find that it rings true.

Today when you hug your kitty or your dog or your horse, or as you drive along considering the sparrows, think about how precious they are to God. It's part of the gift of joy of this day that you are delighted when the animals display the beauty of creation or when they make you laugh or even when they seem to love you more than any person ever has.

—k.m.

October 25
Loved Anyway

They do not say to themselves, "Let us fear the LORD our God,
who gives autumn and spring rains in season,
who assures us of the regular weeks of harvest."
—Jeremiah 5:24

Tyrone is our twenty-year-old cat. He was dropped off at the humane society as an unwanted, un-weaned kitten, too young to survive on his own. That night, the humane society burned, and as they got the animals out, his tiny body took in a lot of smoke. As one of the volunteers, I took this doubtful case home and began to treat him with all the love and medical care I could muster.

Tyrone got through that disaster, only one of many close calls in his life. He was even run over by a Tahoe SUV that he had fallen asleep under. But twenty years later, a cat that was not supposed to make it through his first night still lives, moves, and breathes, fully trusting that his people will make all things better. He has one tooth. He sneezes all the time. He walks like he's put together with rubber bands. But he is alive and trusting and knows to expect love from us. And why shouldn't he, when we've proved time and time again that we will take care of him?

God has been with us through everything. And he continues to be there when we run to him with every disaster, every heartbreak, and all of our pain. He feeds us, holds us, and comforts us, and when we are well, he allows us to run off to whatever playground we choose. He loves us *that* much.

You might be called to love that unconditionally in your life right now, or perhaps you just need to look at all the times God has healed you, protected your heart, and danced with an accomplishment no one else saw, and give him your attention. Maybe a relationship has challenged you to the point of giving up, or maybe you feel like the world is crashing around you. Remember that God has always been there for your bad attitudes, poor choices, and hidden sins. God loves bigger than anything we have done, and he helps us love bigger too. When you need help loving someone, ask God to supply your heart.—d.o.

October 26
Lost Doggy in High Weeds

If you come across your enemy's ox or donkey wandering off, be sure to return it.
—Exodus 23:4

I found Toby, an aged cocker spaniel, wandering in New York City. He had cataracts and worn teeth, but no collar. When I took him home, this dog spent several anxiety-filled months with me. One day, I had a friend walk the dog for me while I was working. She called me and said, "You'll never believe this. A woman just came out of the grocery store, took one look at Toby, called him Lancelot, and he went running to her! She says he is her lost dog!"

I was soon in the company of a young woman, originally from Kentucky, who had moved to the city. She had leashed her dog, which she had raised for thirteen years, to the park fence while she played Frisbee, so he would be safe to enjoy a nice autumn day. As she collected her things to leave an hour later, he was gone. I explained that I had found the dog with no collar and that all the shelters said that a dog of his age would be put down immediately, so I had kept him.

"I appreciate your loving him. I went to the park every day for six months and left food and water where we last saw him," she said.

That day, Lancelot's anxiety ended because he had finally gotten what he was looking for. He just wanted to be home, and now he was.

When we lose something we love, we must never give up hope that God has a plan in the works to help us find what we are looking for. When we find what someone else has lost, we might be a very important part of that same plan. Hope is one of God's greatest gifts. Whatever side of the parable you are on—the searcher, the lost, or the found—know that God wants everyone to find the way home.—d.o.

October 27

Animal Counsel

*Happy are those who do not follow the advice of the wicked, or
take the path that sinners tread, or sit in the seat of scoffers.*
—Psalm 1:1

We should choose our leaders and mentors wisely, only following those who have proved themselves wise and dedicated to God. And you can tell a lot about a leader by the way he views animals in relationship to God. Listen to what some of our revered leaders have said.

Billy Graham said, "I think God will have prepared everything for our perfect happiness. If it takes my dog being [in heaven], I believe he'll be there."

Abraham Lincoln said, "I care not for a man's religion whose dog and cat are not the better for it."

And Martin Luther spoke directly to an animal, saying, "Be comforted, little dog, thou, too, in the resurrection shall have a tail of gold."

Martin Buber was a Jewish philosopher best known for his book *I and Thou*. He said that human existence is defined by the way we dialogue with one another, with the world, and with God. Later, he added animals to that list when he said, "An animal's eyes have the power to speak a great language."

Gandhi linked our treatment of animals with the state of our nation: "The greatness of a nation and its moral progress can be judged by the ways its animals are treated."

Albert Schweitzer, theologian and medical missionary, won the Nobel Peace Prize in 1952 for his philosophy of having reverence for life, which, he says, defines ethics. He said, "There are two means of refuge from the miseries of life: music and cats."

All of these men are known for their goodness, their compassion for humanity, and their influence in the world. If you didn't know before, you can now add "compassion for all of creation" to that list. If these are the men we honor and listen to, then think about this aspect of theology that they all have in common. You might find more truth in the idea than you've seen before.—k.m.

October 28
Beasts of Burden

When a farmer plows for planting, does he plow continually?
Does he keep on breaking up and working the soil?
—Isaiah 28:24

Have you ever prayed and felt worse than before you started praying? We plead with God to protect our children, heal our bodies, fix our finances, and find our lost pets. When we don't see him solving our problems in a timely way, we get discouraged.

Farmers plow soil. It's hard work, and it isn't done in a day. The soil has to be worked and tilled to be ready for the seeds to be planted. Then they have to fertilize, irrigate, and monitor the fields through a growing season before a late summer or fall harvest. Sometimes our prayers feel like that old mule, pulling the plow through stubborn, unmoving dirt. So, we just keep putting our heads down and straining forward. We forget the "waiting for God's answer" part of prayer.

Prayer is not just about talking; it's also about action. What does God expect from us as the extension of our prayers? We might be called to go face-to-face with someone for whom we are praying, admit our shortcomings, and say we are sorry for how we have hurt them or let them down. We might have to call creditors and make amends on financial issues. Prayer is not a list for Santa Claus. It's a petition to God, but it's also praise to God and a conversation with God.

We want to be the garden planted with God's seeds, so we must continue talking to God and waiting to hear from him. Prayer is not the end of that cry—it is the beginning.

If you are burdened with your prayers and discouraged that God has not moved, be encouraged that he always moves when we pray, even if we don't see the movement. God is always with us in the plowing season, in the planting season, and in the praise-filled harvest.—d.o.

October 29
Paper, Rock, Love

One who forgives an affront fosters friendship,
but one who dwells on disputes will alienate a friend.
—Proverbs 17:9

To be content, you have to be in a constant state of forgiveness because someone or something is going to offend every day. If you get through a day unscathed by friend or foe, then turn on the news and forgive the world. But love covers all offenses, God's Word tells us. If life were a game of "Paper, Rock, Scissors," love is the one that beats them all.

A scientist and the author of *The Emotional Lives of Animals*, Marc Bekoff has studied animal emotions and has discovered that animals are generous and forgiving beings. In his book, he tells a story of forgiveness he learned from a moon bear, a black Asian bear with a cream-colored crescent on its chest. This species is endangered, their bodies used to obtain the bile in their gallbladders, which supposedly cures many diseases.

The bear that Bekoff befriended had been abused and brought to the Moon Bear Rescue Centre in China. His name was Jasper. In addition to being squashed in a small extraction "crush cage," Jasper had had a rusty metal catheter inserted into his gallbladder.

Jasper was an unusual rescue; most bears could never acclimate again, but his actions showed that he was willing to see the help for what it was. He had big, gentle brown eyes that stared right into Mark's heart and seemed to say, "All is well, the past is past; I'll let go and move on."

Mark fed him peaches and peanut butter, and Jasper knew things were going to get better. One friend at the Centre said, "Touching the back of his paw one day, I saw his head turn toward me, soft brown eyes blinking with trust, and I knew that Jasper was going to be a special friend."

Mark thanks Jasper for teaching him about forgiveness and the contentedness that comes when we release the hurts we've clung to. Our Jaspers and dogs and cats that need us make us more humane, more human, and they can show us how God intended us to act. If Jasper was able to forgive and trust again after being tortured, then I can forgive harsh words or hurtful actions. Then maybe I'll be as content as he is.—k.m.

October 30
The Grace Road

Then the angel showed me the river of the water of life, as clear as crystal, flowing from the throne of God and of the Lamb down the middle of the great street of the city. On each side of the river stood the tree of life, bearing twelve crops of fruit, yielding its fruit every month. And the leaves of the tree are for the healing of the nations. No longer will there be any curse.
—Revelation 22:1-3a

God promises that our nations will be healed. For all the incurable illness, for all the unsolvable problems, for all the never-ending wars God promises a day will come when all evil is defeated, and love will reign evermore.

When our days are just too hard, resentment lurks to take root. On these days, open to the book of Revelation, allow the text to speak, and find peace and encouragement. When we read about this incredible place where human beings and all living creatures hold the same value at the feet of Jesus, praising and shouting hallelujah, we are reminded that all will be touched by the healing leaves of God's tree of life.

If today has been hard, remember the promises God has made to you. We will live one day at the waterfall created by the river of life. The world will no longer cry with hunger or sickness, because God will heal and nourish us. All humans and animals of every kind will praise God in their own voice. Every knee will bow and every tongue confess that Jesus Christ is Lord. A love hallelujah will echo around the world.

Don't lose heart. Be encouraged! The Son of God himself has created a grace road for you to walk. One day at a time, shine the light on the grace road for someone else, so you can remind each other of the blessings God has promised.—d.o.

Black Cats and Broomsticks

Deliver me, my God, from the hand of the wicked,
from the grasp of those who are evil and cruel.
—Psalm 71:4

D id you know that most animal shelters and rescue groups have a rule that they cannot allow people to adopt any black cats or kittens during the entire month of October? People are warned to keep their black cats inside because cruel people use animals in evil rituals this time of year.

But evil is deceitful; it lets us believe we know everything about a subject, so we become focused on what we believe is bad, while the real enemy comes in the back door and steals our family. Shaking our fingers at witchcraft is easier than admitting our own shortcomings.

The real culprit against animals this time of year is not a particular group but what happens when impressionable people see make-believe rituals thought up by Hollywood and enact cruel copycat rituals to innocent animals.

The warning of this time of year is to watch out for all pets. Dogs, cats, and animals of all species can be in danger if they aren't watched carefully. We aren't being overrun with Satanists or Wiccans trying to steal Tom the cat when you're not looking. We are so busy watching out for some obvious villain when the real one may be in our house, unmonitored and uncensored.

The enemy is cunning, but our God is stronger and smarter than anything that could come against us. God gives us practical ways to protect ourselves. Knowledge that some people don't have our best interest at heart, discernment to see the disguises that the enemy uses, and protection of our boundaries are our best defenses. Keep your loved ones safe and close. Walk through life with bold choices of holiness in all you do in Christ's name, passing the principles down through your family. And above all, ask God to protect the areas you may not see and trust in his faithfulness to do it.—d.o.

Beautiful Mess

May the God of peace himself sanctify you entirely;
and may your spirit and soul and body be kept sound
and blameless at the coming of our Lord Jesus Christ.
The one who calls you is faithful, and he will do this.
—1 Thessalonians 5:23-24

Jack is a big boy, with more Pyrenees than Collie in his mix, and he's a friendly, beautiful mess. He loves his life so much, patroling the neighborhood, keeping the coyotes away, and checking on the neighbors. We've tried everything to keep him in our yard, but he cannot be contained.

Most of the neighbors know Jack even better than they know us, and they love him. They all seem to know his name, which means he's visited enough for them to check out his ID tag and have a friendly conversation with him. Our country neighbors are friendly and appreciate Jack's diligence as the neighborhood watch dog.

One day a new neighbor moved in who did not understand the value of coyote patrol. She showed up at our front door, holding a leash with our dog on the other end of it. Jack had a look on his face that seemed to say, "I tried to explain to this lady that I was just trying to help, but she wouldn't listen."

He willingly got into her car when she asked him to, and she quickly brought him home and fussed at us. It was quite a lecture about how dirty he was and how we were negligent dog-owners. I thanked the lady for her concern. After the neighbor left that day, I realized that I have felt like Jack sometimes. I've tried to do a good job, to be of service, to be a faithful Christian, only to be misjudged by some well-meaning saint who didn't like the way I look on the outside. But I have learned that, as Paul wrote to the Thessalonians, I cannot make myself perfect or holy or blameless. It is God who does this for me. My only job is to be the very best me I can be, and to be real. God does the rest. That's why it says *God* sanctifies us, that is, makes us clean.

"Holy and blameless" is a label God gives us, not one we earn or others can give us. Jesus welcomes us even while we're a mess. We're all a mess, kind of like Jack, but once we come to Jesus, we're *his* mess—his beautiful mess.—k.m.

November 2

Roar Anyway!

The lions may roar and growl, yet the teeth of the great lions are broken.
—Job 4:10

When we imagine a lion, we think of descriptions like "ferocious, strong, powerful." Yet in reality, only 20 percent of lion cubs even survive into adulthood, and if they do, their struggles aren't over.

The lion enters this world as a blind creature, totally dependent on his mother's protection. Born with spots and sometimes even stripes, the cubs are suckled by their mother up to eight months. Then, mother lion introduces the adolescent to meat, and from that day forward, mom's kitchen is closed.

Once a lion grows into adolescence in the wild, a lion has a life expectancy of about fifteen years. But at three years of age, the male begins to grow his signature mane, which unfortunately also makes him a target, and he will be soon sought after by hunting parties as a collectible hide. He could have his symbol of adulthood for only a month before shots begin zooming past his head.

Isn't it amazing how our crowning glory, our gifts, our special talents, and unique qualities given to us by our Creator also make *us* targets? It seems we hardly get out the door, before a well-meaning person gives us some "constructive criticism," and instead of shining outward, we dim inward. Passive words cut deep, and the enemy uses them to inject death into our dreams, hoping that our spirits will be broken and that we'll give up.

You enter the world as a roaring lion, and people get jealous because they aren't using *their* voices to roar. When we say yes to God, we stand out to people who have said no to him. When we do what others have been too lazy to do, they go after the lion, who is *you*!

Well, roar anyway!

If you are in the midst of a creative project, put off phone calls, e-mails, and correspondence with people who generally make you feel bad and ask God to send you a circle of wise counsel. Get rest. Fill yourself with God's Word. Then, God will reveal to you the authentic support network he has planned to help you on your journey.—d.o.

November 3
Enduring Endurance

*Therefore, since we are surrounded by so great a cloud of witnesses,
let us also lay aside every weight and the sin that clings so closely,
and let us run with perseverance the race that is set before us.*
—Hebrews 12:1

Marathon runners can vouch for the stamina it takes to go the distance. Author Bernd Heinrich is a record-breaking runner, and a biologist to boot. In *Racing the Antelope: What Animals Can Teach Us about Running and Life*, he discovers some amazing things about the endurance of animals and humans.

Heinrich submits that we, just like the antelopes and deer, are all natural-born runners. He cites a two-thousand-year-old pictograph from Zimbabwe that shows hunters running, arms raised in triumph. Then, he tells about the Penobscot Indians in Maine, who designated young men as runners to chase down moose and deer. In fact, several other Native American tribes ran down antelope, bison, and black-tailed jackrabbits. The Navajo could run deer to exhaustion. They used endurance to outlast their prey because, even though the prey were capable of much greater speed, they could only sustain the speed in short bursts.

Paul teaches about faith by comparing it with running a race. We suffer sometimes in our faith exercise with trials and the training of spiritual muscles of wisdom, prayer, and trust. Sometimes we have to sweat it out as we face moments of fear and doubt or times of persecution from those who disdain our love for the Lord.

The one who learns to run the race stops making excuses and complaining when life is hard. The one who endures knows there is hope. And God even gives us a personal trainer, the Holy Spirit.

As in running, faith takes practice and patience, but the rewards are great. The result is that God's love will be poured into our hearts. The key is in knowing that God will teach us to persevere and in being open to his lessons, all while our eyes are trained on the goal—relationship with our Creator.—k.m.

November 4
Little Is Much

And God said, "Let the water teem with living creatures,
and let birds fly above the earth across the vault of the sky."
—Genesis 1:20

In an ounce of sea water, nutrition for all of life is found in the tiniest of creatures. In the book *Marvels of Fish Life as Revealed by the Camera*, written by Francis Ward, the diatoms and microscopic plants make up the "pastures of the sea." They feed the fish and mammals there, and eventually all life, including humans. Plankton are all the small vegetation, egg sacs, and larvae among many other microscopic beings that are food for even the largest mammalian consumer, the humpback whale.

This tiny collection of life-forms breaks down into many different types of life, including diatoms, which are single vegetable cells about the size of a pinhead. Diatoms divide approximately five times a day. According to Dr. Ward, if they weren't constantly consumed or destroyed, a single diatom would divide and multiply so often that, in a month, the tiny pinhead would increase to a mass that is "a million times the size of the sun." The sea literally teems with life, a treasure vault with all we need.

Our seas also have a cleansing cycle that preserves the life of both food and feeder, but that system is working overtime right now. God's ocean floor sweepers, toxin absorbers, and carbon dioxide eaters are busy trying to keep up with a constant flow of man's carelessness.

With every hole drilled in the ocean, with every large party vessel spewing waste, and with every deep sea trawl of illegal nets, we disrupt the delicate balance that has served us well for so long. As we're awed by the complexity of the system God created, let us look into his microscope and ask what we can do to help restore the balance of life in the tiniest of places.—d.o.

November 5
Polly want a Juicy Story?

A gossip reveals secrets; therefore do not associate with a babbler.
—Proverbs 20:19

Billy Graham said, "A real Christian is a person who can give his pet parrot to the town gossip." No secrets. Clean, honest living means you have nothing to hide.

I've been wondering what my parrot would tell the town gossip. Would he repeat something I gossiped about? Maybe he would complain about Sunday's sermon and gripe about the preacher. Would he criticize a friend in my voice or repeat something I said I had forgiven? I wonder if my parrot would recite my resentments and regrets and talk negatively about my life and failures?

I know what I would *want* my parrot to say. I would like for it to spout off blessing after blessing of the promises God has kept to me, good things about my family and friends, and statements that reflect my belief in their goodness. I would want my parrot to tell everyone how good God is and how beautiful life is.

However, I suspect my parrot would mention the bills and my worries. I think I talk about them way too much. Maybe my parrot wouldn't repeat my gossip but would gossip about me. If he impersonated my TV shows and music, would I be happy—or embarrassed?

Reverend Graham knew, as shown by his statement, that peace of mind comes with a clean heart. We make life so much harder with our secrets. Let's celebrate the life of this great man by following his Christ-like example and talking about the good things of God.—k.m.

The Eagle Has Landed

These are the birds you are to regard as unclean and not eat
because they are unclean: the eagle, the vulture, the black vulture. . . .
—Leviticus 11:13

How could an animal symbolic of our protective holy Father be the first on the list of unclean animals in Jewish law? We think of the eagle and we remember verses like Isaiah 40:31, where God renews our strength so we can fly like eagles, yet they are considered not fit to eat. Perhaps the greatest reason these birds were considered unclean is because they eat dead things. But God still uses them as images to help us understand a Father we cannot see.

The shadow cast by a seven-foot wingspan is huge to those walking below. God comforts us under the shadow of his wings, so he compares his massive reach to the largest wing shadow understood—that of the eagle.

The eagle flies at breakneck speeds to unseen heights. Our God is immediately at our side, unseen by human eyes, but present whenever we call on him.

When God's Word says he brings us to himself on wings of eagles, the metaphor is one of power, lifting us higher and building us up in God.

Finally, eagle eyesight is the sharpest of almost any animal on earth. He sees everything below from great heights. Picture the eagle that sees all—it's a perfect image for a God who watches over us.

Jewish law said not to eat birds that eat dead things, but God's images pull the best attributes from *all* things, even those that are considered unclean, so we might understand who he is. God extracts the best from all of us too. We have some unclean habits that cannot be used by God. But when God wants to use us, he pulls us up to his level, cleanses, and makes us new through Jesus.

The listed birds eat away whatever is decaying and putrescent; likewise, the Holy Spirit cleans away the dead and decaying old us, and we are made new, clean in God's eyes. What in the world's eyes is an unclean bird, in God's imagery represents the cleansing of sin in our lives.—d.o.

Is It a Dove or a Paraclete?

He whom God has sent speaks the words of God,
for he gives the Spirit without measure.
—John 3:34

When Jesus was baptized, as is told about in Matthew 3, the Spirit descended like a dove. This dove-like gift was God's response to show his love for and approval of Jesus, and all those Jesus would pass the gift to. The heavens opened up, symbolizing that a revelation was being given, and just like in the book that bears that name, the revelation was Jesus Christ. God was showing the world something specific and long waited for. The descent of the Spirit was a foreshadowing that things were, at last, going to be set right, so the dove *hovered over the waters* just as the spirit had in Genesis 1:2. A new creation was on the way.

In the natural world, among the different types of doves are the mourning dove and the laughing dove. How appropriate, since joy and sorrow are sister emotions. The little doves in Jerusalem, brown with blue shimmers, are a beautiful image to represent the Spirit, symbolizing peace and gentle strength.

The Holy Spirit, the descending dove, is God, the third person of the Trinity. He is intangible and present everywhere and is always with us. The Holy Spirit is the one who whispers to our heart that Jesus is real and right.

John's Gospel is the only one that calls the Spirit *Paraclete*. That word expands our understanding of who the Spirit is as he is our Advocate, Comforter, and Counselor. Jesus prepares his disciples for life after he is in heaven by teaching them the importance and role of the Paraclete. From soul to soul, by the revelation of the Holy Spirit, we become witnesses from generation to generation. We are the living testimony that God's story—the story of Jesus—is authentic. The Dove descends again and again on every child of God and keeps the Truth relevant.—k.m.

November 8
Star Light, Star Bright

He is the maker of the Bear and Orion, the Pleiades and the constellations of the south.
—Job 9:9

Have you ever seen animals in the sky? God's connect-the-dots art-work was seen as hunters, bears, water dippers, and various other creatures by the early astronomers as they charted the heavens.

I remember watching the movie *Dragonheart* and being so touched when the old dragon's spirit leaves him and becomes a constellation after his last heroic, sacrificial act. *Dragonheart* is legend, but the early Hebrew people also believed that our loved ones became stars. The passage in Daniel 12:3 says, "Those who are wise will shine like the brightness of the heavens, and those who lead many to righteousness, like the stars for ever and ever."

Loss is painful to the core of our souls. What a beautiful thought that we become stars. What a lovely, artful image of the jewels of God's crown—us. Are you able to think of yourself as a crown jewel for Jesus?

When we think of ourselves as loved, precious, and rare jewels, does it affect how we treat other loved, precious, and rare jewels? If we walk around with a thorn in our paw, we treat creation poorly. When we walk around in pain, we also walk around feeling neglected, unloved, and the opposite of precious, and then we're not able to treat others with the right attitude, feeling either jealous, angry, or self-deprecating when we think of the delight they are to God. Love changes the way we live. Look around your world. How many thorns in throbbing paws do you see?

God sends us images to connect with, to bring us closer to him. Tonight, go to the night sky and let God reveal to you the message he has for you. Or go star-gazing with a friend and share stories of your loved ones with each other. By the end of the night, you might find two people who shine just a bit brighter.—d.o.

November 9
Choose a New Name

But now thus says the LORD, he who created you, O Jacob, he who formed you, O Israel:
Do not fear, for I have redeemed you; I have called you by name, you are mine.
—Isaiah 43:1

Sometimes when we rescue a pet, we don't know the pet's name. Its identity is lost, along with its past. The pet's story begins anew, from that point on. Giving it a new name is an important aspect of its new life.

God deems names as important. He knows that all of us can feel stained and full of regret. We look in the mirror and see someone different than the person we wanted to be, and we can soon forget who we are, the person God created us to be. So God gives us a new name. With that name, he gives us back the identity that was stolen away in the wilderness and confusion. He redeems our life to make us clean and whole.

The passage in Isaiah 43:18 says, "Do not remember the former things, or consider the things of old." Habits that once prevailed begin to fade away as our desires change and line up with God's. The details of our life begin to come together, touched by his grace as he restores the broken parts.

In a moment's time, in the blink of an eye, he makes us new, though it can take us a while to catch the vision of what God sees because he sees the very best we can be.

The most special aspect of getting a new name is that God gives us his name, the name he chooses for us that identifies us with him. He says, "I have called you by name, you are mine." I love belonging to God.—k.m.

November 10
Elephants and Donkeys

How then can I dispute with him? How can I find words to argue with him?
—Job 9:14

When a child asks you to explain what grinning caricatures of a donkey and an elephant have to do with who becomes the next American president, you'll have a hard time keeping a straight face.

Cartoonist Thomas Nance created lethal cartoons that dug deeply into the comfort zones of many political figures. He is credited with stamping the donkey and elephant as mascots to the two burgeoning parties in America. His portrayal of the two parties as ineffective and somewhat stupid remains today as Americans sign up to be on one "side" or another.

As Christians, we are called to look past cartoons in our decision-making process. We are never to treat people as donkeys, or elephants, or us and them. We don't have to argue any side because the one we represent is Christ, and he can defend himself quite effectively. God tells us to leave the heart-changing responsibilities to him and worry more about showing his love in the world, serving both those who share our opinions, and especially those who don't.

A donkey was one of the first domesticated animals that served man, and it has helped man in many ways, not the least of which was carrying Mary, who was pregnant with Jesus, to Bethlehem. An elephant is a powerful, faithful animal that has also served man for centuries, bearing his loads, helping build ancient structures, acting as transportation across jungles, and even fighting for him in armies. So the animals used for the two opposing, almost warring parties in America are both symbols of *service*!

As we talk politics with our children and each other, perhaps less labeling, more praying, and a serving attitude could help us understand what God wants from us and our political systems. God guides our leaders, our country, and our lever-pulling when we give our attention to his ultimate law of love. We lose our testimony of love when we argue and denigrate, especially when someone doesn't share our belief system. We are called to love and serve across the aisles, across the room, across the street, and yes, even across the divider of the voting booth.—d.o.

November 11
Musical Magic

The LORD, your God, is in your midst. . . . He will exult over you with loud singing.
—Zephaniah 3:17

Martin Luther said, "Next to the Word of God, music deserves the highest praise." Music is the language of the soul, human and animal. Their songs bless us, our songs bless them, and God's songs fill us with life.

One summer day, I set up a table on the front porch with my lucky pencil, my favorite legal pad, a guitar, a dobro, and a mandolin. The cats were surprisingly respectful of the instruments once they had sniffed the mandolin and caught their reflections in the chrome resonator of the dobro. I set the instruments on stands to protect them from wagging doggie tails and proceeded to write.

As soon as I began to play an instrument, a peaceful, comforting feeling seemed to link us all, heart to heart. As I wrote, I sang each song to my motley audience for approval, which I was granted with every newly composed tune. But one song provoked an unusual response.

I decided to write a prayer song. When I played it, a simple miracle happened. As I sang, the tree closest to my side of the porch filled with all types of birds. I thought it was mere coincidence that they would come now, but strange that they were feeding so much earlier than usual. . . . I sang on. A hummingbird came to me, though his feeder hung on the opposite side of the porch, chirped, and flew off. Then a couple of big, bright butterflies joined the party, and two more hummingbirds, both to my side of the porch. Three or four butterflies later, I decided this was not coincidence. They liked the prayer-song.

God gives us our song just as surely as he gives songs to the birds, whales, and all the rest. Rejoice in the Lord always, with a song.—k.m.

Pawpaw's Cat

Dear children, let us not love with words or speech but with actions and in truth.
—1 John 3:18

My grandfather adored his cat, Missy. She would come in as he lay down on the floor in the heat of the day (he was Native American, so that was how he napped), and Missy would literally massage his head. She kneaded and groomed until he fell fast asleep. It worked every time.

When he and my grandmother needed full-time nursing care, they moved to a facility together. After going through all the alternatives, from home care to sitters, they finally agreed to a nursing care facility as a last resort. My grandfather was the most worried about Missy. They couldn't take her, of course, so for a while, everyone took turns going to the house to feed her.

I will never forget the image of my grandfather pulling my mother close and saying, "Take care of my cat. Take care of my Missy." She was one of the things that kept him here; he had to make sure that Missy would have a future when he went to heaven.

When my grandfather did pass, Missy became representative of him in our lives. As long as we had Missy, we felt like we still had a piece of him. She was cared for late into her old age; she went gently, and I am sure my grandfather was waiting for her, arms wide open.

The best deed we can do for someone who is in heaven's waiting room is to make sure they know that those they loved will be loved and cared for when they're gone. Encouraging words are lovely, but Jesus spent at least as much time acting in love as he did speaking. So let us put action to our prayers, our promises, and our love by doing, giving, and applying God's commandments in practical ways so all can see our testimony lived out every day.—d.o.

The Night Life

You are the LORD, you alone; you have made heaven, the heaven of heavens,
with all their host, the earth and all that is on it, the seas and all that is in them.
To all of them you give life, and the host of heaven worships you.
—Nehemiah 9:6

A whole new world comes alive at night while most people are sleeping. Someone who is always on a morning schedule may miss the beauty of it altogether. I met a woman who discovered the nighttime magic of nature for the first time because of a less-than-magical reason: her dog was incontinent.

I met this lady at a United Methodist Church women's brunch. I finished singing, and she wanted to share her discovery with me. She said she'd been patiently cleaning up little accidents and dribbles she found in the house, but the hardest part was having to get up in the middle of the night. Her dog would quietly put a paw on her arm in the night when she "had to go," and I almost got the impression that the poor dog was embarrassed and hated to be such a bother.

As their new routine unfolded, the lady began to find the miracles in the quiet, mysterious wee hours of the morning. The stars were different, the air was softer, and one night, as she waited in the stillness, a magnificent owl flew over as though to offer a bit of wisdom: "Notice. Look around you. Isn't it amazing?" Her countenance was as bright as a child's as she talked about how she had never seen an owl before.

As she went on, I realized God had unveiled a world to her, almost like a waking dream. "I wouldn't have ever seen any of this if my dog had not been incontinent," she said. Her worry that she would have difficulty dealing with her new situation became a gift.

Blessings come in strange disguises.—k.m.

November 14
Storm Chasers

Some trust in chariots and some in horses,
but we trust in the name of the LORD our God.
—Psalm 20:7

Horses know when a storm is coming; they like to face it head-on. They don't want any surprises. They create a formation to be ready for what's coming. In fact, in times of bad storms, some farmers gave me the advice to let the horses out of their stalls. I was told, "If a tornado is headed our way, a horse has better instincts than we do. Horses don't feel safe confined in a barn. They feel imprisoned."

An inexperienced stable manager in our area left his horses locked in a barn as a thunderstorm ensued. The caretaker believed the horses would be safer locked in the dry warm barn, but lightning struck, causing a fire, and all the horses perished.

We learn hard lessons in life when it comes to trust. We ask God to lead us, tell us where to go and what to do, yet we find believing the instructions we're given more difficult than we thought it would be. God has given us, like horses, innate feelings of warning that we often talk ourselves out of.

Trust is a hard thing to learn, but it begins one courageous step at a time. With time, we learn God-instincts and begin moving in sync with God's will until we are facing all the storms of life like our horses do—head-on, protected by God.

The safety of the barn may *seem* like the perfect place to weather a storm, but if God is telling you to stand in the rain and to look into the wind, then follow his instructions. The storms of life will come, and they may bring fear and impossible decisions. But God has a steadfast love that he offers to hold us firm. He is the only anchor we need to face any turbulence and survive even the toughest of times.—d.o.

November 15
Big Bear, Baby Bear

Happy are you, O Israel! Who is like you, a people saved by the LORD,
the shield of your help, and the sword of your triumph!
Your enemies shall come fawning to you, and you shall tread on their backs.
—Deuteronomy 33:29

A little bear, a golden-brown grizzly, foraged one day with his mom. He lost interest in his appetite as curiosity took over, and he wandered off. He didn't realize his mama was watching him closely, letting him learn and grow, but keeping him safe. She knew that he needed training through experience so he would be prepared for whatever dangers life would bring.

Soon, he found a bank on a river where the water was easily accessible, so he stopped for a drink. He jerked up when he heard a ferocious sound beside him. It was a mountain lion, snarling and crouching, ready to defend its turf.

The little bear thought quickly, "What would Mom do?" Hearing his mother's voice answer in his head, he stood straight up, paws in the air, and growled with all his might. The lion was unaffected. So the little bear tried again, and this time, a deep, fearsome rumble roared so loudly that it rattled his own chest! The lion froze, then turned and ran quickly away.

"Wow!" thought the little bear, "I'm really a tough bear!" The little bear proudly strutted his way back to drink from the river, never realizing that his mother had come and roared from behind him.

I feel that way with God. I'm the little bear, so full of myself sometimes, thinking I can handle things on my own, when all along it is God who is my strength. He has my back. He never leaves us just because we don't always remember that he's there. How blessed are we, to have the constant concern of the Creator of the universe?—k.m.

A Horse by Any Other Name Is . . . a Mule

Don't let anyone look down on you because you are young,
but set an example for the believers in speech, in conduct, in love, in faith and in purity.
—1 Timothy 4:12

I have always enjoyed attending horse shows. The pageantry of animals groomed to perfection, trained to their athletic best, and treated like royalty is always a joy to see.

I was watching the Tennessee Walking Horse National Celebration one year, and the announcer introduced the Grand Champion Racking Mule, saying that he would be making an exhibition ride around the track. The crowd erupted in laughter at the thought of a mule at a horse show.

The music started, and out of the gates came the tiniest mule with a body like all the horses we had seen, except this horse had a pair of humongous ears. His legs pumped in perfect time to the up-tempo beat of the organ, and he increased his steps to match the speed of the music.

The announcer asked this little seemingly piston-propelled critter to pull out all the stops and go for a running walk. All of a sudden, it looked like the rider was on a mule with a blur beneath him, going so fast you couldn't see his legs move. The crowd went wild, giving a standing ovation for the tiny mule that had made his statement in spite of the laughter, the judgment, and the fact his ears were the size of satellite dishes. He did what he was made to do!

Sometimes we are the lone mule at a horse show. We are asked by God to walk into arenas where we don't fit in, where we don't look the part, and where we honestly might get laughed out of the room. God will equip us to live up to our high calling. God never created us to "fit in." He created us to stand out! d.o.

November 17
Don't You Love Me?

Sir, even the dogs under the table eat the children's crumbs.
—Mark 7:28

There is a strange story in Mark's Gospel about a Gentile woman who approached Jesus, desperate for him to heal her daughter. Jesus' response is surprising. He dismisses her, telling her that "the children must eat first," suggesting that she was not entitled to his healing benefits. Some say he was testing her faith. Jesus was often approached by people with bad intentions, asking for miracles like a dog and pony show, not for the real heart healing an encounter with him brings. The woman passed the test with persistence and a humble attitude. She told Jesus that even the dogs get a few crumbs, and he knew that she meant business. She would trust him no matter what. When she got home later, her daughter was whole.

One day, I met a lady whose story made me think of the woman in Mark. She was compelled to tell me about her parents' dog. "They love that dog," she spewed, and proceeded to explain how the dog could get away with anything. "It brings mud into the house, it runs off, and they'll go to any length to find it."

I knew there was deep hurt behind her words. Her parents, she said, loved the dog more than they had ever loved her as a little girl. They treated the dog well, she said, while they criticized everything she did.

"What kind of dog is it?" I asked.

"I don't know. Some kind of little black dog, a terrier or something." She despised the dog too much to care about its breed. She thought it was getting the love and attention *she* deserved.

For many days, the lady came back to my mind. She told me her parents had always taken good care of her, had reared her well, and had provided opportunities for her. In a way, the lady was begging for crumbs, wanting to be treated as well as the dog, yet she was already in a place of honor as a daughter.

We treat God the same way sometimes, thinking he waits to punish us, when in reality he longs to be gracious to us. We may ask for crumbs, but God provides the finest bread. Even when we would settle for less, God gives his best.

And by the way, the dogs in that Markan story were house dogs, and probably received some pretty delicious "crumbs"!—k.m.

Turtle Fishin'

Not all flesh is the same: People have one kind of flesh,
animals have another, birds another and fish another.
—1 Corinthians 15:39

My grandfather often fed his family from the plentiful catches from his trotlines in Little River. We used to love going with him as he used his boat paddle to lift the line and check the hooks. We would scrutinize the series of lines tied and baited that stretched from one side of the river to the other. It was like having ten fishing poles in the water at once.

Sometimes we would find a catfish, but on one particular day, it was a turtle, a soft-shelled one whose meat my grandfather described as a perfect collection in one animal. He told us that inside that leathery shell was every kind of meat. One part was like chicken, another part like beef, a different part like fish, and yet another part like pork. The few times we pulled a turtle from the water, we feasted. They were heavier and larger than anything I had ever seen, filling the bottom of the center of the boat!

We had the turtle for supper that night. I can still hear my grandfather thank God for that turtle . . . he sounded like his gratitude was from the depths of his soul.

My grandfather understood what it meant to really hunger, knowing that millions in the world are not able to celebrate a meal with their families every day, so he was deeply thankful. He chose to remember those who are starving, especially while he was blessed to taste several different kinds of meat in one meal. If he could have spread those different meats out to the different countries of the world, I know he would have.

This week, look into how you can help stop hunger in our world for men, women, children, and animals. God has a table set for you and me and all of creation. Let's be a part of his plan to fill the table with food for everyone.—d.o.

November 19
Horse of a Different Elephant

If you love me, you will keep my commandments.
—John 14:15

The word *obey* gives some people hives. Maybe it's a rebellious spirit in them, or maybe the word was misused on them as children. No matter what the reason, the word always rubs them the wrong way.

I finally got obedience into the right perspective by being around horses. I saw a trainer one day barely say a word, gently commanding, and I watched as those magnificent creatures obeyed with every move. When I later had the opportunity to hug a horse for myself, I felt the power of their strength. I then realized that those horses could do whatever they wanted. They were physically much stronger and faster than their trainer. So why obey? Out of respect and love.

So often, people go to church or don't cheat on their taxes out of obligation or because they have the slightest inkling that "Mama might have been right." But doing good deeds just to pay our dues won't help in the tough times. If we don't have any respect and love for the one who created us, then how can we expect to feel his peace when times are hard? God's love for us is all about connecting from the heart and sharing that connection in communion with others. Go to church because it makes your heart sing.

We obey with every thought, word, and deed as a natural outpouring of our love for the Lord. His message never was, and never will be, about rules. The message is that our obedience to a loving God fulfills us and that we're more blessed by taking hold of the life he offers than by doing whatever we want. Take a lesson from a good horse.—k.m.

November 20

Strong Heart—True Heart

All kinds of animals, birds, reptiles and sea creatures are being tamed and have
been tamed by mankind, but no human being can tame the tongue.
It is a restless evil, full of deadly poison.
—James 3:7-8

In 1954, J. Allen Boone's *Kinship with All Life* described extrasensory communication perceived between humans and animals based in part on a connection made with the author and an animal film star whose stage name was Strongheart.

The German shepherd was trained in Germany as a police dog, and brought to Hollywood for use in silent movies. The dog worked in several films including the first screen version of *White Fang*. Although he has a star on the Hollywood Walk of Fame, most people remember his successor, Rin Tin Tin, better than they remember Strongheart. His breeding line is still going today, and so is his eponymously branded dog food.

In 1928, Strongheart's accomplishments were forgotten when he was accused of murdering a child. He was finally exonerated when the family admitted to fabricating the whole story. Truth won, but if it hadn't, Strongheart's life would have literally been over. Strongheart won over a nation, had books written about his communication skills and adept training, but even a wonderful dog like Strongheart would have been destroyed with a lie told by manipulative people.

Gossip is a cruel and dangerous evil. Repeated rumors are water-cooler weapons that are just as detrimental as straight lies, even if they never travel back to the subject.

We cannot un-ring the bell, so watching our tongues and our accounts of stories is our *only* choice as Christians. We have to guard our words as surely as we guard our souls, because Satan loves to tear us apart with lies. They occur one small deviation from the truth at a time.

We have to ask God to let the truth shine. Poisoned words almost shattered an animal that had no voice, but the truth shined through. Are we not just as protected by the truth?—d.o.

November 21
No Lazybones 'Round Here

From everyone to whom much has been given, much will be required;
and from the one to whom much has been entrusted, even more will be demanded.
—Luke 12:48b

One of my favorite scriptures when I was a child is about an ant. It's a proverb that says, "Go to the ant, you lazybones!" (Proverbs 6:6). The idea is to look at the ant and think about how it lives. So, I bought an ant farm. They're simple to keep, and you can watch how they work.

Ants are incredible creatures. First, they're very fast. If a person could run like an ant proportionately based on body size and strength, she would be as fast as a race horse. Second, they can lift fifty times their own weight, and they don't waste that strength. Also, ants only live a couple of months, but they make good use of the time. They work together for the good of all, and they work hard, which is why they have survived since the age of dinosaurs.

I've always connected the verse about the ant with the verse about responsibility. To whom much is given, much is required. The more gifted you are, the more work you'll have to do for the good of all, but you'll want to do it, because you're fulfilled when you use your gift. You discover joy when you see how your unique abilities fit a specific role in accomplishing God's plan.

Your gift is like the strength and swiftness of the ant. Whatever our gifts are, they are given to us for a reason, and we have no right to hold them back. If you have legs, walk. If you have a musical gift, sing. Do you have strong arms? Help the weak. Money? Give to the poor. If you have a special love for animals, adopt a kitty. Do as God enabled you, and he will only increase your blessings, pouring out his love and offering more opportunities to take part in his work.—k.m.

Judge and Jury

The violence you have done to Lebanon will overwhelm you, and your destruction of animals will terrify you. For you have shed human blood; you have destroyed lands and cities and everyone in them.
—Habakkuk 2:17

A color picture of an emaciated horse splashed the front page. Her ribs were so prominent that she looked like a skeleton with hair. She was only one of a herd of neglected, starved horses taken from a farm in a rural county. Federal animal welfare agents confiscated as many horses as they could save, but many were already dead, lying in filth, decaying just out of sight of the road. But the world got involved as new homes for the horses appeared overnight and food came in from everywhere.

The owners of the horses declared innocence, saying that the horses had come to them that way, and the men were convicted only of a misdemeanor.

Those men may not have received enough of a punishment to make them stop, but awareness was raised. Horses were saved. Sometimes, that's all we get for pursuing good in a world where evil stands tall. But we can't ever give up.

Have you been the unpopular voice in a group of people who believe that animals are a disposable commodity? Have you spoken up when a social event was really a front for dangerous activity? Keep doing it!

The weight of carrying God's sword of truth can be heavy, but if cruelty to animals enters into society, the cruelty to man is not far behind. Look at the passage in Habakkuk: God was just as displeased with his people's brutality toward animals as their killing of people.

With every word, every petition, every solid stance against what is wrong, we get a step closer to the freedom of spirit that God intended for his creation. Be God's soldier in the army of good, see what is in need of change, and fight for it!—d.o.

welcome to the Family

Let everything that breathes praise the LORD! Praise the LORD!
—Psalm 150:6

I grew up in a Christian tradition that did not include much liturgy, so when I first heard the gorgeous words of doctrine, symbol, and repetition, my heart was deeply moved. I felt I was connecting with Christians throughout the centuries who knew and loved my Lord. I felt something lasting and right about saying the words together as a community of saints.

Have you ever heard a Liturgy for a New Pet? It begins as the minister welcomes the presence of the Lord, not only in the service, but with all creation. Then everyone gives thanks for the wonderful earth, and the people sing a song of praise, not so unlike today's verse from Psalm 150. We have done this in our church. We sang a beautiful old hymn called "All Things Bright and Beautiful," one of several old hymns that honor God's beautiful world and all the creatures in it.

After the praise and thanksgiving, a scripture is shared by the minister. Again, there are many good ones that suit the occasion but one that is especially nice is from Hosea 2:18. It says, "I will make for you a covenant on that day with the wild animals, the birds of the air, and the creeping things of the ground."

I never thought about God's covenant applying to the animals until I discovered that verse. God is in the business of animal rescue!!

The minister prays then that the Lord would make us ever mindful of our part in that covenant, and that we should be devoted, as well, to caring for the animals. The minister might even pray that we feel a deeper kinship with all living creatures.

There is something lasting and true about the good rituals we share in community as the body of Christ. Liturgy is like beautiful poetry that expresses our hearts and connects us with God and each other. How appropriate that we should include our pets, with whom we share so much of our lives, as well as the other animals. Maybe they can't go to church with us, but I expect they would be glad to know that we pray for them!

Perhaps your church does not do animal liturgy, but if you know some animal lovers among your Christian friends, you might want to lead the way in getting a group together for some prayer time that includes *every* member of the family!—k.m.

November 24
Fencer of Men

Run, tell that young man, "Jerusalem will be a city without walls
because of the great number of people and animals in it."
—Zechariah 2:4

Anyone who has ever owned a farm knows that fences are in a constant state of construction. Horses will push through a hole in a fence, trying to get to greener pastures. Cows will move in a group and push down an entire section. And bison have difficulty with any corners in a fenced area. They'll jam into the corner and have difficulty getting out of it. Goats climb fences, dogs dig under them, and sheep get caught in them. Basically, anything that is used to keep anything "in" will have to be fixed sooner or later. But the fences are still very important in farming because they protect the inhabitants from wandering and getting lost.

As children of God, we might need fences, even if we're outgrowing the confines of our current situation. Are you drifting into areas that might be treacherous? God may be telling you that it's time to have your fence mended. He does that by surrounding you with his word and covering you with his love, keeping you close to his heart.

Are you behind a wall, fearing what's on the other side? Our God is a mighty fortress, a strong tower to those who are in need of protection. Maybe you need to ask God to fortify the walls around you so that you feel more secure and safe.

Or, maybe today is the day that God is going to expand your territory!

No matter what situation you find yourself in today, remember that God has a plan for all of us, whatever our needs may be. Never be afraid that your fenced area is too small or too big; God knows exactly what we need, and he's faithful to give us just that. Ask God to reveal what your "boundary plan" is today!—d.o.

I'm Hungry Every Day, Thank You

I give thanks to my God always for you because of the grace of
God that has been given you in Christ Jesus.
—1 Corinthians 1:4

In 1854, Native American Chief Seattle said this: "Humankind has not woven the web of life. We are but one thread within it. Whatever we do to the web, we do to ourselves. All things are bound together. All things connect."

Few would disagree, but many do not live as though this is true, at least not on a daily basis. When the winter comes and the holidays center on kindness and gratitude, more people notice what is important. We then create occasions for good deeds. But we could be supporting a bigger push for humane service more often than on calendar holidays. Kindness should be a rule of interaction every day.

Many never forget those in need. God has a way of keeping their compassionate hearts alive. He moves and prompts, guides and calls, and then makes a way for Christians to help others build a lifestyle of concern for life.

The spreading of daily compassion is how the web of life forms a beautiful tapestry. When we bless each other, we bless the animals too. In fact, I know a cat who lives behind a restaurant and survives on the kindness of the chef. It's always Thanksgiving for her. It could be for all of us.

In *Animal Blessings: Prayers and Poems Celebrating Our Pets*, Kent Greenough tells us to remember to be thankful for pets. Be thankful because the love and time they give us reminds us to take time to enjoy and learn from them. They teach us to love unselfishly, to live each day to the fullest, and how to grow old gracefully. They teach us to die with dignity.

A holiday is just another day to be thankful. Don't worry about how much money you have to spend this season or how much time all the shopping will take. Instead, thank God for the love we have to give because of him. Let's remember and honor our animals, our families, one another, and our loving God.—k.m.

Figs and Wasps

Do not be afraid, you wild animals, for the pastures in the wilderness are becoming green.
The trees are bearing their fruit; the fig tree and the vine yield their riches.
—Joel 2:22

Did you know that in the rain forest, the most important food source for the ecosystem is the fig? The fig is called a keystone species because it is a vital food source to the rain forest menagerie. In some rain forests, 70 percent of the animals depend on the fig as their main food staple.

Bats, pigeons, monkeys, and more are able to feed on this sweet fruit year-round thanks to a tiny species of wasp that climbs inside the fruit, pollinates, and lays eggs, and then moves on to figs in other trees, carrying pollen right along with them. Without them, there would be no seeds, and without seeds, there is no growth. Without the fig wasp, there would simply be no more figs. They are the sole fig pollinators on the planet! This partnership between wasp and fig feeds almost the whole rain forest. God is *so* into the details!

God says, "Do not be afraid," because he *knows* all of the factors. He will take care of every little detail. God desires that no one goes hungry or worries about where their next meal is coming from. He wants us to enjoy the riches of this life, opening our hearts to his blessings and care, not walking around with a spirit of fear. Anytime fear and worry enter the picture, take warning: it is *not* your Father talking!

If God links a tiny wasp with a fig and feeds a whole rain forest as a result, how then must he also be putting together the details to take care of you? Today, live in the miracle of the minute details that you don't have to handle. Let God do what he does best! And the next time you see a wasp, a bee, or even a caterpillar, just remember they are all part of the little tiny details in God's great big picture.—d.o.

Blessing of the Animals

Praise the LORD from the earth. . . .
Wild animals and all cattle, creeping things and flying birds!
—Psalm 148:7a, 10

Many local United Methodist churches have services called the "Blessing of the Animals," as do other denominations. People bring their pets to church on leashes and in cages, and children especially love church on that Sunday evening. It's a joyous occasion!

One often used liturgy was inspired by Saint Francis and Saint Clare. The unique aspect of this particular service is the way it encourages us to pay attention to how we treat our animals. The gathering opens with a welcoming prayer inviting all to join the celebration of the circle of life. Then the minister asks for the Lord's blessing, his *shalom*, on the animals who have been brought to the service as well as the ones outside in the wild, acknowledging that God redeems and renews all life.

The people give thanks for the animals, and there is a time of confession for the ways that humankind has harmed the animals. With humble hearts and repentant spirits, the congregation says together, "We are sorry, Lord."

This attitude is, I think, what the world needs—a repentant heart. Such an attitude shift would change the world for the animals. With our awareness of animals' struggles, and with our faithfulness to care for them as God told us to, we are able to say together with all the earth: praise the Lord!

When you get to church this Sunday, say a prayer of thanks for our animals and reflect on the ways we, as a human race, can care for them better. Let there be peace on earth for the animals, too, and let it begin with me and you!—k.m.

Grateful . . . Except for Broccoli

Let the message of Christ dwell among you richly as you teach and admonish one another with all wisdom through psalms, hymns, and songs from the Spirit, singing to God with gratitude in your hearts.
—Colossians 3:16

Yogi was one of the most perfect dogs God ever created. He was a beautiful, red golden retriever with a compassionate spirit and a sweet countenance that always made you feel better on a stormy day.

Holidays were always special for Yogi because the house smelled like cooking, and the leftovers were fantastic! Yogi would wait for his goodies patiently, and the only indication of his excitement was a single drip of salivation falling slowly toward the floor.

Yogi loved gravy over kibble, and he always seemed grateful for every bite! On one particular night, I added the leftover broccoli, thinking this would really make his tail wag, but when I turned, expecting to see empty, shining bowls, next to Yogi was an orderly pile of green broccoli stalks, sucked clean of gravy. Like a youngster who doesn't like his veggies, Yogi had spit out the part of the gift he didn't want in one big, "Yuck!"

God often gives us gifts that include a side effect of "yuck." Many times, with his glorious "gravy" comes the broccoli of life. We are blessed with a wonderful new job that demands more energy than we've given before. We are blessed with children, who eventually leave us with heartbreaking empty nest syndrome. With every blessing comes challenge.

What do we do when our favorite joy is laced with bits of broccoli? We *thank* God for the broccoli. God invites us to enter the greener pastures, and sometimes the green turns out to be broccoli. We have a choice to spit it out, or we can learn to honestly thank God that he cares so much for us that he gives us nourishing broccoli.—d.o.

November 29
God Is Interested in Cows

I know all the birds of the air, and all that moves in the field is mine.
—Psalm 50:11

In 2010, Billy Graham, key leader of the Southern Baptist Convention and one of the most admired people of the twentieth century, received a letter from a worried mom. Her daughter wanted to devote her life to animal care. The mother was concerned because animal care was not, she said, something God was particularly interested in.

Ever the kind, compassionate man of God, Dr. Graham responded: "Yes, let me assure you that God is concerned about our care of every part of his creation—including the animals." After all, God made them, and ultimately they belong to him: "For every wild animal of the forest is mine, the cattle on a thousand hills" (Psalm 50:10). God is interested in all the animals he made, whether dogs, cats, monkeys, aardvarks, or cows.

Another time, Dr. Graham was asked if the Bible tells us how to treat animals. He said, "The Bible commands us to take care of animals. . . . In fact, the Bible tells us never to treat any part of God's creation with contempt. When we do, we are indirectly treating our Creator with contempt." Strong words, but true!

God cheers when churches take a stand to protect and care for the animals. Their work announces to the world on God's behalf that his creation is valuable and worthy of our ministry.

Fighting for and representing the animals is important. We need to do more! Let Jesus' light shine on the animals, too, so the world will know we are Christians by our love for all of God's creation.—k.m.

November 30
Heavenly Habitat

All the birds of the sky nested in its boughs, all the animals of the wild gave birth under its branches; all the great nations lived in its shade.
—Ezekiel 31:6

We have a friend who walks out her door, and birds come to her, eating out of her hand like she's Snow White. She once stopped traffic at a busy intersection to rescue a chicken. She bent her knees, flapped her pseudo-chicken arms, and clucked. The hen came right to her, and she took it home, safe and sound. A baby starling fell from its nest, and though most people would try to get rid of the squawking, ugly bird, she taught this one to sing and talk. That starling now spends much of its time on her shoulder. What others have called a "trash bird," she calls her treasure, lovingly caring for it every day.

God has given us beautiful music as the soundtrack of life, but not everyone knows to appreciate it as much as our friend, the bird lady. She may be one of the few, but she's certainly not the first to see the perks of paying attention to these animals. Billy Graham said that he used to practice his preaching to the birds on his college campus. And Saint Francis of Assisi had done the same thing. Why did these great men spend so much time among birds? Because they followed Jesus' advice. The birds are constant reminders not to worry and to trust that God will care for us.

If you can't have pets where you live, or you have dander allergies, God has supplied the perfect companion animals in the wild birds. We are blessed to see a wide variety of these creatures as they fly north and south in the varying seasons. Build a bird-feeding area on a terrace, patio, or even at office windows and wait for the flurry of chirping activity. Listen and hear the music of their different, worry-free calls.

Birds teach us the willingness to be cared for. God blesses birds because they welcome his interaction in their lives. Do you need a blessing? Have you been asking? Do you need help in receiving? Watch the birds, and let them show you how!—d.o.

Kookaburras and Gumdrops

You will have joy and gladness, and many will rejoice at his birth.
—Luke 1:14

I always felt a special connection to the kookaburra song we used to sing in elementary school because of a Christmas tradition in my house. My mom used to set out a gumdrop tree every year the day after Thanksgiving, right after we put up the Christmas tree. I always ate the red ones first, then purple, then orange, and hoped she would refill it before I had to eat the yellow and green. The sugar from the gumdrops would gather in the little tray beneath the tree, creating a snowy confection that went with the season. Well, the kookaburra song mentions a gum tree, and I thought it grew gumdrops. Really, it's about an Australian bird whose boisterous laugh sounds almost human.

I always wonder what he must be laughing about, but it doesn't matter too much; I somehow felt happy because he was happy. Laughter is contagious.

The Australian aborigines have a legend about the kookaburra. They say that when the sun rose for the first time, God ordered the kookaburra to laugh its loud, raucous, human-like shriek so that the humans would wake up and see the sunrise he had made.

We want our holiday memories to be about joy and laughter. It's a season of childlike faith, yet our good expectations are often met with unexpected feelings of sadness. I want to be like the kookaburra, one who brings laughter, don't you? Maybe others around us will catch on, spreading the joy to even wider circles. We can bear the light of Christ by sharing our light, kookaburra-imitating heart with others.—k.m.

Barren Dark Creativity!

Now the earth was formless and empty, darkness was over the surface of the deep,
and the Spirit of God was hovering over the waters.
—Genesis 1:2

Polar bears have always fascinated me. These beautiful creatures spend all of their lives in cold, icy climates, most days of which are covered in darkness.

It was out of darkness that God first created. I wonder how the thoughts came to him as he considered the ice caps, the funny penguins, the leopard seal, and the big fuzzy polar bear. When we paint, write, or create, we often have inspiration or influence to get us started. But God started with darkness. From the loving explosion of creativity, everything came into reality perfectly locked in harmony.

Each earthly habitat, even the most unforgiving, has been populated by God's creativity. And from the darkness of God's first creation came the polar bear, perfectly suited for the dark winters in the frozen North.

As we enter the dark cold months of winter, ask God to grow your creativity. Ask him to form new ideas as you spend reflective time with him. When our lives are so full of activity, sometimes the void created in the cold dark months is just what we need to replenish, rest, and rejoice in God's plan for us. Let God inspire you to start new projects or finish one that's been shoved to the back burner.

Maybe the darkness you face is a dark time in your life. Ask God to take you through this dark time, creating in you a new vision full of hope and excitement. If he could create all that we know as creation and so much more than we can imagine out of darkness, just think what he can create out of your own darkness if you surrender it to him.—d.o.

December 3
Shuv, Baby!

You, having been set free from sin, have become slaves of righteousness.
—Romans 6:18

In a Blessing of the Animals ceremony, the writer ascribes words to God. He says, "For all your sins against the creatures of Earth, I forgive you, and I call upon you to honor and protect all my animals."

We need forgiveness. One of the reasons we go to church is to have a tangible way to find forgiveness through worship, liturgy, and sharing honestly with others who have accepted Jesus' gift of love. God is merciful and is always waiting with outstretched arms for every person to receive his grace and his help to do better. He changes us, heart first, and afterward, the actions follow. Asking for forgiveness and repenting is the action that begins to shift our hearts toward God.

The Hebrew verb for repent is *shuv*. To repent literally means "to turn." We turn *from* something, *toward* God. It is in forgiveness and repentance that we are set free: free to make better choices. When we turn toward God, we're not slaves to purposeful bad choices, or even the I-don't-know-what-made-me-do-that choices anymore. Instead, Paul says that we're indebted to righteousness.

We can't undo the mistakes we have made, but God doesn't want us wallowing around in guilt and regret. He never holds our mistakes against us because then we would be enslaved to them. We're free of them, not bound to shame because we're not perfect.

God has to do a miracle within us to free us—that miracle is Jesus' victory over death. The words of the liturgy are a way of making a commitment to God to live like the one who freed us. Then we can set our hearts and minds on better things.

God gives us the strength to keep that commitment. The more often we focus on living like Jesus, the less our thoughts obsess about undoing messes and the more they turn toward prayer, thanksgiving, and service.
—k.m.

Out of the Desert

See, I am doing a new thing! Now it springs up; do you not perceive it? I am
making a way in the wilderness and streams in the wasteland. The wild animals
honor me, the jackals and the owls, because I provide water in the wilderness
and streams in the wasteland, to give drink to my people, my chosen,
the people I formed for myself that they may proclaim my praise.
—Isaiah 43:19-21

As the holiday season approaches, are you starting to feel worried about the strain the holiday might put on your budget? For people in construction jobs, for example, the holidays many times mean time off, which translates to no paycheck. No matter our situation, we often increase our spending and then stress that we've spent too much. And when we're worried, one of the most wonderful times of the year can be lost in a tension-filled life.

God reminds us through Isaiah that he makes a way for all of us when success seems impossible. He makes streams in the desert.

Scripture does not say he will provide a way in the wilderness for the consistently budget-minded or the terrifically organized. Those skills can help us, but we can't ever allow ourselves to think that we've got it all together, so we don't need God. God specifically refers to the wild animals, the owl and jackal that must depend on the Creator *daily* for everything. Without God, we're starving, whether we realize it or not. But with him, we drink of God and taste sweet water when everyone else only tastes sawdust.

Now is a special time of year to give God genuine, heartfelt praise. Give all your worries and your tensions to him, and let him carry you through this season in celebration of Jesus becoming human so that we can taste true life.

We have a scriptural foundation we can cling to as we go into stress mode. As fear creeps in, praise it out. And remember that God doesn't need our offerings to make a way for us; he forges a way out of nothing, through the wilderness and the desert. How will you show him that you believe that?—d.o.

December 5
How Do You Know?

Now faith is the assurance of things hoped for, the conviction of things not seen.
—Hebrews 11:1

Flannery O'Conner said, "Faith is what someone knows to be true, whether they believe it or not." Her statement could be the motto of animal lovers. We have a kind of sixth sense, a way to tune in to our animals that is both inexplicable and undeniable. Science can't yet prove some of the things we *know*. But perhaps, one day, it will.

I think about faith a lot since Josie became a part of our family. The intensity of and message in her eyes is so poignant and sincere that I can almost hear what she's saying. Scientists might tell me I'm fooling myself, but experience tells me differently. Unfortunately, we have relatively little to use as a specific defense in Scripture. It tells us to care for the animals and love them. We can point to scriptural evidence that animals will be in heaven with us, but even heaven as we understand it is one of the things we *just know* about—we don't know exactly what it will look like or how we'll experience it.

But don't fear, because God protects his Word, supporting it with more than the pages of the Bible. The Bible itself explains that we must "rightly divide the word of truth" (2 Timothy 2:15). In other words, use discernment. Ask God for it, and he will allow his Holy Spirit to make the Bible understandable to you. God's Word is in the Bible, but it is also in Jesus, and it is all around and in us through the wind of the Spirit. God's Word is in the witness of the multitudes of Christians who have witnessed Jesus, seen God perform miracles through others, and deeply felt his love.

I remember as a child, knowing that God was with me before I knew what a profession of faith was. Search God's Word with an open, truth-seeking heart, and he will help you find truth, often confirming what you already knew.—k.m.

December 6
Not in My Power

The righteous care for the needs of their animals, but the kindest acts of the wicked are cruel.
—Proverbs 12:10

If you have ever participated in any form of rescue, you have probably been exposed to cruelty. Bill Maxwell, a columnist for the *St. Petersburg Times*, described the way he felt about the tidal wave of evil pouring into the world with a quote from *Gulliver's Travels*: "I cannot but conclude the bulk of your natives to be the most pernicious race of little odious vermin that nature ever suffered to crawl upon the face of the earth."

Evil and sin share this world with us. When staring into the face of teens who have burned a puppy alive, or parents who have tortured their own child, we can feel that hope is lost. How will the good news make any difference to people who participate in such horrible acts?

First, we must see the traps the enemy sets for children of God. The enemy loves to make us blind to our own actions, numbing ourselves to violence and pain through overexposure. The storylines of many bestsellers and box-office blockbusters often are based in cruelty that we excuse because of popularity. Until we can recognize brutality, we won't be able to fight for its victims.

Next, we must reach out to both perpetrators and victims with the same love. Of course, we can't do this without God working through us. Ask God to let you see what he sees. The offender might have been mistreated in the same way. God asks us to be supernatural in our love, not our judgment. Our warfare is with the evil, not the person imprisoned by it.

How do we do that? We must pray without ceasing. We forget sometimes in the onslaught of horrible news that prayer to our listening God is our first responsibility. When we pray against evil, God fortifies our arsenals of love and eventually allows us to see that every person who commits a cruel act was born into this world a precious, naked, helpless child of God. Don't let your hatred of cruelty birth more cruelty in your actions toward one of these people whom God loves and desperately wants to heal.—d.o.

December 7
Rats! There's a Cat on Board!

I hereby command you: Be strong and courageous;
do not be frightened or dismayed,
for the LORD your God is with you wherever you go.
—Joshua 1:9

"Life expands or contracts in proportion to your courage," wrote Anais Nin, a French-Cuban author. Many animals know what courage is all about.

The ones who work in therapy are special heroes. A miniature horse named Magic visited patients who needed comfort in group homes, hospitals, or even hospice care. One day, Magic went to visit a patient who had lived in assisted care for three years and hadn't said a word to a single soul the whole time. The moment she laid eyes on Magic, she said, "Isn't she beautiful?" The patient has communicated ever since, and Magic received the AARP Most Heroic Pet Award.

Another heroic animal lived on a British Royal Navy ship in 1949. The HMS *Amethyst* was hit in an attack by Chinese Communist forces. Simon, the ship cat, was injured in the leg and back, and his whiskers were singed off. They didn't think he would survive, but eventually, Simon recovered enough to wipe out a massive rodent infestation on board the ship. He later caught an enormous rat that the sailors had named Mao Tse-Tung. Simon became known around the world, and he was given the Dickin Medal in the United Kingdom, an award which honors animals in wartime.

Moko the dolphin saved two pygmy sperm whales, a mother and her child. Rescuers had tried to herd the whales back out to sea, and the pair would have died had Moko not come along. She somehow explained to the whales that they were not safe, and she led them out to deeper water.

When God commands us to do (or not do) something, he doesn't just leave us to figure it out. We have the joy to know that God is with us at all times, in every situation, so if we don't feel particularly courageous, we can just ask him for some of his. And boy, does he love to share himself with us!—k.m.

Forgive and Remember

A person's wisdom yields patience; it is to one's glory to overlook an offense.
—Proverbs 19:11

My first Christmas with Sophie, my Great Dane, was an adventure. In her heart, she was a small puppy, filled with mischief, but in reality she was huge in size and with teeth that could destroy an ottoman in a single afternoon. She was a force to be reckoned with that year around the Christmas tree.

Upon waking in the morning, I found a red wooden cowboy boot with its toe bitten off on her bed. She had stolen the ornament from one of the lower branches in the night and chewed until half was missing. One pointed look at her, and she hid the destroyed ornament under her big, blocky head, ears back and tail down.

I couldn't bring myself to fuss at her because she seemed to realize that she had made a mistake. I also could never bring myself to throw away the marred remains of the ornament. Each year it gets a special display, and we tell the story about the fate of the missing part of the ornament.

To this day, that ornament is a precious reminder to me of how God sees the mistakes we bring to him. Even when we disobey, going against his law of love, God's forgiveness is great and beautiful. He looks at the broken ornaments in our lives and hangs them, forgiven and precious, on the tree of life as a testament to his love for us. Our mistakes are not reminders to God of our failures. God forgives us fully and wants to display his glory in us. Our forgiven mistakes represent our true success in God's eyes.

We are the ornaments on the branches of God's Christmas tree, shining in beauty for all the world to see. Forgiveness is the gift that brings us to God's original brilliance, and our honesty about our problems and his forgiveness makes that brilliance shine from our lives into a world that desperately needs light.—d.o.

December 9
French Monkeys in the Trees

We have escaped like a bird from the snare of the fowlers; the snare is broken, and we have escaped. Our help is in the name of the LORD, who made heaven and earth.
—Psalm 124:7-8

An orangutan who lived in the San Diego zoo reminds me a lot of our pony because they're both escape artists. The orangutan, named Ken Allen, became famous for his Houdini impersonations, and just like Geronimo, the ape didn't mind getting caught. He seemed to be bored and wanted the challenge of getting out. He never went anywhere once he escaped; he just waited to be let back in.

In a single day at the San Francisco Zoo, a herd of buffalo, a hippopotamus, and a South American rodent escaped. All were eventually chased down and captured, a couple chases and several hours later.

In 1958, a sea lion from Ontario went searching for his San Francisco homeland and wound up in Ohio near a boathouse.

Twenty monkeys were set free from the monkey house at Le Jardin d'Acclimatation in Paris in 1926. The monkeys swung from tree to tree in a nearby park while Parisians "gleefully chased them all day long."

Why do we try to escape from our safe places? When we feel afraid, why run from our source of help? Sometimes we even bait God by doing something wrong intentionally, just to test if he will respond well every time. Inevitably, wherever we escape to becomes the snare, whether it's a physical place, a relationship, or even a destructive habit. But every time we run away, God is there, inviting us to accept his help and come back to him.—k.m.

December 10
One Sheep, Two Sheep, Three Sheep, Four

The animals take cover; they remain in their dens.
—Job 37:8

Sometimes I wish I were a bear. I would love to pack on sustenance, curl up in a warm cabin, and sleep for days. A sleep-cation sounds like a great way to catch up on some rest and miss the cold, wet days of winter.

Bears aren't the only lucky ones. Raccoons will sleep for several days at a time, wake up and eat, and go right back to sleep. They can lose half their body weight during the winter months. Woodchucks create tunnels underground where they hibernate for the winter.

From grizzlies to tiny dormice, many animals enter a state of suspended activity to allow survival when food is scarce. Did you know that the outdoor ponds with large goldfish can freeze over in winter, and the fish will be suspended in a cold sleep-like state, ready to move as the water warms?

Provision can take many forms, and God has created a system that requires the provision of rest. Where *hibernation* is almost a coma-state in which body functions slow to a crawl, *sleep* is a rejuvenation of our bodies and mental faculties. Our sleeping time is when the little construction hats and metaphoric dump trucks go to work within the system God placed in us, so we can get up the next day, raring to do the work God has for us that day.

Is it time to plan a sleep-cation for yourself? What about planning a day, a weekend, or even the week between Christmas and New Year's Day to have a spiritual sleep renewal? Turn off your phone, hide your to-do list, and unplug your Internet connection. Alert your family and friends that you are taking advantage of the rest God offers and going on a sleep-cation.

Ask God to give you a personal Sabbath, and during it, trust that your family will survive if you ask them to make dinner for a few nights, and allow God to care for and complete you. You might find that the rest does so much for your attitude and your contentedness that once a year is not enough!—d.o.

December 11
At-a-Zebra

Not that I have already obtained this or have already reached the goal; but I press on to make it my own, because Christ Jesus has made me his own.
—Philippians 3:12

We love animal movies at our house. Animated ones, like *Spirit*; talking-animal ones, like *The Adventures of Milo and Otis*; and real ones, like *Black Beauty*. One that captured my heart—*Racing Stripes*—was about a zebra that believes it is a racehorse.

Belief is a powerful thing. The zebra gets faster and faster, thinking he's doing what any other racehorse would do, so his owner, a young girl, enters him into a professional horse race. He isn't afraid, though he discovers, to his surprise, that he is a laughingstock. But he is determined to prove them wrong. As long as he believes he is a racehorse, he is, and besides, the girl believes it, too, and when it comes to faith, that's a majority!

One day, a jealous stallion tells him his true identity. He's a zebra. Suddenly, the zebra is not fast, cannot run, and is paralyzed with fear. The girl and all the animals talk him into trying again, but he ultimately has to find his *true* identity before he can race again. He's not a horse; he's a very fast zebra with a resilient spirit. When he believes this about himself, he can act in that newfound reality.

The zebra is a "little engine that could" in a timeless scenario.

His is the walk-on-water story.

His life is an I-can-do-all-things-through-Christ example.

Jesus is the master of the motivational speech. He helped people know their true nature—what they could be in him. Press on, Jesus said. Take off those rags, Lazarus, you're not dead, you're alive! Jesus knows who he created us to be, and he constantly directs us toward fulfilling life.

The Lord never gives up on us, and when we lose sight of the dream, he will keep it alive for us, lovingly guiding us forward. Sometimes, failure is part of the success, but if we follow after God, he will lead us to win the race!—k.m.

December 12
The Gift Horse

Each of you must bring a gift in proportion to the way the
LORD your God has blessed you.
—Deuteronomy 16:17

As we move into the Christmas season, we are all being called to the baby shower of Jesus, to give a gift to the new King.

What would you bring if a star or an angel told you to head to Bethlehem and see the newborn Messiah? Would you just start walking? Would you go shopping for the perfect baby gift? Would you touch and dial on your smartphone and order something via the Internet? Would you look for something on sale, or would you try to make something by hand? Would you call ahead and ask what everyone else has given, so you could stay in the same financial ballpark?

I love how our pets want to give us gifts. A dog that wants to enjoy a nice walk might bring you his leash, but he is really bringing you himself, his best, begging for relationship and time together.

When a horse, an animal that at the very least *dislikes* having a cold metal bit in his mouth, allows you to ride on his back, then he has given you trust, a gift that is probably the most precious thing he could give.

I've always loved the thought of sharing our talents as a gift to Jesus. But what about the first fruits of our labor? Do we come to Jesus each day, insisting on spending time with him? What a gift that would be!

You have a chance to follow the examples the animal world has been showing us for years. When we rush to Jesus to give him our time, our trust, and our best, we have given him the most beautiful part of ourselves, and the only gift Jesus ever wanted in the first place.—d.o.

December 13
white Bird Black

Where were you when I laid the foundation of the earth?
—Job 38:4

I read about an unusual bird, a one-in-a-zillion fluke of nature, whose story taught me a lesson about the absolutes of life. It's a story of a penguin with a genetic quirk. Without exception, every single penguin in the whole wide world is black and white, right? That is, except for the one completely black one. He was discovered in the Arctic by a fascinated scientist who then tagged the bird and followed him to see if his genetic quirk affected any other aspects of his "penguin-ness." Apparently, only the pigment in his feathers made him different. Otherwise, he's just a regular penguin following the other penguins around doing what penguins do. Neither he nor the other penguins seem to realize he is odd.

I daresay people are not so nonplussed by the unusual. We like our black and white answers, and we search for absolutes. Though change is inevitable, we resist it; when the remarkable happens, we explain it away. Sometimes things we expect to be "black and white," perfectly predictable and unarguably unshakable, simply aren't.

It's okay when we don't have all the answers. God does, and he reserves the right to reveal his plans to us on a need-to-know basis. The beauty of not knowing everything is that it keeps the mystery in the miracles. It also keeps us reminded that we are not God.

Today, look for the one-in-a-zillion penguin among all the others. Ask God to open your eyes to the unusual opportunities he may be sending your way. Ask him to help you see your own special uniqueness—and celebrate it!—k.m.

Hee-Haw Holiday

By day the LORD directs his love, at night his song is with me—
a prayer to the God of my life.
—Psalm 42:8

Have you ever heard dogs singing Christmas carols, maybe in the department store while you're shopping for gifts? On the farm, we've had quite the canine choir for years. They don't sing Christmas carols yet, but they do achieve a bit of harmony on the high notes when the train whistles. One of our donkeys, named Lil' Bit, has even begun joining the dogs when they howl sometimes, and he has the loudest voice of all.

Last night, when I was taking down some food to the animals, Lil' Bit ran up to me and released a humongous "Hee-haw." I showed him the bucket that I hadn't filled with food yet. He shoved his head inside and let another "Hee-haw" fly. It echoed loudly in the bucket, rattling his ears. He pulled back abruptly and shook his head, looking a little disoriented with his own voice so amplified.

Our voices are our trumpet of praise to God. We can lift them in joyous song or raise them in disappointment when things don't go our way. We shift back and forth, excited one day that God let us have a great conversation with someone, then angry or depressed the next day with a negative conversation.

But what about God's voice? When we hear our Father's voice, it is not confusing, like ours, and it doesn't cause fear. We never have to question if God's voice is real.

And God's voice is the song of life. To me, he sounds like my pawpaw. To you, he might sound like a friend, or like a deep-voiced actor. God's voice sounds different to all of us, but his is a song of comfort for everyone.

For Lil' Bit, God probably joins in with a clamorous "Hee-haw." God speaks to every living creature in a voice that is both distinctly his *and* distinctly ours. He speaks so we will listen and so that we can understand. Listen for his version of Christmas carols this season.—d.o.

December 15
Perfectly Good Leftovers

You have put gladness in my heart more than when their grain and wine abound.
—Psalm 4:7

The aardvark, which resides in Africa, looks like a stuffed animal that was created from all the scraps left over from other stuffed animals. It's like a pig with a crazy long nose, but a body like an armadillo, but with a kangaroo tail, and ears like a rabbit. It is a nocturnal creature, which is a good thing to be in the sweltering heat of the Sahara, and it eats termites, which it digs out with its powerful claws and sweeps up with its freaky, long tongue. An odd creature, indeed.

I feel like an aardvark sometimes, as if I've been all pieced together. Those days are not my favorite, no offense to the aardvark. My life doesn't always follow the neat, tidy trajectory I've planned, although not for my lack of trying.

I look at others who seem perfect and wonder what that would be like, and other times I think I've got "perfect" mixed up with "life before turning twenty-one." Relationships, work, finances, and unanswered dreams all conspire to challenge our perception of perfection. But life is not the Magic Kingdom; it's a bumpy road.

God doesn't erase our past for us. Instead, he heals the one we've got. Before saying yes to God, we may be a mess, but God doesn't just piece us back together. He makes all things new, restoring us to how he always intended for us to be, and that includes giving us a new perspective on the old. Aardvarks are cute when they're in Africa, but not so cute when you see them in the mirror. I want God to form me, and I now remind myself, on those days when all I can see is the discombobulated aardvark, that God remembers exactly what he had in mind for me to be. He will fill me with gladness while he restores his precious creation.—k.m.

Provision Pastures

Then they will have towns to live in and pasturelands for
the cattle they own and all their other animals.
—Numbers 35:3

My grandfather used to rotate his pastures. One year, the pasture by the barn would be grass for cattle hay, the next year, it would be soybeans, and the next, corn. And for every crop grown, part would be reserved to feed his cattle. He never thought of providing only for people.

Have you ever noticed in Scripture that when God provided for humans, he always provided for the animals too? He didn't ever act as if human beings were the only part of creation to worry about. In fact, God created the animals first, and instead of leaving them to their own devices, God put humans in custodianship of them. God looked out after the animals from the very beginning.

I've heard the question before: "How can you care so much for animals when there are so many people in need?" God has given "animal people" an answer in his Word for whenever they're asked that question. We are gifted differently and we are called differently.

This time of year, everyone vies for our time, talent, and money to help further their cause. The pastures within us may need to be rotated too. If we feel we must say yes to everyone, we can become too drained to do anything.

God's pastures provided for all his beautiful creation, and you can be a provider with him too. But don't try to do it all at once. If that were possible, we wouldn't need God; but the fact is, we cannot do it on our own. God calls us to say yes to *him*, not to everyone who knocks on our door.
—d.o.

December 17
Laser Beam Love

And the LORD said to Moses, "How long will this people despise me?
And how long will they refuse to believe in me,
in spite of all the signs that I have done among them?"
—Numbers 14:11

Watch kittens follow, pounce, play, and get totally exhausted because they are convinced that the moving dot of light will, one of these times, be theirs! They truly believe that they are in control of the chase, no matter how many times they fail to catch the light.

We are a lot like laser-chasing kittens. In spite of all the times we fail to control the moving targets of life, we still believe that somehow we are in control, that if *we* are just smart enough, consistent enough, or charming enough, we will look the way we want. I'm sure God must shake his head sometimes and ask, "What have I got to do to make you understand? *I'm* sovereign. *I'm* in control. And *I* will protect your future."

In a world that trusts lottery tickets, psychics, and numerologists, we've got a lot to learn. God doesn't want us to put our confidence in the stock market and the media. He wants us to set our sights on him.

When employment rates drop, houses are foreclosed, and families are broken, we can look to God for some real answers. He has given signposts throughout all time to show us how much he loves and cares for us.

Today, imagine God's laser light just trying to get our attention. Let's not chase blindly. Look toward the light until you can see God face-to-face. Trust in God, not the world, when you need a miracle. He hasn't stopped performing them, you know.—k.m.

The Donkey and the Ox

The ox knows its master, the donkey its owner's manger,
but Israel does not know, my people do not understand.
—Isaiah 1:3

The first known nativity reenactment was populated with donkeys, sheep, and camels, and it took place in Italy in 1220, initiated by Saint Francis of Assisi, according to most accounts. The Pope endorsed the plays, word spread, and soon churches were expected to have a nativity of some sort every Christmas. German immigrants are credited with bringing the wooden nativity scenes to America in the eighteenth century.

The donkey always plays a big part, as he brought the Christ's mother, the carrier of the one who would carry the burdens of the world.

According to some scholars, the donkey is also representative of the Gentiles, while the ox represents Israel. Habakkuk foretold of the Savior being manifest between two animals, the donkey and the ox, symbolically foreshadowing the union of the Jews and the Gentiles when Jesus entered our world.

Regardless, God makes a powerful statement. Coming to us in such humble surroundings, in the presence of farm animals, breaks down any thought that we must *do, achieve,* or *BE* something of significance before God can work in our lives. He will come to us, ignoring the boundaries of politics, social status, or housing situation, and he will set up a permanent grace-filled residence in our lives.

As groups protest nativity displays, perhaps the real protest is by an enemy who wants us to forget that God *will* come to us anywhere. With every nativity scene that is removed by legal systems, a new one can be built in the heart of every person, and that display can never be touched by evil.—d.o.

December 19
One Plus One Is One

Again, truly I tell you, if two of you agree on earth about anything
you ask, it will be done for you by my Father in heaven.
For where two or three are gathered in my name, I am there among them.
—Matthew 18:19-20

I have always thought that the two turtledoves mentioned at Christmas time represented Mary and Joseph, because they were God's lovebirds, called to train up the Son of God in the way he should go.

Turtledoves feed in pairs, and their elegance and soft, cooing voices make them the perfect symbol of romance or true friendship. They are migratory and monogamous. The male gathers twigs, and she builds a fragile nest. Pairs even preen each other with love.

In Scripture, the turtledove represents covenant loving-kindness. God can do amazing things with two united souls. Jesus said when two agree, it moves God to action—this is God's ecology of prayer and teamwork. The Bible is full of pairs, from Adam and Eve to Abraham and Sarah, Jacob and Rachel to Joshua and Caleb, and Ruth and Naomi to David and Jonathan.

I will still always think of Mary and Joseph when I think of the two turtledoves. What a beautiful example of what a partnership is meant to be, focused toward bringing Jesus to the world together, as a unit.

Relationships have lasting value when Christ is in the center. So, pray together as friends and as couples. Talk about God and about Scripture. Involve God in all your decisions and conversations. When you share a heart full of God together, the impossible becomes possible.—k.m.

The Savior in Us

Come quickly to help me, my Lord and my Savior.
—Psalm 38:22

Some people rescue turtles, some people save children from human trafficking, and other people save entire regions from starvation by delivering food across enemy lines.

But the job of being a savior is not easy. A mother dies trying to save her child from a burning house. A homeless woman is struck by a hit-and-run driver as she rushes to help her dog that had been hit by a car. A father drowns as he jumps into icy waters to save his two Jack Russell terriers that had been swept off the pier. Being a savior doesn't always come with a happy ending.

But we have a reflex to save, just like we have a reflex to live. It's in our DNA, and we cannot stand by and watch life fade away without trying to do something, at any cost. Life calls to life to be saved. Whether man or beast, the distressed calls for a response because somewhere within all of us is someone worthy of saving.

God believed that we were worth it when he heard the distress of our entire world, calling out to be saved. Though we are told by some people that we didn't deserve to be saved, God's message insistently and continuously contradicts them. *You do deserve to be saved* because you are God's child. God believed we were so worth the effort that he sent his only son to save us from every wrong thing we have ever done and will ever do.

As we continue through the season celebrating the birth of our Savior, let us think of the genetic makeup of our bodies that is like his. As Jesus became man, he walked as part of us. And because of his victory over death, we can walk in this world now as part of his plan to redeem all creation.—d.o.

Disney Dog

I thank my God every time I remember you.
—Philippians 1:3

Tiffany Abigail was a Christmas present to my two daughters. I stuck a little bow on her head, and she completed the picture with licks and doggie smiles. We called her Abby. She was a beautiful blue merle sheltie with multicolored eyes to match her coat. I gave her to them early, just before December, because I knew it would be a sadder-than-usual Christmas. It would be the first one with just us girls.

I was worried about money, but I managed to save enough to take us, including Abby, to Disney World. So that year, we had a Charlie Brown Christmas tree because there was not a penny left for a bigger one.

At Disney, we found the most wonderful kennel, and though Abby was not thrilled that we were leaving her there, she was clean and safe. We came back to give her hugs just about every hour, and at lunch time we took her out of the kennel and had a picnic with her. No matter how fun each ride was, my six-year-old constantly reminded us, "We have to check on Abby again after this ride, okay, Mommy?"

It's funny to think about it now, but the thing that makes that year stand out from all the rest to me wasn't the sadness or bitterness of our situation; I remember that Abby was there. She made us laugh, and now that Christmas is a precious memory we share.

Our pets are an important part of our lives. They can give us comforting reminders in the midst of family tension or when the sad memories come. They bring us laughter and smiles as they join in on the celebration and festivity of the season. We miss Abby, but every Christmas, I thank God for her because she was the best Christmas present our family ever got.
—k.m.

December 22

Drinkin' from the Cocoa Pot

Though you have not seen him, you love him; and even though you do not see him now,
you believe in him and are filled with an inexpressible and glorious joy.
—1 Peter 1:8

One of my favorite traditions at Christmas is to get everyone dressed up in pajamas and load them into the car, hands warmed with cups of hot cocoa, to see the Christmas lights while listening to Christmas music. My father started it when I was little. Back then, we rode around a neighborhood called Christmas Card Lane. Not only were there lights, but the whole community created, lit, and displayed a beautiful wooden Christmas card. Looking back, our tradition was simple, and maybe a little cheesy, but it was the best time ever!

As an adult, one year, I found myself unable to get enough time off to travel back to Louisiana for the family Christmas. That was the first year I had ever experienced the loneliness of the season without my family. I picked up a little silver tabletop tree, but even that didn't make it feel like Christmas.

Then it hit me. The *tradition*!

I donned pjs and dressed my dog-boys up with Christmas-inspired bandannas. Filling a cup with cocoa and grabbing some holiday CDs, we went in search of Christmas lights. For the first time in my lonely first Christmas away from home, it *felt* like Christmas.

Christmas is an experience that can be very different from year to year. Our lives change, our families shrink or grow or just change, and just when everyone else is happy, along comes an unexpected blue mood. Those moments can steal the beautiful gift of Christmas from us, convincing us to ignore the celebration of our Savior's birth. We need to hold fast to the traditions that help us defeat those thoughts and remind us of the joy we have in Christ. For me, filling my gratitude cup with cocoa and taking a ride with the dogs was one way to experience joy this season. Find what will delight you!—d.o.

December 23
Possum on the Half Shell

She said to her mistress, "If only my master would see the prophet
who is in Samaria! He would cure him of his leprosy."
—2 Kings 5:3

We were coming up the driveway one night, and the headlights shined on an unlikely critter for our neck of the woods. An armadillo scurried across the gravel drive headlong into the tall grass. Tennessee has been getting a few armadillos, but they are really a more southern creature.

Referred to as turtle rabbits by Native Americans, armadillos are fabulous swimmers, able to inflate their intestines and hold their breath for up to six minutes! They can sniff out their insect dinners as much as six inches below ground too.

Also, I was surprised to learn that leprosy infects about 20 percent of the armadillo population in Louisiana and Texas. Leprosy may sound like an extinct disease, but it is still around today. Armadillos are believed to have caught the disease from humans five hundred years ago, and now they are giving it back. But, we don't have much to worry about if we aren't trying to make armadillo chili. These so-ugly-they're-cute animals like to stay to themselves. Leprosy doesn't do anything to harm the armadillos, but it can be debilitating, even fatal, to humans by attacking the immune system and crippling victims.

I cannot imagine what those with this sickness must have felt when they were suddenly healed by Jesus' touch. Finally, they had a chance to prove to the world that their hearts were always yearning for goodness, since now their bodies matched. The word must have traveled like lightning when loved ones of afflicted people found hope in a touch.

The lesions on someone afflicted by leprosy are obvious—those people know they need to be healed—but soul wounds are harder to spot, and harder to accept. We may be emotionally falling apart, but we fail to talk to the one who could and would heal us, whether because of pride, fear, or something else. Ask God to heal what your hard, outer shell is trying to hide. Ask for him to look past the armor you walk around in, and *unbreak* your heart.—d.o.

December 24

Will It Be a Talking Donkey Like on Shrek?

While they were there, the time came for the baby to be born,
and she gave birth to her firstborn, a son. She wrapped him in cloths
and placed him in a manger, because there was no guest room available for them.
—Luke 2:6-7

Playing taxi for grandchildren, while challenging at times, can be the best opportunity for collecting "funniest things I've ever heard" statements. Granddaughter Amelia was three and grandson Music was almost six when we were driving around discussing the delivery of two donkeys to the farm.

"What are their names?" asked Music.

"Are they boys or girls?" asked Amelia.

"I want to name the boy," Music added.

"Will they be talking donkeys like on *Shrek?*" Amelia asked. It was a very appropriate question since she had been introduced to donkeys through the popular movie series, and she had never really seen one in person. If you were in her situation, at three years old, you might very well expect every donkey to smile and sound like Eddie Murphy.

"No, these probably aren't talking donkeys. They might just be hee-hawing donkeys," I told them.

The first living creatures to cast their eyes on the newborn king, other than Mary and Joseph, were animals. No one really knows what animals were surrounding the manger that night, but we do know that a donkey carried Mary to Bethlehem, and we do know that they had to be somewhere animal-related because Jesus was laid in a box that was normally used for animal food. Now whether or not they could talk . . .

Some people do say that since that first Christmas, animals are blessed with the ability to speak—the Christmas Miracle, I told the kids.

"What did the animals say on that one night?" Amelia asked.

Music turned to her in a very mature, older brother way. "They said . . . 'Merry Christmas, Jesus!'"

Even if the "Christmas Miracle" isn't exactly historical, Christmas Eve is a perfect time to remember that God can take the most forgettable among us, allow us to witness the most beautiful gift humankind ever received, and even use us to help that gift reach the recipients. He gave a donkey such an honor, and he will do the same for us.—d.o.

The Story

For a child has been born for us, a son given to us.
—Isaiah 9:6a

Today is the first day of the twelve days of Christmas, and every year on this day we remember the first year, the first physical fulfillment of the Savior who had been promised hundreds of years before.

The Spirit has kept the story alive through the generations. Those who knew Mary and Joseph must have talked. The shepherds and the innkeeper must have told it over and over again—how the angels sang, and how the sky changed, and how the astrologers and scholars came from the Far East to see this baby, who turned out to be Jesus, our Savior.

And others probably repeated everything about their encounters with him during his lifetime on earth, probably recounted every time they ran into him at the market or talked about those crazy miracles he performed. They went home and told the kids, and the kids told their kids, and those kids told their kids. The eyewitness accounts of his life were so widely spread by so many, they would be viable in a court of law. Too many people were there. Too many people saw him. The story just wouldn't die.

Many worry over the lost message among all the lights and shopping, but don't be alarmed. God can still protect his message. And we will just keep on telling it.

As we tell and share the story, it lives on in our hearts, in our homes, in our communities, and in our world. Merry Christmas. God loves you.
—k.m.

The Right Thing

So Christ himself gave the apostles, the prophets, the evangelists,
the pastors and teachers, to equip his people for works of service,
so that the body of Christ may be built up until we all reach unity in the faith.
—Ephesians 4:11-13a

Did you know that almost every species of gorilla depends on their favorite food, the small bulbs of the wild onion? Scientist Dian Fossey devoted her life to these massive, endangered creatures, working in and around Rwanda for some eighteen years to map the behavior of the primates. You may have seen the famous picture of Dian reaching toward an ape that mirrored her movements and reached back to her. That photo left an indelible mark of interspecies communication.

Fossey fought against poachers and regimes who sacrificed harvested gorillas for body parts, zoos, and tourism. She was called, and she obeyed. After apes were killed in a raid, she even took a machete from the hands of a poacher and displayed it on the wall in her cabin to remind her that her enemy was real and her fight necessary. On the evening of December 26, 1985, an intruder entered her cabin, and she was killed by a poacher's machete to the head.

She is now buried in the cemetery she had created for the apes, beside Digit, her favorite gorilla. Her work to protect gorillas is still in place today, and though she started as a scientist, she became a friend and activist, literally battling to help save the great ape from extinction.

What in our world are we called to stand against? If you are being called to action by God, trust him that you will be equipped for the call. No matter who you were, where you have worked, or who you have been, God will give you the exact skills you need to complete it.

Dian's final entry in her journal, written on the night of her death, was, "When you realize the value of all life, you dwell less on what is past and concentrate more on the preservation of the future."—d.o.

December 27

Heroes

He saved us, not because of righteous things we had done, but because of his mercy.
He saved us through the washing of rebirth and renewal by the Holy Spirit.
—Titus 3:5

I was asleep one night in a house I shared with two roommates, one down the hall from me, and one downstairs. Bill, our downstairs renter, had blown out a candle on the fireplace mantle and gone to bed after us. He didn't realize a small spark from the wick had blown to a dried flower arrangement in a basket near the candle.

My schnauzer, Winston, woke me by barking like crazy and finally pulling the covers off me completely. By the time I was awake enough to realize what was happening, the place was filled with smoke. I called to Trish down the hall, and we both worked to get Bill awake and out of the house just as firefighters arrived. Smoke was heavy, but we were all safe, thanks to a little dog that would not let up. He forever will be my hero.

God's mercy sees our every need and loves us so much that he sends help when we send up distress signals, or in my case, even if we don't. And his aid is not dependent on whether we think we deserve it or not. God knows that we *don't* deserve his love based on anything we've done. God chose to love us, save us, give us worth.

In fact, in our weakest state, God's mercy flows freely. When we are struggling the most, God knows just which life preserver to throw out.

If you are in need of mercy from God, ask him for it and trust that he will answer. If God is calling you to show mercy to someone, then forgive and love as God does—regardless of the apparent worthiness of the other person. Ask God to enlighten you to the call for mercy around you so that you can be someone's hero. And open your arms to accept all the mercy and compassion your father has for you, too!—d.o.

King Sulemani and the Whale

Great is our Lord and mighty in power; his understanding has no limit.
—Psalm 147:5

In Swahili legend, a great king, named Sulemani, had fed all his own people, animals, and spirits, so he sought God for the chance to feed all the creatures on the earth. It was a huge job, but he felt he had the power to do anything.

So God granted him his request. One whale came to the king and ate not only all the corn he had saved for himself, but also all the corn portioned for everyone else.

"You are very big. How many beings are like you in this world?" the king asked.

"Oh, seventy thousand more just like me, and just as hungry," replied the whale.

The king ran back to God, threw himself before him, and begged to be forgiven for asking to feed all of God's creation. Then he thanked the whale for the very important lesson. From that day forward, the king never tried to take over God's job of feeding all creation.

Have you ever tried to take God's job? We often bite off more than we can chew, thinking that we can handle it, or that nobody else can do it right. We get involved in too many events or committees, and we begin to feel pretty important.

Stress and being stretched too thin are side effects to trying to do God's job. We show up to do our good works and leave exhausted, unable to enjoy our families or any quiet time with God. God loves a missionary spirit, but not when it stems from a need to prove our goodness. It is easy to fall into the trap of worshiping the good deed—or just as bad, ourselves—rather than God.

Worshiping God and loving others is our job: that is enough challenge for any of us.—d.o.

December 29
Koala Sam

This poor man called, and the LORD heard him; he saved him out of all his troubles.
—Psalm 34:6

In 2009, Australia was plagued with a series of wildfires considered some of the worst in history. But out of ashes came a story that moved people to tears. As a firefighter moved through the smoky ruins, he saw a koala moving carefully on her scorched paws, weak and parched. In a moment of compassion, he offered her a drink from his water bottle. To his surprise, this wild animal caught on, and began to drink right from the bottle.

This little koala that rescuers named Sam became a symbol for the survivor spirit of Australia and of the problems koalas face in our world today. In fact, as updates were joyfully posted about the koala with bandaged feet, her reunion with the firefighter who saved her, and even a friendship Sam developed with another rescued koala, the world was informed through her story that a disease called chlamydia was attacking and killing Sam, as well as her species. The doctor working to help her heal took Sam into surgery only to find that this courageous survivor had masses of tumors. To spare her more pain and misery, the compassionate staff helped her peacefully be euthanized. Today, to Australians she remains a symbol of a species desperate for our help.

God heard Sam's cry and rescued her through the firefighter. Because God made a way for Sam to survive and connect with the right people, research is now growing to stop the disease. We can now see that he planned to use Sam to save other suffering koalas all along, as in her passing, she made the world aware of a disease that is causing the tremendous shrinking of the koala population.

God answers prayers in many ways. He says yes. He says no. He says not yet. But he always hears our cry from whatever our wildfires may be, and tells us to come home to his merciful arms.—d.o.

December 30
Leftover Angels

Suppose one of you has a hundred sheep and loses one of them.
Doesn't he leave the ninety-nine in the open country and
go after the lost sheep until he finds it?
—Luke 15:4

They were cleaning up and putting away holiday decorations at the pet supply store, gearing up for a new year of squeaky toys and Greenies treats. The hustle and bustle had definitely left things in disarray. I saw an artificial tree being dismembered. From a few of the limbs hung pictures of animals. I watched as an employee took a photo of a dog, yellow with a long pink tongue, from a branch and throw it away.

A young man in a red store apron looked up. "Can I help you?"

"Are these the ones who didn't get adopted?" I asked.

"Yeah that's all we had left."

I reached down into the trash for three pictures and shoved them into my pocket. I left the store with a few extra treats and headed to the shelter. Finding the leftover angels at the shelter, I passed out belated gifts to them.

There's no fuzzy, happy ending to this story. Each year, millions of little angels who need our help go unnoticed. Pictures of children, teachers and classrooms, the elderly, and pets in need are hanging in department store displays as written invitations to us to share our love with them.

God never leaves leftover angels hanging without hope. He seeks us out, individually and lovingly, making sure that our needs are met through one another. In a world of lonely angel trees, we are God's hands, feet, and hearts. What leftover angel will you reach out to today?—d.o.

Another New Year's Eve

In everything set them an example by doing what is good. In your teaching show integrity, seriousness and soundness of speech that cannot be condemned, so that those who oppose you may be ashamed because they have nothing bad to say about us.
—Titus 2:7-8

As strains of "Auld Lang Syne" waft through my head, I often feel a little sad. It is hard to imagine the death of a year, even amidst the celebration in the birth of another. We have to realize in that human moment that what we have done with this year is all that we can do. We have to accept our accomplishments and limitations and move into the new year with acceptance and truth, believing that God's goodness has prevailed this past year and will continue to prevail this next year.

Have we done all we can do? Have we followed God's plan? These questions are answered by God's eternal grace. When we are frustrated and feeling like we do not have value, or that we've failed, we have to remember that God is bigger than our perceived mistakes. God's plan is firm, and he will bring it to pass.

Take courage as you go into the vast unknown of a new year. God is not disappointed in you. God believes in you, his good and faithful servant. Let us link arms, join forces, and carry on with a belief in God that is just as great as his belief in you. This knowledge allows us to overcome evil with good. Let our testimonies shine brightly with the light of Christ so that our enemies can have nothing bad to say about us. God bless you in your past, your present, and your future, which in Christ Jesus is always as bright as the Son.—d.o.

Acknowledgments

Danielle, Shea, Will, Music, and Amelia—Thank you for your joy, your sharing, and your childlike spirits that bless us every day.

Faith, Campion, and Mama—Thank you for your belief and example that all things are possible through Christ Jesus.

Janice and Bob (Mom and Dad)—Thank you for allowing me to have pets growing up and showing me how much they can bless you. With all the fish, gerbils, dogs, and even a pet squirrel, you helped me know the joy of animals.

Landra Anderson—Thank you for your encouragement, prayers, and feeding us during the writing of this book. You are our angel!

Lane Wilkinson   Thank you for your friendship and support in every way! You are truly God's gift. Also thank you for our new mascot schnauzer, Pepper Jane! You have blessed us more than you know.

Jim Oliver's Smokehouse, Monteagle, Tennessee—Thank you, J. D., Betsy, Marla, Gwen, and family for being our inspirational writer-getaway destination, keeping us warm, fed, and inspired!

To Andy Parrish—Our angel in heaven who now watches over Big Sky Heaven Blue. The animals miss you so much and so do we. Take care of the fur babies as they cross the bridge.

Joe, David, Steve, and Shannon—Thank you for being the farmhands, errand runners, and feeders of the flock on our travels.

The Tuesday Night Prayer Group—Thank you for being our prayer family covering us, loving us, and supporting us through all.

And most of all . . .

Charles Ford (Daddy Charles)—You loved all God's creatures with such a sweet appreciation. Thank you for setting such a godly example and walking the walk you talked. Thank you for being more proud of being a daddy to little girls than anything else you ever accomplished. Thank you for making all your "adopted" daughters feel unconditionally loved. Your joy in mockingbirds, sparrows, dragonflies, deer, dogs, kitty-cats, horses—as well as your tears at seeing the Grand Canyon—are just a few of the ways you praised God with all your heart. We will always take you with us in our hearts and in these pages.

About the Authors

Kim McLean and **Devon O'Day** are hosts of FoxNews Radio's *Plain Jane Wisdom* heard nightly on www.wlac.com and on WSIX Nashville's *Country Spirit Show* on Sundays. They have collaborated on songs recorded by Pam Tillis, Lee Ann Womack, and many others, as well as a book/CD project purposed for pet bereavement called *Goodbye, My Friend* (Thomas Nelson Publishers). Both are on the board of Come to the Fire Women's Conferences and travel extensively in ministry with music, message, and testimony. Together, they created the Sweet Tea Tour with music and a legacy collection of recipes called *My Southern Food*.

Kim McLean is an award-winning songwriter with more than three hundred credits including songs heard on NBC's *West Wing*, CBS's *Cold Case*, ABC's *Hope & Faith*, and more. Her duet with Dolly Parton "Angels and Eagles" has become a Mother's Day prayer anthem used seasonally and for children's charity fundraisers around the country. She is the creator of the quadrennial missions theme for the Church of the Nazarene of the Cross, as well as The United Methodist theme for Peace with Justice Sunday. Kim McLean holds a master's degree in biblical theology and is an ordained elder in the Church of the Nazarene, travelling internationally as a musical keynote/Bible speaker, predominantly within denominations of the Wesleyan tradition. A Greensboro, North Carolina, native, she is lead composer of music for Come to the Fire Women's Conferences.

Devon O'Day is an award-winning songwriter, author, and career radio broadcaster. Her book *My Angels Wear Fur* (Thomas Nelson Publishers), a collection of short stories and essays of rescued animals and their spiritual lessons, is in its sixth printing. Devon is a graduate of the University of Louisiana-Monroe and took continuing education classes in creative writing from authors at New York University while she worked as a plus-model for the Ford Agency. Hailing originally from Pineville, Louisiana, Devon O'Day has been behind a microphone as a radio host both locally and nationally since 1977 on shows including Gerry House's *House Foundation* in Nashville, *Country Hitmakers*, and Bravo Network's *The Road*, and *Impact Songs* for television. Her voice has been heard on all major networks, on radio specials and commercials for Garth Brooks, Gaither Homecoming, and the Dove Awards, as well as KFC, Hilton Hotels, The United Methodist Church, and countless audio books for Zondervan, Thomas Nelson, and The Upper Room.

Websites include:

www.KimMcLean.com
www.PlainJaneWisdom.com
www.PawsToReflectBook.blogspot.com

Kim McLean/Devon O'Day
P.O. Box 3
Kingston Springs, TN 37082

plainjanewisdom@gmail.com (Also on Twitter, Facebook, and LinkedIn)